WHAT TO
EXPECT
WHEN YOU
WEREN'T
EXPECTING

Best wishes on whichever path life takes you! Hope these words give you a smile. ~Jyl Barlow

WHAT TO
EXPECT
WHEN YOU
WEREN'T
EXPECTING

PARENTING TALES FROM THE
MOST UNQUALIFIED (STEP)MOM EVER

JYL CJ BARLOW

atmosphere press

For Rich, you are all that is good. Thank you. For your endless patience, for believing in me when I didn't believe in myself, and for loving me always. I know there were many days when I was a terror. I was probably just hangry.

For my mother, there are not enough pages to fill with words of adoration for how you managed our circus. Apologies for my part.

To my (step)children, I chose to be your mother. I would do it again and again. Never forget the place you have in my heart.

FOREWORD
by Rich Barlow

A long time ago, in a southern state far, far away, a boy met a girl. There were unicorns and rainbows, glorious Instagram posts, inspirational Facebook posts. No voices were ever raised in frustration over the state of the dishwasher, and they lived happily ever after.

This is not that story.

This is the story of a woman who built a relationship with a heartbroken man and his two devastated children who then found their way to happily ever after through hard work, tears, and compromise—but mostly through unfailing love.

I was first married at a young twenty-one (my ex-wife was nineteen) while a student at Valley Forge Christian College. VFCC was jokingly known as the Northern Bridal Institute due to the number of marriages that came out of its august doors. We were young, stupid, and ultimately not ready for the responsibilities that we were unknowingly assuming.

As a child of divorced parents, I vowed never to follow that path. My father has divorced and remarried seven (or eight?) times. My mother remarried and divorced once—on fairly unfriendly terms. I was 110 percent committed to making my marriage a lifelong event, no exceptions. I even insisted that we never use the word "divorce" in our home for years.

I hadn't considered having children until I was a decade

into my first marriage. As with so many others, when 9/11 happened, something changed in me. My daughter was conceived shortly after, and our tiny family settled into a comfortable routine. Four years later, we had a second (surprise!) child—a son.

Then, with two children under five years old, it became obvious that the wheels were coming off my first marriage. With differing interests, the divide between my children's mother and me grew at a rapid pace. Though we tried to close the gap, it was not long before the writing was clearly written on the wall and, after twenty years together, we divorced.

I had no intentions of becoming an "every other weekend" father. With my personal promise never to divorce broken, I stood firm on an equal custody schedule, at minimum. We started with a 50/50 split that was updated to sole custody to me within a year.

I swore that I would never let another woman into my life.

And then one night, out of the blue, I met Jyl. She was zany, lovely, infuriating, and, ultimately, the perfect woman for both me and my children.

I have watched her struggle with heart, mind, and soul to find her place in our family. I have witnessed the depth of love she has for both me and our children.

There were moments when I was sure she might give up on this (step)mothering path, for fear that staying would kill her spirit. There were moments in which she fought to love, unconditionally, two children who were not interested in receiving it.

Still she persevered and today, we are stronger because of it.

This is that story.

A story bravely written. A story that, even after living through it, fills me with wonder and awe.

A story which I am so proud to have told.

~ Rich

Many of the names in this memoir have been changed.

Because of that, for the first time in my life, I was able to choose the name of my children, an exercise that ended up being quite an unexpected special perk.

Maybe it's your turn for something good.
  - *Unknown*

Come to me with secrets bare, I'll love you more so don't be scared.
  - *"Come to Me," Goo Goo Dolls*

TABLE OF CONTENTS

on the topic of (step)momming than I was when I started on this road just under a decade ago.

Reader, if you bought this book, then you may feel unqualified (or frustrated or lost) as well. Or maybe you just need an ally. Maybe you just need to read about the failures of another (step)mother who struggled. Maybe you will wonder if my children are actually still alive (as in *"if **her** (step)kids survived, mine will as well!"*). They are.

What's in the box? An ally. A (step)parenting sherpa. Yes, I am your Sherparent.

Oh yes, the shortcut.

Try to remember that your worst days may turn into your best stories. Mine have.

And, for the love of Carol Brady, find a counselor.

Which Way's Up?

It'll be funny someday, right?

Probably. But not if you try to do this alone.

Get a counselor, you moron!

Did that sound too harsh?

I don't care.

Do it.

CHAPTER ONE

The Truth Is, I Have No Idea What I'm Doing

MY QUALIFICATIONS: MOSTLY NONE

(Step)mom.

Is that you?

Is that going to *be you*?

There is so much advice I could give on this topic but if I had to narrow it down to a one-word blurb, the most helpful thing I could tell you, knowing all of the things I've learned in nearly a decade as a (step)mom, it is

RUN.

Like the wind.

Yes. Flee. Skedaddle. Abort.

Just turn around and change your plans. Trust me, your life will be so much easier.

The truth is no one really dreams of marrying a man who comes with pre-made kids and an ex-wife who can't get her shit together. When I met Rich, my husband-to-be (and got those stupid love-at-first-sight feelings), I had no idea how much baggage he had in the trunk of his Chevy Trailblazer. As the details began to trickle out of his griefcase, I hardly even flinched because frankly, I was a moron.

Just under a decade ago, Rich and I were married (good-bye, Barbie townhouse). It was actually *before* then that I became an accidental mother to his seven-year-old boy and ten-year-old girl (hello, emotional chaos). It's not that I didn't *know* there would be children involved in our relationship. It's that I didn't heed Rich's many messages that his ex-wife would never be able to maintain life as a single parent. He told me this approximately 724 times while we were dating. He told me that the result would, without a doubt, end with him gaining full physical custody of Max (seven) and Amelia (ten). He told me that so that I would have total clarity in that—should we make our relationship permanent—I would land smack in the seat of driving the mom bus.

It's not that I wasn't listening. I was just set on Scoff Mode.

How hard could step-kids be, after all?

I should have listened. I should have run for the hills. I should **not** have jumped in with both feet and an over-inflated ego. Precisely what Rich predicted would happen did happen. Within five months of unloading everything I owned into a storage unit three hours north of my home, I became a full-time caregiver in Rich's home. I had hardly arranged my shoe collection before Max and Amelia became dependent on me—ME, the one with no qualifications. I threw myself into it the only way I knew how: schedules and lists, which promptly led to confusion and tears. We boarded an emotional roller coaster with seating for four. Outbursts and anger were common, laced together with thin threads of sweet moments, always at risk of snapping.

Before I had moved, I'd asked my therapist her thoughts on stepparenting. The summary of her response was, "*Oh, just acquiesce all kid-related items to the biological parents.*" Perfect. I could do that. It wasn't until much later (and three years into our marriage) that I learned the hard facts. Marriages involving existing children only succeeded about **thirty** percent of the time. In other words, *"Just relax, it'll probably be over soon."*

Maybe this wasn't going to be so perfect.

Just over a decade ago, I was *thoroughly* enjoying the life of a single girl, back in my beloved Tarheel state. I had an active single-girl social life. I played tennis, volunteered, frequented the gym, and took naps with my dog and cat whenever the mood struck. I worked (in the days that required going to an actual office), traveled, and dedicated one weekend a month to visiting my parents. My day-to-day life had very few surprises. There were no visible road bumps in my future. I preferred this simplicity, as it is how I remember much of my childhood.

I have always had a very close relationship with my parents, likely born out of a few cross-country moves and then nurtured via life as a competitive gymnast. While other kids my age were exploring the boundaries allowed to teens in the eighties, I was riding shotgun to and from practices or meets. I never did all the crazy, rebellious things, as I was too busy obsessing about perfection.

Daydreaming about weddings or journaling about cute boys at school never crossed my mind. I never imagined names for my future children or practiced a signature with someone else's last name attached to my first. Fairy tales and love stories just didn't hold my interest. There were many things I wanted to accomplish, but "dating" never made the top ten.

It wasn't until my senior year in college that I had my first boyfriend. He had grown up as competitive in cycling as I was in gymnastics, so we were both relationally immature. "Marriage" did work its way into our conversations after several years together, but really only because that's what we were supposed to do next, *right*? We stayed together for five years until coming to the awkward end of realizing that we were only together out of habit, rather than desire. Our time together wasn't *bad*, but neither of us knew the right way to end it.

Even then, in the aftermath of that relationship ending, my twenty-nine-year-old uterus never screamed out for attention. Having children seemed like a really exhausting way to eliminate all the fun from my life at a time when I was single (!) and free (!) and on my own schedule (!). My thirties flew by with concerts and cruises and brunches and beaches. When I finally did reach the age of "uter-use it or lose it," I didn't have a lot of interest in dating. Did I say interest? I meant suitors. There wasn't a line at the door. Well, shit.

Still, I was mostly unruffled. I'd also spent my twenties dealing with various misdiagnosed forms of mental health hiccups and I'd been told multiple times that, in order to carry my own child, I'd have to come off any serotonin lifts. For years I associated pregnancy with nine months of panic attacks and depression. Of course, today that is no longer accurate but, back then, the thought of voluntarily following that path instilled terror. Besides, if I really wanted a child, there was adoption or, yes, marrying into them.

I had always had an inkling that I might inherit someone else's kids. I know that sounds strange. I assumed it was due to my fascination with the blended families I tuned into on television: *The Brady Bunch, Diff'rent Strokes,* and *Silver Spoons.* Then one day, my mother threw out that she had always imagined me marrying a man who was hoping for someone to help him raise his kids. Was that strange? Maybe. But hearing it from her gave me great relief. Yes, that would be a perfectly acceptable way to gain my own family.

Today, my made-for-me family includes Rich, my husband of nearly seven years, an eighteen-year-old (Amelia), and a sixteen-year-old (Max). When we met at a work dinner in 2012, Rich's handshake sent very cliched sparks through my body and I knew instantly that this was the person I'd been waiting for - though, for what, I wasn't sure. Rich and I didn't start out by thinking we were seriously dating. I certainly had no plans to give up my easy-breezy life for a man who was extricating himself from a marriage. He showed up carrying with him all sorts of emotional baggage: backpacks, suitcases, storage lockers, and change purses — unsure of whether to hold onto it like a badge of honor or to launch it all over a cliff. We started out thinking we were having fun, with no strings. When we began to really like each other, it was petrifying. Imagine our surprise when we realized that we had fallen in love.

I write this memoir as a second wife. I write this memoir as a spare daughter-in-law. I write this memoir as a mother to someone else's children, neither of whom wanted an ancillary parent added to their lives.

With no biological children, my knowledge of nurturing was fairly low. Max and Amelia were well established as tiny humans when I came into their lives. What was not established was my pulse as a caretaker. When I spoke to mothers with children of their own, they often responded to my parenting struggles with challenges with, "*Wait, how did you not know that?*" "How" was because I had no idea what I was doing. "How" was because a few teenage years as the neighborhood babysitter did not prepare me for a life as a full-time (step)mother. My vision of what a mother/child relationship should look like came from my relationship with my own mother—a very tight bond nearly devoid of conflict.

In addition to my lack of mothering qualifications, I had no idea how to be a wife. Rich had a Rolodex of mistakes he wouldn't make again, and I came with an empty notepad that I would soon fill with mistakes. There were times when I wished that we were experiencing the challenges of marriage together, rather than with his head start. It is hard to be the "first marriage" person in a marriage in which one of you already has a road map. There were times when it felt like I had gained a mentor when what I really wanted was a fellow new student. I didn't always want to live with someone who could predict my failures and how they would fit into our script.

I am a (step)mom. I have no idea if my experiences apply to biological moms or to stepdads or elephants or donkeys. I only know this role from my own perspective and who it's allowed me to become. I can recall every mistake I've made, and I know that they all come with a box of hindsight to be unwrapped over several glasses of Malbec. I know that I have taken many of those failures more personally because I have no biological children to look to for comparison. Nearly every stumble came with a gurgled question as to whether or not it was just "normal kid behavior" or if it was specific to my role as a (step)mom.

My life may or may not translate perfectly into the lives of other (step)mothers. My hope is that, whether our paths are identical or not, my words will still offer a feeling of camaraderie. Despite it being a well-hidden, whispered-about role, (step)mothers are prevalent in the world. Those who take on that role should announce it proudly. It is then that they will find allies at every turn. Those women who have walked this (step)mothering path before will become a lifeline. Knowing those women will diminish the feelings of isolation, lessening the frustration and panic that comes with feeling utterly lost.

I have had success, yes. Sometimes only by pure luck, sometimes because of what I have learned as a (step)mother.

When I begin to question my qualifications or sense the bubbles of insecurity, I tell myself this:

You Are Enough.

Corny? Yes.

Written on my office wall in twelve-inch letters? Also, yes.
Because I am.

And, reader, so are you.

MY QUALIFICATIONS: REVISED (*TOO SOON?*)

Not long after joining the (step)momming club, I realized that
the word "(step)mom" is often totally inaccurate. Therefore, I
would like to veto the use of it unless actual clarification is
needed. It is very outdated. It comes with a lot of connotations:
that this person is the lesser parent or that this person is uninvolved or that this person doesn't know what it's like to be
a *real* parent. I often refer to myself as my kids' mom and I
mean it. I am aware that I am not their original mom, but I
have yet to discover a moniker that holds the same weight as
"mom" while also indicating that I came into the role through
circumstance. I also hate the term "bonus mom" as if the kids
won some sort of prize through divorce or death. *Hooray!!
Your parents' relationship tanked! Please choose a prize from
the middle row!* So, yes, I will often refer to myself in the following pages as Mom unless there is a distinct need for clarification.

Historically, (step)moms (*okay, already a distinct need for
clarification*) have gotten a bad rap. I have no idea when all
stepmothers instantly were tagged as "evil," but it's a reputa-
tion that lives on. It does make sense, I suppose, to a child's
brain. Phase I: Parents are together. Phase II: Parents are no
longer together. Phase III: Enter a strange lady. Surely, the
strange lady is the source of all the bad things involved in
Phase II. Me? I wasn't even a whisper in Phase II. Well, maybe
a whisper, but nothing more than a woman who accidentally
fell for a man with two children. There was no intent to marry.
There was certainly no intent to meet the kids beyond a wave

as their arrival matched my departure.

What were my qualifications? None. Really. I'm not a counselor (see above ...). Trust me, I wouldn't have had a half dozen counselors on speed dial if I had any working knowledge of how regular humans work, let alone those involved in blended families. I'm not a teacher or doctor or life coach. I'm not even a woman who had her own children prior to taking on the role of (step)mother. When I say I started this with zero qualifications, I mean it.

Today? Yes. At the very least, I am the proud owner of one qualification.

I have walked this (step)mothering path. I have learned on this path. I have felt like a moron, I have felt like a hero. I've dealt with emotional agony, and I've experienced spirited highs. I have recently started to see the light at the end of the tunnel, and I wish more than I could say that I'd known someone who'd found that light before me to guide me there.

THIS ISN'T A LOVE STORY.

Don't get me wrong, I'm madly in love with my husband. He's truly my best friend (cliche), my soulmate (cliche #2), my lover (gross word), and the one I want to grow old with (cliche #3). Right, so he's my best friend that I also sleep with, in the biblical sense (*we all know there are levels of best friends*). As we begin rounding the corner to a decade of knowing each other, I still have no idea how I scored this guy who is so cute and sweet and generous and kind. I always thought the concept of "love at first sight" was a stupid thing that happily-in-love people made up to make their single friends feel better.

"*Sure, yeah, that sounds great,*" I'd think, "*there's someone out there just waiting for me to walk in the room, and bam!*" Really? Sure. I assumed all the preachers of love had stock in

Hallmark or, at least, provided cute sayings for them to paste on their overpriced cards. Yet, here I sit, a near-decade later, deeply in love and a believer in all things typed out on pink cards with pictures of birds sharing a worm or toddlers dressed as adults holding hands or those craft store wooden boxes with hearts pasted to them (shakes fist at sky).

Still, as a former frequent flier in the single-gal club, old feelings occasionally creep in. Like being a little pissed that when sweeping me off my feet, Rich also swept away my plans to become a crazy cat lady who dressed too young and lurked at concerts geared toward the college set. He also swept away my plan to never know the excruciating pain of stepping on a Lego. Or debates over bedtimes (kids) or a reasonable amount of covers for one person to have over another (Rich). He swept away a pretty simple life—though, in hindsight, it did look very similar to the life of a retired person.

When we were dating, Rich began to look at me differently. At the time, I didn't really know why. When I figured it out, I was both touched and honored—proud, but also preparing for my exit—as I realized he was searching my soul for signs of a mother. He knew that, should we make our relationship permanent, he'd be handing over his two most precious people, Max and Amelia. I'd become a (step)mom (*okay, that sounded easy*) but, more than likely, an actual mom (*wait, now what?*). Again, this was not something he hid from me. He told me this often with a mixture of both urgency and warning.

Here's how my brain worked: *So? I could totally be a mother! How hard was that? Clothing, food, school—check, check, check, I'd get it done!* My brain also tends to live firmly in the "*it will probably never happen*" zone. Rich would very clearly state that he would have full custody of his children and I would think, "*right ... but maybe not.*" Nothing was in stone— so, really, just put those suitcases in the back seat. But, even if it **did** happen, *"the kids would just slide in and instantly love me, right? They could just see me as their dad's friend, right?"* I seesawed back and forth from polishing my rose-colored "Motherhood? No problem. Easy even" glasses to "Nope, there's no way this guy can predict the future." And, again, even if it did happen, well, I'm not sure what I *thought* I was signing up for. The fact that I had pets, knew how to make spreadsheets, owned a tiny crockpot, and lived by the schedule of one who has OCD led me to believe I was completely qualified. Overqualified even.

Oh, what a funny, funny person I was. Funny? I meant naive.

One morning during her custodial week, the kids' mother packed them in her car to drive them to school. While delivering them, the local sheriff placed a padlock on her apartment door—a final step in an eviction that had been in the works, unbeknownst to Rich, for months. When she returned and found herself locked out of the apartment that she had rented for her and the kids, Rich leaped into action. That morning, the children left for school from their mother's house and never returned permanently. That afternoon, they returned from school to Rich's house, where they would stay forever. This was the same house that I had moved into months prior in a long thought-out decision that also felt a lot like throwing caution to the wind.

Rich and I were still figuring out how *we* would live together and, suddenly, there were two tiny, emotionally wounded children on the doorstep, without so much as a toothbrush. They were confused, wondering why the school principal put them on the bus instead of in the pickup line. Panic? Yes, please, table for four. The house suddenly seemed smaller and more unstable as the four of us orbited through its rooms, gauging where our space was. If I could go back, I would have left immediately. Not permanently, but long enough to give Rich and the kids time to process and grieve without the oddity of a fourth pair of eyes staring at them. Instead, I felt this incredible pressure of "It's my time to shine!" We overdid the normalcy. *Just another day when you come home from school. Just another day when we ask about your homework. Just another day when we all eat dinner together. Just another day when we start the rotation of baths. Just another day when we go to bed at night.* It was a terrible way to handle it. And I say that not from a guilt-filled place—I say that from a place of the unlearned. We would have done it completely differently if only we had known.

It was shocking to learn that owning a house, a car, a dog, and a crockpot did not equate to an instant ability to be a mother. It was shocking to learn that spreadsheets made into chore charts did not equate to the boundaries that kids thrive within, something I had read about somewhere in a quick search of what to do when surprise children arrive. It was shocking to learn that cooking for one (and healthily!), did not equate to cooking for four (three of whom had spent the previous year downing comfort food while their lives flip-flopped). It was shocking to learn that I could not force the installation of bedtimes after only six hours together. After only half a day, I was absolutely emotionally and physically exhausted. I was also the only one in the household in bed at 10:00 p.m., well before Max and Amelia would finally sleep.

The one-day transition to motherhood was not smooth, as the reality check smacked me far from my typical success as a perfectionist. My entrance to the portal of parenthood—with a clipboard and an assumption that I'd grow into Mary Poppins overnight—was a disaster.

There is love in this story. But it is mainly a story of chaos and joy and tears related to finding it.

This story is one of throwing four people into a blender—but three of them are ice cream and syrup and Oreos, and one of them is broccoli.

This story is one of fighting—both literally (oh, we've had some epic verbal battles) and figuratively (so many opportunities to throw in the towel...).

This is a story of hiding in the bathroom with the shower running so no one could hear my sobs. This is a story of me standing outside another bathroom, waiting patiently by the door, while someone else took their turn with not-very-well-hidden sobs.

This is a story of laughing so hard that we could (and can) share a look for days and get right back to uncontrollable belly rolls.

This is a story of storming out. And storming back in. And staying. Forever.

This is a story of how I misjudged a smooth entrance to motherhood.

This is a story that jumps back and forth between where we started, where we are now, and how we got there.

This is a story of how we are going to be bonded forever.

Oh, okay.

Fine.

This is a love story.

Which Way's Up?

Lost and Found

Why would I share more than one story of misplacing my own child? To prove that YOU REALLY ARE DOING AN AMAZING JOB.

I'm one thousand percent sure that this happens all the time to other parents. I'm one thousand percent because almost no one looked at me funny when I lost him that first time. Nor the second time. Nor any of the times since. Is this something parents brag about? Not really, especially in today's land of cyber bombs. Looking totally inept keeps such stories of failure tucked away, hidden from others who would likely hear it and respond with, "Oh, yeah, that's happened to me multiple times, no big deal."

How did we keep track of our children prior to being technologically tethered to them at all times?

I know my parents did it. Mostly.

There was that one awkward instance when my brother and I declared our independence by heading off to find a new land with all of our important belongings packed into my Red Radio Flyer, determined to start a life devoid of people trying to be the boss of us. We were six and ten. It ended with our giving up on our newly established home (set up behind the 7-Eleven that was located across the street from our schools). This was 1970-something. We did want to run away, yes, but we did not want to miss out on a perfect attendance award. Sadly, we were caught almost immediately when trying to shoplift a plastic magnifying glass (we'd need a way to start a fire to cook hot dogs, right?) and sent packing. While the owner of the store did not call the police on us, our parents had, after finally admitting that their two kids were, in fact, *lost. We thought the scariest part of our day was realizing we would likely starve to death. It turned out that rounding the corner home to the site of patrol cars capped that only to be quickly demoted by the whooping that followed the relief of our return.*

Disappearing children is not a new thing, no. But it is terrifying, nonetheless.

My first go at losing Max happened almost immediately after I had moved in with Rich and the kids. I was still a part-timer in the parenting force and after a few weeks or a month or I can't remember how long, Rich asked if I would be comfortable alone for a night (with the kids) as he had a business trip approaching. "Oh sure," I probably responded, full of "I've been a parent for a few weeks or a month or I can't remember how long" confidence. We rehearsed how it would work. Rich would drop the kids off at school on the way to the airport and I would remain staged at home for approximately six hours preparing myself to stand on the front porch and wave at Mr. Gary of Bus #56 as Max came down the stairs in return to his homestead. Mr. Gary would see a completely capable person awaiting this second grader and pull away while Max and I reunited with a moment that would probably (not) include him running across the front yard and into my open arms. Would I be blasting Journey in the background? TBD.

The bus typically appeared around the 3:00 p.m. mark so I began my pacing of the front porch at 2:45 p.m., just to make sure I was ready, sitting casually (or should I stand?) on the porch steps with my left ear trained to the sound of an approaching bus. And, right on schedule, I did hear the sound of an approaching bus. Sure enough, Bus #56 meandered towards the house, slowing. I stood up and began an early wave just to give Mr. Gary the "everything's A-OK, nothing to see here" vibe in advance of the drop-off. The bus, however, did not stop. Mr. Gary waved back as he sped back up and continued the route.

What the shit? What the actual shit, Mr. Gary?!

I realized I was still waving as I watched the bus turn right at the next street.

That can't be right.

I also realized that I had no idea what else I should be doing, beyond waving and staring. And also sweating.

A lot of thoughts went through my head, actually. For example, how did I lose this kid on my first try? And also, what the shit, Mr. Gary?

I was still trying to work through this when the bus came back down the road minutes later, slowing again, to my relief. Right. I had just forgotten that on this day, Max would be bounding down the stairs on the return trip. Right? No. Mr. Gary's window slid open, and I heard him yell that Max wasn't on the bus today! "Oh, right!" I said, waving again as he drove away. *What? Why did I say that?*

This was not how we'd rehearsed it.

As I walked back into the house, I began to text Rich a red alert. Then I remembered he was likely sitting in a customer meeting and how that text might read (MAX IS LOST WHAT DO I DO?). Yeah, probably not the best update for him to get while several states away. I went with the much more casual "Hey, what's the name of Max's school again?" while simultaneously trying to Google "local schools" for a hint. The answer came back from Boston, "Rural Point, why?" "MAX IS LOST" still did not seem like the right response. "Just wondering! ☺"

What I was really wondering was how attached we really were to this eight-year-old vanishing act.

I rang up the school, praying that I wasn't about to be asked to enter a number for seventeen different routing options. The second prayer was that there was a Press 1 For Lost Children option. Instead, a real live person answered, and I started down a long, dark path of who I was and that

I had just moved here and that this was my first time getting a child off the bus, and that he didn't get off the bus and ... at which point the voice interrupted and asked, "Ma'am, are you looking for Max?"

"Yes!!"

"He's sitting here in the office. There was some confusion about pick up."

THANK YOU, SIX-POUND BABY JESUS. I drove NAS-CAR-style the three miles to the school, ready to scoop up a weeping grade-schooler writing in his journal about his newly discovered feelings of abandonment to show a counselor much later in life.

Max was not weeping. He was having a great time wrapping up the day with the office staff. Evidently, there was an announcement to his class that "Max would be picked up today." The announcement was meant for the other Max in his class but, being second-graders, neither paid attention to the last name. Or perhaps all of that rehearsing inspired him to throw a wrench into the day and really test the abilities of this new face in his life. He was not weeping at all. He looked fine.

I was not fine. My nerves were frazzled. I began apologizing profusely for dropping the ball on my first catch attempt. No one seemed to mind, just a little confusion on pickup. But I felt awful like this was a preview of how I would forever be rated as a mother figure.

As we made our way out to my car, I continued the apologies, throwing in an offer for ice cream, if it would help. I'm not sure exactly what it was going to help, but I knew I needed it. And, as luck would have it, eight-year-old boys apparently always need it. Off we went, back past the house to the nearest ice cream parlor, which is when panic number two arrived. While we were standing in line waiting to order our cones, it suddenly dawned on me that I was now pushing not being home at all for the SECOND bus delivering the SECOND child from the SECOND school.

Make that two scoops. Stat.

Seven years later, I have added several locations to the places in which I have lost this Artful Dodger:

+ *At Target after a flu shot. Max was so devastated at having to face a needle that he ran off in the middle of the shot, leaving a trail of blood down his arm. This was the last thing we saw before spending thirty minutes scouring the store, trying to find him. If the pharmacist hadn't witnessed the run, we probably could have kept it very hush-hush.*

+ *At Kohl's. During the years 2014, 2015, 2016, 2017, 2018, and ending in 2019, which is when I realized it was easier not to take him. Which was after I realized it was easier to let him run wild in the store with strict instructions not to leave the building but also realized that finding him when I was ready to leave was going to be just short of impossible and almost always required an assist from the store intercom.*

+ *There was that one weekend when he was at a friend's house with plans for his (bio)mom to pick him up. He went cell phone dark, ignoring all texts from three parents, finally causing an awkward phone call to the hosting parent during which all three parents learned that he'd told her (the host parent) that a longer visit was all worked out. It wasn't. None of us knew what was happening or where he was, only that he knew better than to make up such a story. Or at least he would know better very, very soon.*

+ *Name a cruise and we've misplaced him. Kind of. We always give him very clear instructions about not jumping overboard before sending him off. But to a child, "very clear" is often "very open" to interpretation. But sometimes parents need parent time (wink, wink) which may involve an approved "go, explore the ship, but be back in an hour ..." Pro-tip, make sure said child understands how long an hour is.*

✦   *On most soccer fields. All the time. Literally. They all look the same when dressed in a navy top, black shorts, and navy socks. I do cheer for every goal as if it were my own kid who scored it. Because it may have been. I don't know. I've missed more than I've seen. Which are zero. I'm quite terrible at being a sports mom.*

I'm not sure if I'll ever recover from that first attempt at bus duty. The kids have arrived home on the bus probably about 1500 times since. By my count, I've missed less than five arrivals, without notice, since. It doesn't matter much anymore as they have keys and common sense and I'm (mostly) sure they won't burn the house down, but I do like them knowing that I will be home when they arrive. Even now, I set an alarm while running errands to ensure that I will leave Target in time to make it home before the kids. More than once, I arrived at the start of our long driveway just as the school bus began cresting the hill. Typically, I throw the car in park with a casual, "Oh, I just thought I'd pick you up today" surprise (wink, wink).

I've been racking my brain for ages in order to share a companion story of a time when my older child became lost, but I cannot think of one. Is it a younger child thing? They see you've yet to permanently misplace the previous children, so their sense of security is higher? Or is it a boy thing? Do they just not feel any low-level panic when their parents disappear from their view? Do they feel a sense of freedom and space and anticipation when they realize they are riding solo, feet off the pedals, a breeze in their not-so-lonely hair? Does it awaken their sense of exploration?

Is that really what happened to Lewis and Clark?

Were they just supposed to go, explore a bit, but be back in an hour?

Wink, wink.

CHAPTER TWO

Remember Where He Came From

HE HAD A WHOLE OTHER FAMILY

It took me quite a while to appreciate that before I was even a blip on the radar, my husband had a life without me. That life included his own parents (at the very least) and possibly siblings, aunts, uncles, cousins, and grandparents. When he and his ex-wife married—he duplicated that entire set of relatives via her lineage. When their kids were born, they were born into that combined ancestry—and, likely, the focus of everyone's attention.

Divorce didn't end that.

Or at least it shouldn't have.

Until I was in the middle of a blended family, I'd never thought about the extensions in the lives of children who are carried through a divorce. I'd never thought about how far beyond the couple that the "we're getting divorced" conversation went. Yes, I knew it affected the children. But it also went up a pipeline to parents and the grandparents. That conversation went across the rails to siblings and cousins and aunts and uncles and godparents and neighbors and schools and church members. And, at a time when the focus should rightfully be placed primarily on those immediately affected (mom, dad, kids), everyone outside that circle is both ripe with advice and panicking about what will happen to their roles in the lives of all these people they have come to love. While the affected parties are working towards an amicable (that's the goal, right?) ending to a relationship, all other parties are clamoring to find out what kind of new beginning is starting for theirs.

There is grief. Parents hope for happy marriages for their children, not for marriages that start out great and peter out years down the road. Nobody ever sits at a wedding reception, fork in hand, thinking *oh, I hope they have steak at the next wedding as well!* And I suspect that in most cases—even in divorces whose landings are stuck perfectly with no drama or argument or sore losers—the family members on either side feel a strong loyalty to the afflicted. I can't say that I've ever heard the parents of a divorcee say *well, in fairness, **my** kid **was** the asshole in that relationship.* Even if both members of the couple defend the other to the very end, pleading with all to continue getting along and resist blame, well, people are people. When a divorce removes a member from the circle, there is a hole that is likely not acknowledged. Status quo for humans. Pretend the difficult things aren't there.

As I strolled into my relationship, I had no inkling that there was anyone that really cared about what happened to my husband's first marriage beyond him and his ex-wife. Naive? Table for one. In my case, because the movement from one relationship to the next seemed so, so fast to his family, there was no welcoming party present upon my arrival. My third-wheel position was assigned to me quickly: an extra body at family gatherings, *that girl he's dating now*, tucked back in a corner trying to figure out if there really was a place for me in this family's well-established world.

Because my husband and his ex-wife, for the most part, kept the demise of their marriage behind closed doors until it was right out in the open, most of his family didn't really understand that the end had been brewing for years and years.

What they saw as a rush to the next relationship was really a slow burn that started five years prior when the living-to-gether-separately stage was reached, occupying one house but no longer sharing sweet conversations, meals, or a bed. What they saw as a rush had years of effort and failure and denial and resignation behind it. What they saw was one face substituted with another at birthdays and holidays and graduations and weddings.

I suppose our situation was more challenging, as my husband was not very close with his extended family. If he had been, any low hums regarding the end of his first marriage would have been replaced with low hums of a new friend a few hours away and then of that friend becoming more than a friend and then of that friend thinking very carefully through her options and if she was doing the right thing or not. Instead, they saw one wife disappear from family events and a new girlfriend take her place shortly after. I suppose a reaction of leeriness is to be expected. Was I a rebound? Was I in it for the long haul? Did I just hop on the gravy train as it came through? Without knowing all the details of the divorce, how could they possibly trust that I would be any different? It's a bit of a spongy ground—truly, they didn't need to know all the details of the divorce or the events leading up to it. But then, how could they know that it was actually the right path?

I did not have a very slow entry into Rich's family circle. On my few visiting weekends, I did meet his mom, but that was it. When I moved to Richmond, it was just weeks before Max's birthday. I'd never hosted a kid's birthday party yet here were six of them hopping off the school bus with Max, followed by the arrival of various family members, all coming in and out of the front for the rest of that Friday evening, arms laden with presents. The focus was on Max. It was his birthday, after all, and it included an extra dose of "make it good as his parents just got divorced!" The focus was not on the short blonde hiding behind Rich, wondering just how one recovers from the resulting hurricane of seven seven-year-olds on a sugar high.

Adults came and went, nodding to me when introduced. There were no blurbs of *"So glad to meet you"* or *"Finally nice to put a face to your name"* or *"How are you finding this new town?"* Certainly no *"You probably are totally overwhelmed. Want to get a breath of fresh air?"* I lost count quickly of how many family members there were and how I was ever going to remember who belonged to whom and where they lived and were these people going to be my new friends and I hoped they liked me.

I'm not sure what the proper way is for regular relationships to be introduced to extended family, let alone relationships that begin after a divorce. As of today, I have yet to meet any of my children's significant others. I assume, as my children begin to dabble into dating, I will have to resist the urge to get too attached to any boyfriends or girlfriends, knowing that they will likely not last for the long haul. But as adults, how does that even work? In my husband's case, his first wife **was** someone he met as a teenager, whom he, admittedly, was led to marry so that his very Christian college would permit biblical relations. And that is not to say that the two weren't in love—they were, with lots of common interests—but at the base of it, they were still teens with teenage brains and probably with no business getting married. Still, the marriage lasted most of twenty years (though no one is sure if the last five should count).

During that twenty years, Rich's family came to know his ex-wife very well—the good and the bad. Prior to the birth of the kids, the good was on the heavy end of the scale. After the kids, for lots of reasons that I'm not sure I'm qualified to name, the scale started tipping heavily to the bad. My armchair diagnosis is a combination of being married to someone who had done a presto-change-o in a desire to have children at all (they'd both started the marriage in the "No kids" category but after 9/11, Rich changed camps) and how that would have sent me into a total panic when the first baby actually arrived.

I have thought of this because having children was something that Rich and I discussed. I was completely fine not having my own children and declined his hesitant offer to reverse his vasectomy. What would I do if he suddenly felt sure that one more child, my child!, was exactly what he wanted? If I agreed to it, and I likely would have, I would have then been shocked if getting pregnant was quick and easy. I would have been terrified if the runway was shortened due to dumb luck, leaving me no time to lean into the idea of being a mother slowly. The terror of "Holy hell, we just had a baby" would have quickly been silenced when Rich's family swooped in to lift this baby onto every pedestal available. Rich tells me that this is exactly what happened when Amelia was born, that she was celebrated as if she were the Dalai Lama, the Pope, and Mother Teresa all wrapped up in one perfect swaddle.

As I became absorbed into the family, I spent most of my initial time wondering why I wasn't feeling the same level of excitement and joy and love for these children that Rich's family did. Would I have felt the same way had I birthed them myself? Would I have watched the trail of well-wishers pass while wondering why I wasn't overjoyed at every tiny breath? I have no doubt that Rich's ex-wife loved (and loves) her children with all her heart. I also understand what it feels like to be surrounded by my husband's family as they watched me try to force my own love for them to meet their levels. I felt like I just couldn't grasp that rush of joy that everyone else had when the kids entered the room. I have felt like a failure while watching blessing after blessing bestowed on these children while I waited for my own existential bond to form. Was this the (step)mother's version of postpartum depression?

Grandchildren are the center of the universe in Rich's family. I often feel like the spouses are merely tolerated, but only because they come with the children. Grandchildren are the focus of every holiday, every birthday (whether theirs or not), every vacation, and every dime saved. I often wonder if anyone would notice if I skipped the circus of Christmas rather than take my relegated place in the background. I think of Rich's ex-wife and I wonder if she, too, felt like an outcast. She was a regular presence for fifteen years, though not so regular for the last five years of their marriage. Did the family notice that change? Were they concerned or caring?

I have now witnessed a decade of wonder in which, when something is the slightest bit off with one of the grandchildren, the elder family members immediately swoop in as if piloting rescue helicopters. This is not always welcome. When I first witnessed this phenomenon, it gave me comfort. I saw an emotional safety net for the entire family; myself included. I realized later that I was incorrect. The safety net was not available to me. I asked Rich if the safety net had been in place for him or for his ex-wife when they began to struggle with their marriage. No, not really. I wondered if that was because the extended family just didn't notice or if it was because it was easier to focus on the children with hope that the adults would figure it out.

I could not imagine that the finality of Rich's marriage ending was not revealed before the snowy night on which police cars were called to referee false accusations of domestic abuse. But, if so, if Rich's extended family simply *hadn't* noticed the drawn-out end to his first marriage, then perhaps the time, for them, before his second marriage, was not adequate. Would Rich's family have had time to process that a segment of their clan had fallen apart? There was a rush to the sides of the children, but, according to Rich, not nearly enough support for the adults. I wondered if anyone asked him what *he* needed to recover. I wondered if anyone asked his ex-wife, the mother of those blessed grandchildren, what they might do to help *her* move forward.

According to Rich, he had mentally checked out of his marriage years prior to meeting me, giving him time to resign, recommit, resign again, and grieve. The kids tell us of having an awareness of things turning sour within their home, but only on the surface. Rich met me at the exact right time. He was ready for a friend and confidante. His extended family, on the other hand, had no time to fully process the divorce. They were still learning what had happened as bits and pieces trickled out at the same moment in which I appeared on the scene, excited to meet this group that I'd heard so much about. In hindsight, Rich should have given his extended family a more appropriate time to heal and, perhaps, a clearer debrief. Instead of chatter about this new life Rich was building with his kids, there should have been chatter about how different the holidays or birthdays would look in the future. Rich certainly didn't expect (or ask) his extended family to say "goodbye" to his ex-wife, nor did he implore them to rally around me. The thought that Rich should guide this transition in his little family's status never crossed his mind.

One could argue that my presence in the children's lives was really only the business of Rich, his ex-wife, and me (oh yes, and our counselor). Instead, Rich was bombarded with questions immediately when my existence was announced. *What about the kids? What will happen to the kids if this relationship gets serious? What would Jyl's role be in their lives? Would she be able to step up as a mother? Would Rich continue to curtail his work schedule in order to be home with the children, or would Jyl be doing that? What about their (bio)mom? Where was she going to fit into all of this? Were Jyl and she going to share responsibilities and communicate about the children? Had Rich thought through all the brick walls that might pop up if he fast-tracked into a second marriage? Why would she move in so close to Christmas? What about her family? Does anyone even know what she likes?* It was as if, as Rich's first marriage was fading out, his family was watching his ex-wife slip out the back door, quietly. What they missed was me slipping in the front door.

Two states away, there was another family going through the same thing— Rich's former in-laws. I'm sure there is no blueprint on how to handle in-laws during a divorce. We did find out much later the ways in which the break could have been handled from our household. Just after Rich and I were married, Rich received a phone call from his former in-laws wanting to know how their grandchildren were doing. It had never occurred to Rich (or me) that they would love updates and, as the children were with us full time, we should have taken the initiative in supplying them. In the melee of the separation and the divorce and the dating and the remarriage, we never thought to share with Rich's former in-laws. They didn't know what grade the children were in or that Max was playing soccer and Amelia was playing the upright bass. They didn't know how tall the children had gotten or that we had joined a swim club or where we vacationed over spring break.

For some reason, this made me feel awful. Was this something else I had missed in the non-existent guide on how to have an instant family? I immediately set up a Facebook page with only two members: us and them. I promised to update it regularly with pictures of the children and updates about their lives. I resisted the urge to ask why? *Why was this my job? Was this normal?* For years, I cropped myself out of any pictures posted, lest it seemed like I thought I deserved to have moved into their daughter's spot. I was paranoid about how they might feel, seeing pictures of me laughing and smiling and loving the children.

They, too, were grieving the dissolution of the marriage.

They, too, were so sorry about how the family had fallen apart. They had loved Rich as their own, and then he was gone. They had loved Rich and their daughter together, as a couple, and now I was in her place. The strain of divorce extends so much further than I had ever imagined. The least I could do was have compassion for this second set of grandparents, as they also processed it.

I was in a strange position. Rich's family, local to us, seemed to want nothing to do with me. Rich's former in-laws, two states away, ate up any news about the kids with appreciation. On occasion, I would receive tear-filled phone calls from his former in-laws filled with appreciation for jumping in so willingly. I would feel proud and accomplished, but then, later, that would switch to anger. *Why was this my job? Why wasn't my husband handling this? Why wasn't anybody **but me** responsible for this?*

I did have to go to my counselor, Rachel, for that answer as I leaned to the side of my husband's dislike of phone calls, emails, notes, or anything administrative. Rachel told me that it was important to remember that Rich was still very much the man who had divorced their daughter. They were more likely to reach out to me, a relative stranger, than him, who hurt their own child. It was important to all parties that the children maintain a relationship with their (bio)mother's family but, at that time while everyone was still healing, it was only me who could handle it.

Did I always handle it well? No. I'd see that pictures from our family outings were then posted on Rich's ex-wife's social media, as if she were the one who created the memories. This would spark arguments between Rich and me, as I felt that she was taking credit for my hard work. I'd make promises to shut down the page, stop playing the role of the great communicator, and leave it up to everyone else to figure out. Rich would bring me back from the ledge, reminding me just how much what I was doing meant to the grandparents. He'd remind me of my quest for compassion and how I might also need to give some to **her**.

Yes. All true. But I still hated it.

I didn't realize that there would be so many times within this made-for-me family when I would have to stop and think about how my actions (or non-actions) would affect the children. *Be the bigger person? Ugh? Really?!?* I didn't always want to be the bigger person. Who does? There have been many times in my normal life when my interest in being the bigger person was zero, let alone this new life with children. I may seem destined for a Nobel Prize on the surface: sharing stories with in-laws I didn't even know, passing along dates of school activities or start times for soccer games to people who could *easily* access the information without my assistance. When I weighed that against what would run through the kids' minds should family members miss those big events, I carried on. Well, I carried on after assigning Rich to the task and then realizing that schedules, etc. really were in my wheelhouse. I did not always maintain these bridges between relatives peacefully, but I did maintain them silently. I dreaded hearing the voice in my head saying, *"You have to do this for the kids."* I dreaded hearing Rich's voice saying, *"We need to remember how that will look to the kids."* The kids. They are innocent bystanders that I had committed to protecting indefinitely.

Yes, it did seem like it was not "my job." But, in committing to their father, I also committed to caring for them. That was something I was unable to grasp until they were in my care, full time, looking to me for guidance and love.

No, I did not get a welcoming party from their extended family, but it is likely because they were just not ready to throw it. I wondered why nobody seemed happy that Rich was happy being with me and that the kids were happily getting to know me. Shouldn't that have counted for something? I wish someone could have told me then to simply be patient.

And that, while I was patiently waiting, to focus on the kids and building my relationship with them. In the end, that is what would count the most.

MONSTER IN LAW

Remember that whole section about my husband having a whole separate family before I came into the picture? While I'm not going to narrow down all of the players, I am going to touch on my experiences with my mother-in-law. Some are lucky to gain a mother-in-law who sings their praises, offers constructive assistance, and leaves the steamroller parked (*Reader, if that is you, tell your mother-in-law "Thank you" right this very minute*). That has not been the case for us and has been the source of near separation more than once. I'm not kidding. This topic is one of the few where being stubborn has saved my husband and me. If I did not have a stubborn streak; if I did not have an unlimited desire *not* to let her drive me away, I would have packed my bags years ago.

My husband had already been dealing with his mother's interjection into his marriage and parenting skills for nearly twenty years prior to my arrival. He had learned how to put her unwelcome words aside, as if hidden in a box, long ago. I thought he was unfazed by the flow of disparagement, but he actually had given up any more attempts to reel her in. I was shocked to encounter a woman who watched my every inter-action with her grandchildren with a microscope. I was shocked to hear her putting me down in lieu of offering sup-port. I did not (and will not) understand how she carried such malice for me, someone who had only good intentions in mar-riage and (step)parenting.

When my husband's first marriage was ending, it was his

mother whom he often turned to. He has no siblings, wasn't close with his father, and, naturally, sought comfort from his mother. She walked the tumultuous path with him. When the waning marriage reached the point of separation, she welcomed Rich into her home while he picked up the pieces of his shattered life. The unintended sidebar was that she felt vindicated in predicting the divorce. As Rich says, his mother may not have caused the end of his first marriage, but she certainly did not help save it. Rich's mother seemed to jump on any cracks in his first marriage, even alerting him to suspected trouble, where there was initially none, causing tension between him and his ex-wife. By his own words, Rich spent the last quarter of his marriage defending his marriage to his mother as she offered a continuous narrative on what his ex-wife was doing wrong. Because he was so occupied with coming to her defense, Rich then (admittedly) missed the actual red flags.

After Max was born, Rich's ex-wife began spending frequent nights out with new friends while Rich stayed home. If Rich were away for work, his mother would heed the call to watch the children. This pattern increased, causing a rift and an eventual total breakdown of Rich and his ex-wife's relationship. Rich's ex-wife drained their shared bank account after each payday, had at least one affair, and abused prescription drugs. Rich's mother witnessed it all.

The night that the family refers to as "the bad night" ended with both children loaded into a police car. Rich's ex-wife accused him of abuse, in front of their daughter, which caused Amelia, nine at the time, to bolt from their home into a snowy night wearing only pajamas. Several police cars arrived with a K-9 squad to track her down. When she was found, both Amelia and Max were loaded into the squad car as Rich and his ex-wife were ordered to take at least a twenty-four-hour breather. Rich's mother witnessed it all.

While his mother had endless empathy for the children, Rich felt her anger towards him as if she was silently saying, "*I told you so.*"

As Rich began putting his life back together, he met me. It was before the ink was dry on the divorce, yes, but it was purely a relationship built on the here and now without much thought on the future. Today, we call it Rich's recovery relationship. We lived three hours apart and were simply enjoying each other's adult company with no initial intentions for anything beyond that. Still, this put Rich's mother back on high alert. She had just spent years watching her grandchildren's lives get blown apart. She voiced fear that he was more concerned with rebuilding his own happiness than her grandchildren's.

I was confused as to why this woman whom I'd never met would not like me. I was independent, successful, and full of good intentions. She perceived me as a gold digger latching onto the insecurities of her newly single son. This was foreign to me, that someone would dislike me at all, let alone before they even met me. I had heard from Rich how *different* I was from his ex-wife. I couldn't calculate, then, why his mother would be so unenthused for him to be with someone (me) who was the complete opposite of this woman (his ex-wife) whom she held great disdain for.

As Rich and I realized that we were developing a relationship that was not only wonderful but worthy of making permanent, his mother became even less on board. Though Rich and I waited an entire year to bring his children into our relationship, his mother felt it was unnecessary. When I began to form positive relationships with the children, she voiced suspicion of my motives. When I finally packed my things and moved north, Rich's mother was not welcoming.

Of course, Rich and I did make mistakes along the way, but we always did what we thought was best at each stage in our relationship. Still, each time we faltered, his mother was there, ready to pounce with another look of, *"I told you so!"* I often told Rich that I felt like she was standing on our porch, peering in the window, hoping to see cracks in this relationship too— and providing her an ideal moment to swoop in and protect her grandchildren again.

I tried so hard to build a relationship with my mother-in-law. I asked if we could have a standing lunch date in order to get to know each other. As I had moved to a town in which I knew nobody, she seemed like a logical first acquaintance. And, by getting to know her, I'd have the added benefit of gaining insight into raising the children. After our first lunch together, she declined further dates.

As I got more involved with the children, I'd periodically seek out her advice. I made the mistake of voicing my frustration with the behavior of the kids one evening, and she took that as a personal insult to them. Rich was out of town on a work trip and his mother had him pulled out of a meeting to alert him, as I'd said the children were *"being jerks."* She was shocked to hear Rich reply that, yes, sometimes the kids were jerks. At Rich's suggestion, I included his mother in as many activities as I could. She would often follow each event with a phone call to Rich telling him what I'd done or said wrong. She even suggested letting the children move in with her rather than continuing to let them live with me.

This went on until, eventually, the three of us (Rich, me, and his mother) landed in a therapist's office where we spent months hashing it all out. We spent months deep diving through six years of assumptions about each other, debunking each one with hopes of a fresh start. Our relationship seemed to finally settle until two more years had passed and she asked to speak to Rich and me. Neither of us had any inkling what was to come until we were sitting in our living room with her as she told Rich that I continued to be the worst part of her grandchildren's lives. She included a not-so-veiled request that Rich end our marriage by indicating that she would no longer have a relationship with him if I was still involved.

This while I was sitting across the room from her. In my home. None of us knew that the children were sitting on the stairs listening to what we now call Grammageddon.

It was the best and worst thing that could have happened.

I felt amazing. After years and years and years, I was freed. The weight of trying to please her left me as I finally understood what Rich had been telling me for years: Pleasing his mother was unachievable. For the first time, I felt like our home was *our home* and not just the house where her grandchildren lived. This was not the first time we'd been summoned for this type of conversation, but it was her most pointed attempt to create a split between Rich and me. Yet, this time, instead of feeling beat down, I felt uplifted. Her words woke up my confidence. I was a good parent. I was an amazing parent. I knew she was out of line and incorrect in assuming otherwise. I also knew that I'd never let her opinion cause me to question my ability to mother my (step)children again.

At the same time, I felt awful. My husband felt defeated by his mother's inability to support either of his wives. He felt that he had failed *me* as he failed to convince his mother that my love for our family was genuine. He felt the final nail in the coffin of her acceptance and trust for him. I felt awful for each time that I had urged him to defend me to his mother, now understanding that it was all pointless. I had been asking him to do the impossible, though he had told me many times that it was just that. We'd both spent the bulk of our first decade of marriage dealing with unnecessary stress because I didn't believe him when he told me that his mother would never change.

I wasn't the only one who felt oddly invigorated after Grammageddon. The kids were old enough to realize that something unfair was happening to someone they loved dearly. They began to voice realizations that their grandmother had been manipulating them for years by asking leading questions, always trying to get them to say something about me that would confirm her suspicions of my character. They became less eager to spend time with her, as they were no longer willing to deal with the prodding. They quietly upped their support of me, making sure I knew that they believed in my love for them.

A secondary fallout was that the children now had past memories stirred up, though these related to years of disparaging remarks about their (bio)mom. They recounted the numerous times that their grandmother reminded them of the (bio)mother's shortfalls. At younger ages, they likely didn't have the mental capacity to understand what was happening, but after Grammageddon, those tucked-away memories flooded to life. They then sat on the same couch that my mother-in-law had, voicing guilt for not standing up for either of their mothers when their grandmother spoke unfairly about us.

Clearly, there were no winners in Grammageddon, but it did point me to a more final understanding of how the entirety of Rich's past relationship with his mother landed me in her target zone. Right or wrong, she placed so much of what occurred throughout the unraveling of her son's first marriage into his second marriage, with no cause. Yes, we do struggle at times, but no differently than any other family. We are relatively normal, actually.

It saddens me because, after so much work to build our family, she does not reap any of the joy that we now experience day in and day out. We are a stronger family because of what we have been through together. We will continue to thrive because we persevered. While my mother-in-law continues to look for cracks in our familial armor, she is missing out on our amazing successes.

REMEMBER WHERE HE CAME FROM

I was washing the pizza stone recently, and I thought, *wait, when did we get a pizza stone?* Which is when I remembered that we didn't get a pizza stone. It was something that came to us via my husband's previous marriage. I bowed up a little thinking, *"how dare he keep this reminder of his past?"* which is when my grown-up brain kicked in and started listing all the kitchen items that I had brought with me. I brought them and there was never a complaint pointing to the reminders of my single days moving in with me. Was I really going to be upset about a pizza stone? Five years ago, maybe, yes. But now, with all that time under my belt, no. The reality is my husband has a past. Present tense. Yes, his past was past tense, but it will always be here in the present with him, shaping who he is today and how he approaches so many things that live in our world together.

As the new wife, I completely underestimated how much that baggage would affect our lives together. Both the physical stuff (things "they" had bought together that carried memories) and non-tangibles (memories and stories and events) seemed to constantly trip us up at the start.

I'm certain that my husband also didn't know how much of his past would create roadblocks in our present. I won't go as far as saying that the past should not be a roadblock at all—I think that is impossible—but it is a full-time job figuring out ways to allow it to reside in the present without causing tension. I will go as far as saying that this is certainly different for males and females. My husband could have cared less about my past, never once flinching when I brought up old boy-friends or pulling out a T-shirt that I'd gotten on a trip a year prior with people that were not him. In the meantime, I was trying to hide knickknacks that the kids had bought with their mother behind items that I had brought from my single life.

Bigger than the knickknacks or the stories, though, were the kids. They were the most important thing that Rich brought with him from his previous marriage. And what came with the kids in the most gigantic griefcase of all? The guilt he carried for putting them through the divorce and upending their world. My husband knows for sure that the path taken to get to today was the right one. My husband knows that the divorce was an absolute necessity to find a life where he (and therefore the kids) could find happiness again. My husband knows the divorce should have come years before it actually did and that, maybe, they had wasted too much time remaining married because they were afraid to upend the kids' worlds. The griefcase carries a lot of compartments for guilt. It will take a long time to unpack. It will take a lot of permission-to-dismiss for that guilt to be eased. It will never really go away, always lurking with feelings to be brought to the surface.

We all have pasts. The past that arrives in a second marriage is just much more neon and annoying and in your face.

For quite some time, I thought the answer to the "guilt roadblock" was that we should have taken more time between marriages, though it was an option that we were not able to take (because, hindsight, right?). I also suspect that unusable solution allowed me to place the roadblock fully on Rich's plate. *If he had had more time between marriages, he could have worked through all those feelings of letting the kids down or watching them suffer or wanting to make up for the not-so-great years.* In my mind, when he and I were tasked with making a significant decision involving the kids, those guilty feelings would begin to swirl around in his head and heart and create another emotional dust storm. It was easy when I believed that the roadblock was fully attributed to the guilt on his plate.

I eventually realized that my role was to help him through the guilt. I also realized that the time to do that was NOT during those significant decision-making moments. I was honestly too new to parenting to understand parental guilt, and he was too far into it to understand why I couldn't tap into it. In the meantime, we both wanted to strangle his ex-wife each time we went from calm to catastrophe because, really, this was all her fault, right? Of course, yes, that was just a defense mechanism used to hide our real feelings of anxiety; we really weren't going to strangle anyone.

Where did the guilt appear in our household? Many places. One of those most common was in disciplining the kids. It was a frequently ridden merry-go-round driven and deeply affected by that guilt. There was an underlying whisper that because the kids have already been through *so* much and had handled it as valiantly as they could, they should get a sort of hall pass on ever feeling uncomfortable again in their lives.

I came into this new household from a life of single-girl luxury. The thought of having to take the helm (or even a share) of an entire household was overwhelming. And I really do mean the household. I had lived by myself in a three-bedroom townhouse. The only one I had to follow up with or clean up after was **me**. Which meant managing a kitchen for one, a living room in which I was the only occupant, and the master bedroom in which the most clutter was a bed that was half unmade. Fast forward to four people, two of whom were under the age of ten, and I was slapped across the head with the real definition of clutter and disorganization. Looking back, of course, I now realize that in comparison, none of us were actually even that messy. It was really just typical kid clutter—backpacks and shoes and toys—but it was still total culture shock. And, yes, it actually **was** devastating to step on a Lego for the first time.

The thought that I was now responsible for keeping a house three times bigger and three times fuller than my previous one was almost too much. My go-to coping strategy was a walk back to how I was raised: with a list of chores. I don't think I was a month into the new arrangement before I brought this up to Rich. *Couldn't we give the kids some responsibilities?* He balked. Maybe my suggested to-dos were too hard; off to the internet I went where I found lists and lists and lists of age-specific chores. I re-approached. He balked again. We took it to our counselor; she did not balk. We were guided to write down a quick daily duty chart for the kids and I felt myself able to breathe a bit better. I was getting help. We presented it to the kids. They were not impressed. They were also not interested. We leaped on another merry-go-round of the kids forgetting the daily list, me being frustrated, and Rich trying to wash it all away with excuses for them.

I know now that it wasn't at all that Rich wasn't invested in teaching the kids to care for the space around them. Nor was he turning aside from giving them responsibilities. It was that his approach to those things included years of emotional grief and guilt. His first wife did not keep a clean house. He had never felt that the kids should be put in charge of the piles of laundry she'd leave lying around or to monitor the counters for crumbs and grease or to know that the rugs should be vacuumed at least once a week or that there shouldn't be dirty dishes left on the side tables. And he was right. But he was also projecting a code red situation brought on by a poor house-keeping trigger and applying it to what I thought was a fairly simple request: that I not spend every night running laundry, making beds, and cleaning up piles of toys while I was learning to cook for four (one who had a chicken nugget, mac and cheese fetish), juggling school folders, continuing to work full time, and telling myself over and over that I chose this.

When I would tell Max to go back upstairs and make his bed, Rich would hear the start of that previous cycle clicking into place—that this request would lead to Max not only making his bed but also taking over the day-to-day management of the house. I did not understand that. And he did not understand that that was not my intention. And neither understood that it was something we should have talked about because neither of us knew yet that there was something to be unpacked. This may all sound like my husband was not involved in the home management. That is not true. But he'd gone from a situation in which he was traveling five days a week and not involved in it, during which time he knew the lack of housekeeping was "off," but during which time there was really nothing he could do about it. And, not knowing any better, he also assumed that when a woman was handed a house and children, her body would magically become flooded with mom hormones. Which is now hilarious as, well, that clearly didn't work in round one either.

Guilt-gate was exacerbated by Rich's mother's involvement. She got wind of the chores and raised her own red flag. She was right on board with coddling these two tiny victims of divorce for as long as possible. Her approach was not to recognize the win of raising responsible kids; it was to feed Rich's feelings of guilt by making offhand comments on why I expected them to do all the work. They weren't being asked to whip out a twenty-foot ladder and spit shine second-story windows; they were being asked to spray a mirror with Windex and run a paper towel over it. This did not result in a clear mirror most days, but it did instill the groundwork for lessons down the road. We accepted our roles of the adults who would come behind a child attempting to vacuum and *really* vacuum, but we did it in secret, allowing the kids to experience those take-pride-in-your-work moments.

It has taken nearly a decade for Rich to start letting go of some of that guilt he carried into our marriage, as there are so many benchmarks to which he can attribute it. He did not protect the kids from watching their parents' marriage devolve (guilt). He wished he had separated from their mother more quickly to stop the relational bleeding (guilt). If he had done that, the bad night never would have happened (holy guilt). If he had known the kids were responsible for themselves whenever he was out of town, Amelia would not have felt pressured into taking on a mothering role for her little brother (guilt). If he'd paid attention to the finances, he'd have recognized that his (ex)wife was not paying the bills and was leading them into debt (guilt, with a side of feeling stupid). If he'd paid attention to the mail, he'd have seen the threatening letters from the banks, credit cards, and utility companies (guilt, with a side of feeling stupid). If he'd been more available to the school, he'd have found out that sometimes the kids smelled unclean or had not been eating well at home or didn't seem to be getting enough sleep or were afraid that something was wrong with their mom (guilt). If, if, if ... he would have **protected them**.

Which is the bottom-line source of all the guilt he came to me with, **them** in tow.

He was not going to make that mistake again. Ever.

And he very innocently overshot the mark. I've used chores as an example, but the effects of guilt extend on and on. It is a constant "ding" that pops up in my husband's belly whenever he sees that the children are struggling or disagreeing or pushing back.

We've had battles over punishments and grades and restrictions on electronics and whether something I was seeing in one or the other kid was something that should be addressed, and 99 percent of the pushback I'd feel from him was his fear that his kids would, again, feel he did not protect them. The trickle-down was him not wanting the kids to be uncomfortable, an inability to tell them *no*, and certainly not wanting to appear to be choosing my side over theirs. He aimed to be cool and laid back and secure and to provide a home in which everything was fine at all times with a complete absence of triggers for arguments. Any potential moments of strife were brushed under the carpet as quickly as possible, which usually left me standing alone, jaw dropped, and feeling very much like an outsider.

In the early years, I mistook most of it for him just not wanting to do the hard parts of parenting, leading to a frustrated outburst of *"You are so lucky that you found me so that I could do all the dirty work!!"* And, for years, that thought really did clang around in the back of my head. I was building a life as a taskmaster and a disciplinarian in response to my own loss of stability, and it was unintentionally easy for him to let it happen because of that guilt. It's taken nearly a decade for me to understand that what I really had was a husband who was a father to two children who were ripped out of their happy life and for which he felt entirely responsible. I had a husband who was a father to two children for whom he felt immensely sorry and from whom he never wanted to see a sad and confused and angry face looking up at him again. I had a husband who had an impossible task to separate out the feelings his children carried from the divorce versus the feelings his children carried from just being regular kids.

As we look back now and classify our mistakes, the word that constantly pops up is "time." All of the feelings planted throughout the process of divorce don't actually start bearing fruit until the next phase starts. We landed on that next phase with a naive assumption that all would be fine going forward because we were starting this thing where we were putting that jumbled puzzle of lives back together. The rose-colored glasses were thrown on—we knew where we wanted to get as a new family, but we had no idea just how many hiccups and speed bumps and giant potholes were sitting in our way. We lost patience with each other constantly because we did not know we were supposed to have an extra-large stock of it at the ready. I liken it to a Saturday to-do list: It looks like it should only take an hour, but three have passed when it's finally complete. We approached the blending of our worlds in terms of months when, in order to do it successfully, we should have been thinking in terms of years.

Yes. There is baggage. But do not immediately dump it all out onto the floor upon arrival. Uncover it in pieces slowly and as a team. Remember what your goals are, together, and be deliberate about getting there in a way that doesn't exacerbate the pain that was already tied around his ankles like a heavy ball and chain.

And, for goodness' sake, if things get heated, walk away briefly. Take the time to write down a reminder of what your goals are. Write down where you are going and why. Take the time to write down what your other half is likely *feeling*, rather than how they are acting.

Take the time to ensure there will be more time, together, down the road.

Which Way's Up?

Bread Wars

Before: *For as long as I can remember, once each year, my father cooked one thing. Well, maybe that's not entirely fair. For much of my childhood, he did fix dinner for a whole week during my mother's annual trek to visit her own parents' home. It wasn't a perfect week, like the time he attempted to perfect the hamburger by pre-stuffing them with ketchup and mustard. Do not try this if you value your children's baby teeth.*

My father's actual shining moment came each Thanksgiving when he was assigned the stuffing. I'm not sure at what point my dad started taking his stuffing duties so seriously, though likely with the birth of the interwebs and infinite recipe access. These birthed weeks of planning: digging through recipes, planning out the grocery needs, and an early Thanksgiving morning wake-up call.

The stuffing ritual is what I remember the most about our family's Thanksgiving. There was really no telling what would be in the stuffing beyond bread. Some years, sausage. Some years, walnuts and apples. Some years, oysters. Some years, raisins and wild rice.

As Rich and I prepared to host our first Thanksgiving together, nerves were high. I had basically just unzipped my suitcase and hid my shoes under the bed of my new home and, here we were, preparing dinner for both sides of our respective families. Oh, and it would also be the first time our respective families would be meeting each other. Obviously, on "our" side of the familial fence, we went the obvious route of winning the hearts of new relatives by providing a zany stuffing dish.

Thank you, Daddy.

It wasn't until the following Thanksgiving that I learned

that it was not actually the stuffing that won anyone over (okay, it's funny to write now, knowing that there are still hearts to be won). It turns out that while everyone was nodding and smiling and digging in, many were in the midst of an emotional tailspin because there was no Stovetop on the table.

Err, what?

Yes. There has never been another discussion about what kind of stuffing would be served at Thanksgiving and there has certainly never been a suggestion lobbed to our household to bring that particular dish. While I do miss my dad's stuffing, it's probably a blessing that my parents have spent the holiday at the beach ever since, the distance north deemed too far (if the only option is Stovetop—kidding).

I have silently supported my beloved husband's strong opinion on Stovetop. I felt his panic just last year when we did our Thanksgiving shopping too late and found the Stovetop aisle completely empty. I trudged along in the spirit of saving the week while we went from store to store in search of hope. I stopped asking, "Is it not still Thanksgiving without Stovetop?"

I had been edging closer to rebellion for years. Last year tipped me.

This year, I went over. A few weeks prior to the big day, I came across a recipe for Chorizo Cornbread Stuffing. Come again? My favorite meat? With delicious, sweet bread? Sign me up! This was my chance! My one moment in time! In my drooling excitement, I forgot myself and blurted out my plans to grace the table with this delight.

Father Pilgrim was not amused.

Father Pilgrim had a very strong reaction.

For a recap on the "No, actually, it is not Thanksgiving without Stovetop," lecture, please dial 1-800-I-LIKE-IT-DRY. I'm not sure my eyes have returned to their normal *size brought by the shock of the pushback I got when suggesting (innocently) to make a non-boxed, flavored stuffing.*

I backpedaled and dodged and weaved, finally landing at "but we can bring both!"

I realized this would be an ongoing conversation. And it was. Daily. For two weeks.

There may have been some bantering about my superior stuffing and the possibility that I'd be the new Belle of the Turkey Ball. During one slightly heated conversation, I called his mom so she could confirm that it was fine to bring a second stuffing option.

Does that sound like I told on him? Yes. I told on him.

I started my prep work on Thanksgiving Eve, trying to get chorizo-yum as close to complete as I could so that I could hide it in the refrigerator before Rich came home. It was a good plan, except the kitchen gave me away with the lingering scent of chorizo and cornbread.

I held my breath and waited for the fallout.

No fireworks. He even asked about timing and my oven needs and how I would be placed into the timing of cooking on Thanksgiving Day.

Perhaps we would survive this tribulation.

After*: The Stovetop was better. The end.*

My gawd, woman, is there a lesson in here? ***Fine. My stuffing made its debut on the same island as the rest of the food (at Rich's grandmother's home). It was, however, quietly moved to a less prominent location quite quickly and probably by someone who had no idea what it was, other than **not Stovetop.*

Did it hurt my feelings? Yes.

In an unrelated discussion, I did hear someone say, "But we've done it this way for years."

Oh.

Traditions are a wonderful thing and should be altered

with caution.

Should there be some flexibility in them, especially with the growth of a family? YES.

I think of Rich's first experience eating oysters. I wouldn't have known it was his first time (though I was with him) as he jumped right in, later telling me that, in his words, he didn't want to look like a pussy. He has so many stories like this, where he went against his family's grain because he wanted to do something different for himself.

He does not come from a clan of adventurous people. That is foreign to me.

I do come from a clan of adventurous people. That is foreign to him.

I have learned that there **is** some comfort in knowing exactly how a holiday will go: who will arrive when, who will cook what, who will tell which story, and who will sit where. He has learned to jump into crazy town and see where the wind takes you. That works for us.

But that doesn't mean it will work for our extended families.

Do we have nice family get-togethers? We do, and they are getting better now that we understand the difference in dynamics.

His people are Stovetop: always easy, always the same, always delicious.

Mine? A bit more complicated, a bit more out of the box, and also quite delicious.

CHAPTER THREE

Standing Down

STAND DOWN

Are these your kids? Yes. Well, maybe. It's a loaded question, actually, affected by so many variables. How old are they? How much involvement are you expecting to have? How much do you want? What about their biological mother? What's their relationship with her? Where do they reside most of the time? What is your husband's role in their upbringing? Is he super hands-on or does he just go for the every-other-weekend flyby? No, there is no easy answer to that question of whether or not these are or will become your kids.

The only place that offers an easy answer is love. Kids just want to be loved. The more love that kids can stuff into their tanks, the better. The more people providing that love, the better. If you are willing to get basic and sit among that established population that is filling their tank then, yes, those are your kids. Or they will be. You just have to have a whole lot of patience to get there. Unfortunately, having patience when entering a blended family situation is mostly impossible. You are more likely to want to show some immediate control with your mom qualifications by launching into a list of ideas of how you could make things better. Maybe your grandma was Mary Poppins or your dad's best friend was Dr. Spock. Maybe

you have a doctorate in early childhood development as it re-
lates to children of divorce, and you did your studies in the
same school that your new kids attend. Maybe you've been a
mother to your own kids for years. Maybe you just think you
have way more common sense than anybody else.

None of that qualifies you for anything at all when the children you inherit are products of a previous relationship. You
may have been a parent prior, but you haven't been a parent
to these specific children. Those positions are full. It doesn't
seem fair because it isn't. It's also not about you. You will be
told frequently to think about what the kids have been
through, what they are going through, and how it might affect
them going forward— all very important reminders to tuck
into the back of your head. What you won't want to think
about, and likely won't be suggested, is what their mother has
been through, what she is going through, and how it might
affect her going forward. If you come in hot, wearing a Super
Mom cape, all parties involved will immediately be turned off.
And while you might think you don't care whether or not the
ex-wife likes you, you should. And if you think you don't care
what the kids think about you, you may have gotten on the
wrong ride.

It is absolutely backwards to ask yourself to walk a mental
mile in your kids' (bio)mom's shoes but do it anyway. She is a
mom, but she is also someone's ex-wife. She fell in love with
the person you are now married to. She built a life with the
person you now share a bed with. That life that she worked so
hard for was not supposed to disappear. Even if she and your
husband peacefully agreed upon *"Oh hey, this just isn't working"* as a marital conclusion, I have no doubt that it is **still**
devastating and shocking and full of second-guesses. Very few
people start a marriage with the mental safety net of *"Well, we
can always get divorced later ..."* That's reserved for the Hol-
lywood set.

There is grief for all parties, including the ex-wife. And her grief is not just her own, it is grief she holds for her kids, as well. It doesn't matter how young they are (or old) or how much happier they will be without the tension or strife. When kids are added into the dissolution, the level of devastation rises. She will feel defeated. She will never whisper this to her ex-husband and, certainly, not to you, but she will feel like a failure. At being a wife. At preserving her happily ever after. At protecting her children from sadness. She will try to start her new life but will feel pulled to help her kids do the same.

Men tend to dig into work or a hobby or anything they can to shield them from real emotions. Women tend to throw themselves on the couch and wallow. But with kids? There are still schools and sports and lessons and groceries and appointments; there is no time for wallowing or hobbies as both parties try to maintain a sense of normalcy for the kids. Perhaps she has to get a new job, a new apartment, a new car, find her own insurance, and while she is trying to navigate all of that— SURPRISE!— you show up. Imagine. She is probably shocked and feeling replaceable and bowing up with a strong need to mark as much territory as possible.

And there you are, the new girl, flitting around her with the face of new love, a perpetual smile of bliss. Though you are certainly not trying to rub it in anyone's face, it is rubbing. Leave space for her to breathe. Be kind. Show grace. Yes have boundaries, but with a sprinkle of compassion. You may feel like you've won the jackpot, but she is feeling like it is her jackpot. Imagine her watching as you come around more and more frequently and begin to enmesh yourself into her ex-husband's life which, yes, includes her kids. And imagine her kids liking you so much, like you are a new toy or puppy or candy. Any time she spends with her kids is time she is hearing your name over and over, salt in a very raw wound. She's probably thinking not great thoughts and wondering how you could possibly be this much fun and also, what happened to her life?! Your arrival marks the final bell to the end of her former life, the one that she thought she'd live until *death do us part*. All she's got left from that former life is those kids. And there you are, wanting to capture their attention and volunteer at their school and wear a Soccer Mom shirt at their games.

Can you imagine?

That is why you need to stand down. Slow your roll. Stay behind the scenes. Quietly settle in.

It can get ugly fairly quickly if you rush in to be the savior of the hurting children. Yes, your husband will be your champion as you turn their frowns (that he's pegged as his fault) upside down, but you must ease in slowly.

Invest your zest into taking some time to examine how those children are actually feeling. We often think of the grade school set as malleable and resilient and not really aware of what is happening. Not true. They are very much aware that their lives have gone a bit awry as they learn that parents don't necessarily live together forever. Sure, they probably knew that from other kids— the likelihood that they are the first ones at school to be children of divorce is slim—but their understanding of what that meant probably ended at *oh, some kids' moms and dads live in different houses.* It was something that happened in other families that were weird and peripheral. Now it is happening in theirs. They may be tired of hearing *you'll understand when you're older.* Even the simple bits are too complicated to rectify. But now they have parents in two houses and some stupid calendar or whiteboard with color coding that is supposed to make everything all clear.

It's not clear.

And there you are, this *friend* of your dad's that keeps showing up. Yes, you are always so happy to see them, but you also want to take them shopping and buy things that they typically don't wear, or you want to cook them meals full of things that you don't know they don't eat and are moving the prized chicken nuggets to the trash. This is not the time to approach with a plate of broccoli. You may feel the trepidation and wonder why you aren't making inroads. It's quite simple, really: They just want their mom and dad to live together again in the same house they lived in before. Really. If you could make that happen, you would be a real hero. Then they would eat the broccoli.

That is why you need to stand down.

It is the advice that I *wanted* to take. Instead, I was thrown into the deep end of parenting from the high dive. I don't think our story is the norm (I hope not) and I write this from a *"years later ... things are in a better place"* perspective. I write this as we finally feel a small glimmer of confidence that our kids' mother is getting her life back together. It took us all years to get here. She had so many challenges that went on for years after the divorce, ranging from evictions to arrests to prescription medication abuse. Because my husband traveled (and we didn't have the blessed gift of hindsight), I was often left to pick up the pieces. I certainly didn't want to, and my husband never insisted that I swoop in, but when given the details of whatever the latest situation was, I often landed on *okay, here is our best option, and here is where I will shine should the kids ever get wind of this.* Which sounds like I was aiming for a trophy. What I really was aiming for was peace. I did not know very much and did not take enough of the advice I was given, but I did hear from someone early on to always show grace when I was able to. That one stuck with me. That became my mantra in dealing with sticky moments, that someday, way down the road, the kids would remember that I had shown grace. Even in those times when I had every right and opportunity to look away or walk away, I had, instead, chosen grace.

REMAIN STANDING DOWN

I know. Didn't we already discuss the ex-wife? We're going to do it again.

Growing up, you likely didn't think, *"My fairy tale? Oh, my fairy tale involves getting married and my Prince Charming will have come to me via a previous marriage involving a now-ex-wife making me wife number two (or three, or four ...) and he will have a whole history and memories and maybe even kids from that previous marriage."* Neither did I. I was more in the realm of *"Oh, hey, it'd be cool if I get married, but also, eff that, maybe I'll just stay single forever."* Most people land somewhere in between. Having an ex-wife is not an ideal bonus prize. At best, it is slightly awkward. At worst, you are often placed in the middle of one situation or another in which things are not great with that ex-wife and that not-greatness seeps into your life. You thought you could be an innocent bystander (or maybe even a voyeur) to the ex-wife drama, but, nope, you are a participant. It is a tightrope full of moments where you want to offer a rather loud and ugly opinion (and you will) but on which you really have to learn to control your thoughts and words (and you will). If you aren't able to speak calmly and reasonably and without all the emotion that will bubble up, you will find that you are placing that ex-wife right smack in the middle of your relationship with your husband and, oh yes, your kids.

First and most important rule when it comes to the ex: Never, ever, never, ever —and I can't stress this enough— never, ever disparage this woman in front of those kids. Ever. These may be your kids too now, yes. But where did they come from? Her. And who did they belong to first? Her. And who will bow up immediately when you suggest her darlings clean up after themselves or suffer a consequence? Her. It sucks. If you've landed in a situation where the ex-wife carries the entire mom load, leaving you on standby as a sort of hip, cool friend, that's awesome. If you've landed where I did and find yourself being given the mom reins with a no-returns policy, it is very difficult. I was given the reins, the carriage, the horses, the wheels, and the barn where it was all stored—I did not ask for any of it. I really thought I was going to be a part-timer. I completely ignored my future husband's many hints that we would have the kids full time. And by hints, I mean, he blatantly told me that he would definitely, absolutely, without a doubt have his kids full time.

I just wish he'd been clearer.

My husband's ex-wife and I are just starting to have a relationship that doesn't involve rolling eyes or snarky comments. We have spent eight years orbiting around each other. I really thought that we would be this magical parenting force, bouncing ideas off one another or sharing our frustrations. Have I mentioned my collection of "Best at Being Naive" trophies? I could not go to her with my stress as she had her own, though I didn't account for that. At the time, I thought she just didn't like me or didn't want me involved with the kids, all very self-centered assumptions on my end. I did not put enough thought into how hard it must have been for her to recover from the divorce and the subsequent loss of custodial rights.

On the flip side, my husband was also a child of several not-so-great divorces (as opposed to the awesome ones) and his experiences as a child offered a road map of what not to do when interacting with or discussing the ex. He had spent much of his life listening to his mother bitch about his father (in fairness, he deserved much of it) and his father bitch about his mother (in fairness, she deserved some of it). And so, when he found me turning red with rage, he'd always reel me back in and divert me from the kids' earshot.

Children have a loyalty to their parents, *no matter what.* I know this because my husband's father ran the range of being a pagan, a meth maker/dealer, landing in jail, insisted his child come armed when visiting (like, with an actual gun), and contributed zero to Rich's upbringing. I think of this tiny boy being sent off to see his father twice monthly and being handed a weapon to tuck into his sock upon arrival. I think of that tiny boy being left to sleep on a couch, alone all night, while his father was out running the streets of the city. I think of the stories of that same boy witnessing a shooting or nearly having to pull a trigger himself for protection. And then I look at this beautiful grown man (who, frankly, has no business being as good as he is) and I'm shocked that his stories often conclude with how he always went to bat for his dad, *no matter what.*

That is how strong that biological bond is.

And he hasn't only recently gone to bat for his dad, it is a narrative that can be found at all stages of that tiny boy's life. Loyalty to the end. If his mother, aunts, teachers, or pastor ever whispered a pointed comment about his father, Rich was right there to defend this man. Children are programmed to love their parents. When I met Rich, he didn't have much of a relationship with his father, but he didn't *not* have one either. By then, Rich understood that he was cut from a different cloth and his father kept a healthy distance while being filled with pride for his son's accomplishments. I was a bit insistent on meeting this man though, at that time, I'd only heard about a tenth of the stories. Therefore, I could find very little wrong with him. As our relationship progressed and more bits and pieces of his childhood came out, I would often look at Rich with the wondering eyes of *why*?? After all that this man had put him through, why did we even keep his number?

And that's the rub. Biology wins. Always. Rich may have hated his father or not understood him or felt totally let down by him, but that tiny boy would never breathe a word of discontent about his father, nor would he put up with anybody who did. I'm weirdly fairly grateful that Rich had the childhood that he did. Without the comparison of his early years and that loyalty level, I'd probably not have believed him when he counseled me not to cross that line of disparagement with our kids. He would say those same words: *They may hate her, they may not understand her, they may feel let down by her, but you can never, ever whisper a word of discontent to them about her.* Even if the kids' loyalty does fade, this will remain true. I know this because it happened with one of our children, during which a statement was made of "*I love you more than my real mom.*" Even then, I had to withhold any participation in any derogatory chatter while trusting Rich when he assured me that if I did not, I would absolutely lose the trust of the children.

I liken it to collaborating with a friend who seems inches away from breaking up with a boyfriend whom you've never really liked. You sort of get amped up with victorious adrenaline as excitement builds that your friend is finally going to see what you see of this awful relationship. You spend a night out verbally beating the shit out of her boyfriend only to find out weeks later that the two have gotten engaged and, oops, now your friend is no longer speaking with you because you said such nasty things. "*Hello?*" you think, "*you were there too?*"

It doesn't matter.

You want your kids to remember how supportive you were of them. You do not want them to remember that your support also included unkind thoughts towards their other mother. You will remember that in your effort to support your kids, you were trying to create an alliance— creating a cool mom vibe of *oh, yeah, I totally get you.* Your kids will remember that when they were struggling to have a relationship with their other mom, you were feeding on that struggle with excitement for the benefits it offered you. You will think you hid your facial expressions. They will remember that daggers shot out of your eyes towards someone they were born to love unconditionally. Still, you will think that they will move on and really see you for what you wanted to be to them. They won't. You must remember that and have each conversation with them carefully and with the intention not to make a mutual disdain for their (bio)mom the thing that you can finally bond over. For that, they will never forgive you.

STAND DOWN. OVER THERE. ON THE SIDELINES.

One of the neat things about (step)momming is feeling a huge need to be involved in everything. Or at least that was how it was for me. Admittedly, anxiety, fear of failure, and being new to the gig all played roles in my insistence that I was involved in all things school/sports/medical related. I grasped at anything and everything that might allow me to put my stamp of momming on the kids. That and a combination of my husband's frequent inability to keep me in the loop on all of the above (this is a common man-trait called Out of Sight, Out of Mind). If an email came to his mailbox from the school, he would read it, thinking briefly that he needed to let the other parents know, and then go back to whatever he was doing. Gone. There were many times when his ex-wife felt slighted for not getting the information, and I think she felt it was because I was the one holding it hostage. The reality was that I wasn't getting the information either. There are almost constant adjustments on which information needs to be translated to whom, especially in the beginning of blending families. There is also this tendency to want to control all communication and decisions through one house. I suppose it falls into the subconscious feeling of *but I'm the better parent.* The unintended output is that the kids see and hear and feel the tension that is produced through these accidental power plays.

Schools are tricky. Once I wrapped my head around the reality that in a single school, there are probably endless blended families, it became logical that the school had a preference of one parent contact per child. I'm not talking about In Case of Emergency, I'm talking about the daily/weekly communications from the teachers to the parents. I did not understand that because I came into this fully prepared to stay forever and be very present in the school. I knew my intentions, just like probably every other person who has dated someone with school-aged kids. The school presents itself like an easy "in." They always need volunteers, chaperones, room moms, and snack deliverers. I was surprised when I was turned away at the door with a not-so-subtle *sorry, no girlfriends allowed.* I was also pissed. I knew that the kids' (bio)mom was not doing any of the school things. Nor was my husband, as his work schedule didn't enable it. How dare they pass on my perfectly capable copier hands? What the school knew, and I didn't, was that they also provided (and I hate these words) a safe place for the kids, the very kids who were adjusting to a separation and divorce and being shuffled around. What the school knew was that significant others don't always stay. Or even often stay. What the school knew was that the kids were trying to settle into some sense of new normalcy and that my appearance at recess might throw some chaos back into that process.

I did get in eventually. *Eventually* meaning the literal second after Rich and I were engaged. We were engaged on a Friday night, on Monday, the "We'd love your help!" floodgates were opened. I felt so arrived. I also overestimated the difficulties of hopping into a building with hundreds of young children and being able to figure out how to do anything useful, including run the copier. I didn't know that there were aller-gies or that I shouldn't mention Santa not being real or that kids would swarm me like the weakest member of a parenting pack. But my kids were thrilled to have a parent participating, often showing me off like their newest toy when I made an appearance. Their teachers became my lifeline that first year as I sent email after email asking about the normalcy of certain behaviors or if all kids did the same things that mine did. Did all boys wash their rocks in the washer? Did all girls go bana-nas on their first attempts at makeup? Exactly how many ep-isodes of *SpongeBob SquarePants* were there? While they may have thought me completely underqualified, they canceled that out with an appreciation of my dedication to learning how to mom.

All that being said, the communication stream did not change. The school stuck to their guns on the one-parent con-tact. This became incredibly awkward when three parents showed up for third-grade orientation as every parent present thought theirs should be the listed name on all documents. To avoid a catfight, Rich quickly put his name down while mum-bling that he would put an auto-forward so that all emails would travel from his inbox to mine and his ex's. It was a su-per simple solution that could have saved a lot of tension if we'd been prepared for the idea going in. It was still tricky in the beginning, though, as the emails were forwarded to a (bio)mom trying to maintain a place in her kids' lives and a (step)mom trying to figure out if she had a place at all. The emails triggered us both into action, though in very different ways. I would jump on every form that had to be filled out, sign my name everywhere, communicate with the teachers, and don spirit wear. Rich's ex-wife would mostly reach out to Rich to find out when there were events, appear sporadically, but always be upset if she did not get a personal invite. I'd go through phases of making sure she had gotten the message to refusing to be the person in the middle. Truthfully, I did not feel comfortable communicating with her, and my husband was well, male, and therefore genetically underqualified to relay details.

We eventually learned to stick to the basics, which was leaving it up to Rich and his ex-wife to figure out how to communicate back and forth with each other. If that meant he got a lashing for forgetting, then I just stood back and let it happen. I was not unsympathetic: I often stood back thinking *but couldn't she have just looked at the school's website or read the forwarded emails or know that around every single holiday, there would be a school event?* I was new and yet had figured all that out within weeks. It took a long time for me to excel at keeping my thoughts between my husband and me. Even longer to excel at keeping my thoughts to myself. Both were critical as each time I got sucked into micromanaging their co-parenting relationship I, in the end, would be the one who somehow got burned. Getting burned is a common theme in (step)momming and, for me, it most commonly happened when I thought I was simply trying to help, yet it was received as massively butting in (a misunderstanding that is not limited to ex-wives).

Unless there is an actual, real-live emergency that leaves you absolutely no choice but to communicate details to your husband's ex, stand down. And I mean that. It took a few years of misinterpreted messaging for me to finally get it: If the message came from me, it would be met with suspicion and mistrust and the assumption of an ulterior motive. That's not to say that some of my messages didn't deserve those assumptions, but oftentimes I really just wanted to make sure she was in the loop. The problem was that the loop I wanted her to be in was the one related to my family. And half of my family belonged to her. Once I had my Oprah moment, I made a strong effort to leave the back and forth between her and my husband. After that, the first real communication I initiated solo was when my husband had a heart attack. I did not want to reach out to her at all about that (he belonged to me now) and within the shock of learning that his heart had nearly gone kaput, I put much of the blame for it on the stress that she had caused him. The last thing I wanted to do was reach out to her for help. But I knew the kids needed her. They needed their mom. They needed a mom, and I was not in a place to handle their grief while also trying to handle my own. That is the *level* of event that I refer to when I tell other stepmothers to leave the day-to-day communication between exes. Once we got past that terrible weekend, we slipped back into our corners, and I let Rich take over again.

Removing myself from whisper-down-the-lane also meant setting aside my desire to be an amateur detective. Yes, I did hand the communications responsibility over to my husband, but I filled the void by taking sneak peeks at his phone to see what they were talking about or by standing just out of sight while listening in to their phone calls. There was no suspicion of unrequited love. It was strictly so that I could make sure what I requested to be filtered out was getting filtered out. I was the family organizer. I needed something to control in this new crazy life, and the calendar was an easy thing to latch onto. It did seem much easier, in the beginning, to pick up my phone or shoot out an email to map out the kids' summer plans directly with her—and I did the first few years—but if something slipped through the cracks (and something always will), the assumption was that I'd done it on purpose to cut her out or be secretive or keep the kids' schedules jammed up enough that she couldn't see them. I realized I could not be the one on the receiving end when she felt slighted by missing things in our day-to-day world. I realized that my husband had to take those hits. And, if I felt like I'd reminded him thirty-two times to tell her something, I needed to go for numbers thirty-three and thirty-four and thirty-five. What I didn't need to do was jump in the middle, as it would make her feel like I was adding her to my list of things I wanted to control, and it would make him feel like I didn't trust him.

There will be sports and shows and ceremonies throughout the course of your shared kids' lives. In the beginning, if you do attend, it will be as *dad's friend*, probably, and your appearance will be for the finale. As you become more enmeshed in this blended family, your participation level in these events will increase. And, as the kids reach their busy years (the ones that occur when regular parents tend to over-schedule everything and divorcing parents tend to extra-over-schedule everything in an effort to keep their kids' minds off of what is going on at home), that participation will skyrocket. You will be tagged into taxi service, delivering children to and from school, to and from practices, to and from birthday parties, to and from appointments. You will spend time in the crafts aisle picking out crayons and colored paper and glue sticks, all to be brought home so you can spend time helping with art projects, science fair entries, or Valentine's Day cards by the dozens. You will develop a sense of inclusion. You will become critical in the success of these events. And when the big day comes, be it a game or an art show or a graduation, you will have a completely false expectation of having earned a front-row seat.

(Step)moms? We typically do not get the front-row seat. And excellent (step)moms will not ask for it. Is that fair? No. Does it feel awful? Yes. Is it important? Yes.

But probably not for the reason you think.

You deserve credit. You deserve a share of the accolades. You deserve so much. When you deserve so much, it is because you have become an integral part of your child's life. The irony is that as your involvement grows and your kids' love for you grows, a byproduct is an increase of stress for them when it comes to the events portion of their lives. What was previously an easy equation (four tickets to the school play equals one for mom, one for dad, two for grandparents) now becomes a shell game (four tickets to the school play equals one for mom, one for dad, two for … whom?). If you watch closely as your child leaves a field or a classroom, you will see their eyes dart from you to their (bio)mom, unsure of whom they should hug first. Being on that list is a total win for you, but for the kids, it is a nightmare. Regardless of their age, they do feel a split loyalty, which breeds a desire not to hurt anyone's feelings. For me, it was soccer. I noticed with each game that Max would come more and more slowly across the field to where the parenting pack was standing. I did notice his eyes darting from his (bio)mom to me, and the second I saw it, I knew. My response was unexpected (mostly to me—it sounded so grown up). I slipped off to the car and waited there. I did that for the remainder of the season, still greeting him with a hug, relieving him of the choosing. He arrived at the car incredibly relaxed and bouncy each time.

It did suck. Typically, it was I who signed the kids up for things and bought uniforms and got them to and from practices. Of course, I wanted to be recognized for all of that work. But the right thing to do was to stand down and eliminate a stressful moment for those that did not ask for this.

That snapshot has carried onto many things in our lives. It hasn't gotten easier. It is one of the ways I have learned that multiple things can be true in my path to (step)momming. Each year, when Mother's Day rolls around, we start across that tightrope of loyalty. Obviously, I want it to be all about me as, in our situation, I *am* the primary mom. But what I *have* to do is offer the day to my husband's ex-wife so that my kids are not sick with anxiety over the right thing to do. I typically spend the day sulking and sad because I am sans kids on the holiday. Initially, this would confuse my husband, as he couldn't understand why I was sad when I was the one who sent the kids off with their mother. There are two truths. I can be proud that I've alleviated their angst, AND I can still be sad that I sent them away. There have been similar tongue-biting moments sprinkled through the years. Major holidays? Those are pretty easy as they are often dictated by the custody agreement. Minor moments? Those are difficult. Who got to hold our daughter's hand when she was having teeth removed? I made the appointment, got the paperwork for braces going, did all of the dentist drives, but when the anesthesia wore off, it was her (bio)mom whom she saw first. Who got to sit inside the spotlight at graduations? I was most involved with teachers. I helped navigate homework, I picked up and dropped off, but it was her mother who sat right next to her at the party we hosted at our house.

As I write this, we have one in college and one in high school, both at ages at which they can certainly take over the role of communicator. For my husband, letting go of that responsibility has been much easier than it was for me. He doesn't have the emotion tied to it—that need to prove how good he is at parenting—because he has always been part of it. His role has been pared down, mostly, to telling his ex-wife that the kids are old enough to reach directly out to her.

And they are—yes, we've asked shrinks and teachers and other parents. It presents its own challenges as teens are historically bad at communication. The lucky ones do not get a crash course via navigating two separate households created by divorce. Ours have an unfortunate, near-decade-old feeling of having to communicate with a parent who doesn't necessarily want to be involved. Their level of motivation to invite or ask or keep her in the loop is fairly low from a years-long low burn of feeling rejection, intentional or not, from their (bio)mom. We try not to get too involved in that; it is something they will have to reconcile either on their own or with her. In the meantime, we are encouraging in letting them filter down the information while not being (too) annoyed if they do not. There are many other places to "teach" them to be their own advocates in a more direct and demanding way; this is not that.

It is a balancing act, but one that will best be navigated by the (step)mom standing aside.

WHEN YOU CAN'T STAND DOWN

Steer clear. Imagine how the kids feel. Leave the communication up to the husband. Imagine how the ex-wife feels. Take it slowly. No, slower still. Do not become a detective. Be the bigger person.

Unless you can't. Did I really just say that? Yes, there are exceptions.

In olden times—like, maybe prior to twenty years ago—divorces and custody were fairly straightforward. A couple got married, had kids, grew apart (or whatever), filed for and were granted a divorce, and the kids went with their mother. The father had visits every other weekend, so twice a month, typically, with occasional dinners on special days. Holiday schedules were pre-determined and noted in the custody document somewhere. If the mother remarried, her spouse would inherit that primary custodian relationship with her kids. If the father remarried, his spouse would inherit the twice monthly weekend visits. In other words, the father's new spouse would have very little action or involvement with his kids.

Of course, I just wrote all that with basically zero knowledge of how divorce worked when I was a kid. I can't actually remember any of my friends being children of divorce. Surely it happened, right? Was it just so smooth in the late seventies and early eighties that there was no chatter among the grade-school or middle-school set about how confusing the whole shit show was? I'm sure that's not right. Or was it because the post-divorce formula was so straightforward that it relieved all parties of that stress of knowing how things were going to turn out? Today, the formula is still prevalent, but it is also much more likely to be tossed out the window than decades prior. Custody is no longer something that is auto guaranteed to go to the mother. Today, there is a much more even split as fathers have gained more agency in the lives of their children, divorce or not. It sounds great on paper, all that love to go around for those kids, until one realizes that the result will be kids shuffling from house to house following a schedule put together with a scientific calculator.

We started out that way, with a fifty/fifty customer split. It was awful. A judge with any sense would have made each week a clean switch. Instead, in an effort to allow the kids to feel included in their own destiny, the judge asked for the input of two grade-school children in creating a schedule that looked something like this:

Sunday Evening through Wednesday Morning:
Father's home

Wednesday Evening through Thursday Morning:
Mother's home

Thursday Evening through Sunday Morning:
Father's home

Sunday Evening through Wednesday morning:
Mother's home

Wednesday Evening through Thursday morning:
Father's home

Thursday Evening through Sunday Morning:
Mother's home

Essentially, each morning before the kids got on the school bus at one house, the parents would have to coach them into knowing which bus they would have to take in the afternoon to get to the correct home. Did I mention they were seven and ten? If you're wondering how many times they flubbed it, the answer is soooo many. Never their fault, of course, neither really had a firm grasp on bus numbers, calendars, or, well, divorce. They never got a chance to settle in anywhere because, by the time they *did* begin to relax in one home, they were transferred to the other. I got a quick understanding of the unicorn divorces that ended with the kids having "custody" of the physical house while the parents shifted back and forth to their own apartments. At least the sense of consistency would go to those who were too young to figure out what size suitcase would allow them to carry all of their baggage.

We absolutely hated the schedule. Everyone hated it, kids and adults. It was the one thing we all could agree on, but we carried on for months for fear of rocking any more boats. My guess is that if things hadn't changed due to their (bio)mom's implosion, she and my husband would have gone back to revisit custody within the year. Except there was great fear in that as the possibility that Rich would then have to relinquish most of his time with the kids was basically written in stone for, in our state of residence, the motto remains *when in doubt, give the kids to the mother.* This was a shocking realization for me. I'd grown up thinking that fathers just didn't do that, that they wanted the kids to be with their moms. I had no idea that the majority of fathers got totally hosed by that outdated formula. I had no idea that most fathers did want to live with their children full time and were willing to adjust their work schedules to do so. I had no idea that most judges didn't care. On the flip side, in the land of judges that do care, their genius approach was to ask the children. *What!?* As shown by our wackadoodle schedule, neither child was brave enough to pick a side, so they tried to work the week out to benefit both parents an equal amount. Their tiny kid brains froze up for fear of any hints of leaning loyalty or preferences on living room layouts.

My crash course started quickly: Divorce sucks for everyone but mostly for the kids.

Stand down. It seemed like such a straightforward method.

It was not straightforward. It was actually impossible. We had a very different story than most and it left me little choice but to *not* stand down. I wish I'd had the balls to speak up back then and just say to all who counseled me to Stand Down. *Ms. Counselor, I cannot stand down; what else ya got? Yes, Mr. Teacher, I would very much like to stay out of it, but since I can't, will you work with me?* Because I was new to the ENTIRE parenting game and not just the "step" part of it, I brought with me a total lack of confidence, including an inability to recognize and insist that my situation was different. But I suppose everyone's situation is different, right?

A few things play into the difficulties of standing down, the primary of which is the inability of most men to plan, multitask, think ahead, or organize. I love my husband dearly. But if left in charge, it's quite likely that neither child would have had a haircut in the last decade. Men are very one-track minded. Eat. Sleep. Sex. Work. Oh, hey, how about those kids? Because so many custody arrangements now give a rightful chunk of responsibility to the fathers, that means that if there is a next wife (or partner), she will get a bigger chunk of the planning, multi-tasking, thinking ahead, and organizing in her stepchildren's lives. Even in a perfect world where the biological mom *is* maintaining all the extras (sports, appointments, teacher communications), there is a likelihood that the maintenance of the calendar will fall onto the (step)mom. That makes standing down nearly impossible. But not totally. On this very basic *filling-in-the-squares* example, I quickly learned that my returned input was not appreciated. If something came to our calendar and we already had plans, the message that *the kids are already booked* did not have to come from me. I thought it did because I was the calendar keeper. I took the role of the messenger for months and months before finally buying into the idea that if the information came to me via my husband, it could go back to his ex-wife the same way.

Does it always work? Nope. But the blame shifted off of me, so, in that case, yes. It has and will continue to happen: The (bio)mom made plans with the kids. The details then either never made it to their father or the details never made it to me (aka, the calendar keeper). In the meantime, I was creating our own plans and, bam!, we had a problem. I would immediately bow up with anger born from the double booking somehow being my fault. I would then become more irate because I knew that it would likely be my plans that would go by the wayside, especially if the kids were in the loop on their (bio)mom's plans. I would blow up knowing that, in the end, I would be the one who would stand down in honor of our long-standing insistence that the kids could see their (bio)mom whenever she asked. There were several risks if I got persistent, most pointing to their ingrained loyalty to their biological parents. The kids would assume that a cancellation of their plans was my fault whether or not that was true. The kids would be put in a "you have to choose" situation, something that is rarely acceptable or fair, that would also be linked back to me. The kids would think that we were trying to keep them from their (bio)mom. Again, untrue, but try explaining a whole communication blunder to a child.

We have tried many ways to keep it all together. And by we, I mean, we ... my husband and me. He has been very willing to try all the methods such as a shared calendar or group text between *all* parents or to turn over the plan making to the kids when age appropriate or a traveling notebook or letting me participate. Nothing has ever worked consistently. I have been accused of over-scheduling in an effort to minimize my kids' time with their (bio)mom. It is absolutely correct in that I am a well-in-advance planner, but that has been my pattern for decades. In our home, we can generally fill out a year-long calendar before the end of January with vacations, camps, concerts, and sporting events. This has not been ideal for last-minute, fly-by-the-seat-of-your-pants members of the extended family. I am not a free spirit, nor have I ever been. Our kids are not either, though perhaps to a lesser degree than I am. In my goal of standing down, I have learned to stand up a little by reaching out to their (bio)mom first before sending out details about just about anything we have scheduled. I have learned to give her time to respond with any of her own plans prior to inundating her with our calendar invites related to the children. I have learned to include words like *flexible*, and *we're thinking about* ... to indicate some leeway in our world, whether or not there is any.

Our situation was different.

I could not stand down. From the start, the transitions between homes have been head spinners. When Rich and his ex-wife were advised to take a twenty-four-hour breather by the sheriff, Rich was forced to take what he could grab in the minutes he had to vacate his home. The kids looked on, having no idea what was happening or what would happen next in this sudden change. When Rich gained back control of that home a year later, he discovered total disarray, as if his ex-wife had forgotten to pack or plan in her need to make new living arrangements.

It was another quick change.

Shortly after I arrived, there was yet another quick change. While the kids were fully involved in the hunt for a new "it's a fresh start!" home, their (bio)mother's eviction from her own apartment sent the kids to our home full time. We had strategically planned the move while the kids were to be at their (bio)mother's to dampen the stress. Instead, over the course of one week, we went from unloading a U-Haul to an emergency custody hearing and erasing the custody entirely. All heads were spinning, and I could not stand down.

My husband was firmly planted in a job that required him to travel every other week, again strategically scheduled to occur while the kids were with their (bio)mother. I could not stand down because the kids needed me to jump in with both feet *immediately*. They needed me to become their ally while we tried to plug hole after hole in the collapsing emotional dam. I could not stand down because that was not how I was built.

This has been a recurring theme. There have been years of events or moments where my relationship with the kids and the ex-wife would have benefited with decreased involvement (on my end) but in which increased involvement (on my end) was critical to survival.

You cannot always stand down.

In a utopian remarriage, I would not have had any participation in discipline. I would not have had any need to check grades or homework. I would not have been the assigner of chores. I would have spent my time catching up on work or TV, maybe playing tennis, while the kids did their chores or homework under their dad's watchful eye. If that sounds like the (step)mom getting to skip all the icky stuff, YES, PLEASE. The (step)mom should get to skip ALL the icky stuff so that she is not forced directly into the role that Disney wrote just for her. In a perfect world, the (step)mom resides firmly in the fun zone. That does not always happen. I could not stand down. I was not in the fun zone. There was no way for me to even locate the fun zone because I was so busy trying to keep my head above water while transitioning from a single, dog-

owning, forty-two-year-old who'd never had kids to an engaged forty-three-year-old with two new-to-me kids in the
course of about five seconds.

The ongoing advice to remain away from the meat of actually raising those new-to-me children? I could not. I had no
choice. It has caused me endless nights of missed sleep with
worry and feelings of failure that I am only now starting to
recognize as actually quite okay. This is the path we landed on,
and we did our absolute best. Over the years, I went from all
out panic to working my way into the hang of things to learning to stand down while still standing my ground. I often ask
myself if, somewhere down the intellectual road, the kids will
look back at my actions and reactions and think good things.
Will they see grace? Not always. But the more I dig in, the
more strides I make. I hope that the overarching picture of me
as their (step)mother is one that represents an ability to be
kind and thoughtful and look the other way when what I really
wanted to do was shoot daggers out of my eyes, back the bus
over someone, or pack my bags. Or perhaps all three. My hope
is that as they discover the faults of their (bio)mother, they
will also start to erase those faults that were placed on me because of her actions. Although, truly, I would really like them
to remain oblivious, as I think that innocence is vital. The
longer they can envision their (bio)mother as living on a pedestal, the better. I know that the discovery that she launched
herself off that pedestal will be very painful. My faults? Oh yes,
there are many (so many) but they would never have been ex-
posed if their (bio)mother had been able to, well, mother.

Standing down while standing your ground? It is tricky. It
feels terrible, it involves allowing someone undeserving to
steal your spotlight, and never admitting that you owned it
first. When that someone is the actual mother of your kids and
the spotlight is shifted because you allow it, it is very hard to
reconcile your role as the other mother. You give away the

wins because you don't want the kids to feel stressed or torn or sad or like they are choosing sides. The accolades do not come to (step)mom martyrs, especially in the beginning. I know this because I love accolades. Love them. I do not respond with an "*Oh, you don't have to say that ...*" when someone compliments me. I own it. It is very unnatural for me to let someone else get a pat on the back when I've done the dirty work. I suppose that was the signal to my heart in defining how attached to the kids I'd quickly become. I wanted to protect them. I wanted to protect their hearts.

I had to do so by standing down. Even when I was standing up.

Which Way's Up?

Shit Nuggets

Things that come out of human beings are not my favorite thing. I don't have a least favorite, as it is an absolute tie between throw-up or poop-out items.

Sure, I get it, "everybody does it," and all that blabbidy blab. I just don't want to be a part of it. I don't want to know any more about peoples' orifice situations than I want them to have a high level of interest in mine. I am the girl who waited all day at school to use my home bathroom. I am the girl who cannot perform beyond a number **one** *if there is someone else in a public bathroom, let alone a number doody.*

In fact, if I'm having any kind of emotional anything, I can't go at all. I get so annoyed when arguing with my husband on a full bladder as I know that until he realizes that I'm right, I will have lost all ability to relieve the pressure on my bladder. I spent the first half-year of our relationship clenching my cheeks together, hard, praying that this man, who I was quickly falling in love with, would go do his own bathroom business so that I could skedaddle to another bathroom to do my own business before he became the wiser. I spent our first sleepover urging myself to stay awake lest I farted in my sleep, and he (gasp) heard it.

I can't really explain how shocking it was to learn that he knew I pooped all along. Or how mortified I was when he informed me that I tooted my own horn the entirety of our first sleepover night together.

When I was dropped feet first into motherhood, I learned quickly that children often mismanage their "I have to poo" runway. I learned this via my first skid mark sightings and quickly implemented a house policy on handling such incidents: Throw those shit-stained underoos in the trash. This directive was later clarified with a second directive: No, do not throw those out in the inside trash, throw them out in the **outside** trash. March those stained underoos right out the door and dispose of them. No, my dear, sweet husband, I will not be trying to remove the soils or allowing them to dance around in the same pristine water that my perfect clothes are floating through.

I have the same policy for sharts, though my new family was much more on board with that one. Apparently, in their minds, skid marks were just a result of a wiping mistake and not a big deal, while sharts were not something one could return from and certainly not something which we talked about while making eye contact.

I believe it was three years into our marriage when my mother-in-law came to live with us while in between apartments. This was a brave move on our part as she was still not quite on board with her son being married again nor her grandchildren having a (step)mom. We set some pretty clear boundaries, which she graciously agreed to follow, and off we went into this multigenerational experiment.

What could go wrong?

One evening, while she was living with us, we had a horrible spring thunderstorm that knocked out our power just before we all went to bed. This was not uncommon in our neck of the woods, but the power was typically restored within the hour. Not this time. The hours ticked by and that adult I-have-a-fridge-full-of-food-going-bad pit in my stomach feeling began to develop. The power remained out for nearly twenty-four hours.

We were new enough to our house, having only moved in a year or so prior, to not have a real gauge on well-water life during extended power outages. At some point in those twenty-four hours, the topic of "how many flushes" we might have before our toilet tanks would run dry. An un-written, quickly created rule of *don't flush without permis-sion from an adult* was developed. It seemed easier than trying to explain to two children about which cases counted as flushable. Still, as we neared the end of a full, powerless day that did include eating solids, it was evident that, yes, everybody would likely have to flush at least once.

My mother-in-law was staying in our guest room, which had its own bathroom. She typically kept the door closed to her bedroom for both privacy and to keep our arks of animals out. The morning after the power went down, she left early in the morning, before anyone was up (including the power, pulling her door closed behind her). During her stay, I really did my best never to open that door as I wanted to keep a firm separation of our worlds until a day arrived when we felt more comfortable to-gether.

Which is how it came to pass that I sent my (step)daugh-ter into the room to grab something for me ... and, as she was a child ... she did not close the door upon exiting. Be-cause, you know, kids.

I'm not sure how long it was until the following events took place.

I was sitting on the couch trying to come up with some-thing entertaining to do while I told myself that I really didn't need coffee to survive. Our newest addition, still a puppy, jumped up on the couch to greet me and I reached out for an intake of sweet puppy smell. I retracted my offer for snuggles **SO FAST** when I was hit with a horrific stench. Awful. Not a sweet puppy smell. Worse than you are imagining. I jumped up, covered my nose with my shirt collar, and went on a fearful dash while trying to pinpoint the odor.

Had an elephant dropped a deuce in the foyer? Were cows migrating through our yard? What was happening?

Which is about when I realized, no, it was much worse.

My little innocent sweet ball of puppy had actual shit in her mouth. Her mouth. That was the only explanation. But how? And where? Did I mention worse? It was the remnants on her puppy smile that gave it away. How?

She'd come into the living room from the direction of the guest room. What?

I saw that the door was opened.

But, what?

Had this animal gone bobbing for shit nuggets?

That had to be it, right? An unflushed toilet mishap?

I followed the dog as she bounced her way back to the source of her glory and whipped into the guest bathroom only to find ... nothing. The toilet bowl was definitely empty, yet, why were my nostrils telling me things were getting worse? I then heard the unmistakable sound of a grocery bag ruffling, flipped on the big bathroom light, and, well, was still super confused—but now with a churning stomach.

And then I saw it.

At my feet, in a torn-up Target bag that my sweet puppy was still nosing, was well-used toilet paper and a pile of poop. Confusion quickly turned into confusion plus horror. Why was there a bag of shit in the bathroom?!?!? The dog had eaten the bag of shit?!?!?! Where did this come from?!?!? There was shit smeared across the floor?!?!? Who was going to clean up this shit?!?!

And then, the worst of it all.

The shit belonged to my mother-in-law.

This is where my hindsight always kicks in.

I should have just retreated.

I should have just left a note.

I should have stayed single forever.

Instead, I went into high speed, cleaning up the crime scene mode. I wanted to eliminate the entire room before my brain could really process what I was doing. Dry heaves? Yes. And also, wet heaves. I called out to the guilty but also innocent child for help, but also so that she could join me in this place that no person should ever be. There was no way that I wasn't going to have someone to share this story with.

Our minds must have immediately begun the process of sheltering us from the memory as we came to minutes (hours?) later while both running our hands under scalding hot water and debating the possibility of below-the-elbow amputations. The dog continued to bounce around the house smelling like she'd had a sewer Slurpee. I praised the lawd that both dogs were due at Doggy Daycare that very day and packed them in the car for an early arrival. I made record speed to drop off, handing over one well-behaved, perfect dog and one puppy who very clearly had poop hanging from her beard. Hey, if you have time, she might need a bath ...

Hours later, post-Xanax, I rang my husband.

He was three hours away at a meeting and my first words to him were, "You have no idea just how big the owe is right this second." As I was explaining the course of events, he went into man mode, trying so very hard to come up with some kind of logic behind the surprise bag of doodies.

I did not want man mode.

I wanted the Level of Owe to be acknowledged and feared and for flowers to arrive immediately.

I also kind of wanted to burn the house down. Or at least the guest wing.

In the end, we concluded that his mom, who is a VERY neat person, couldn't stand the idea of leaving poop in the toilet. With an early rise time, she likely forgot that it would've been her first flush (or maybe not, we'll never know) and, therefore, permissible. We don't know if she pooped directly into the bag or fished in lieu of flushing. Our assumption is that she meant to take the bag with her, *but then it slipped her mind. Our other assumption is that she is still wondering what happened to her missing bag of shit nuggets.*

We also later discovered that our well has a backup generator.

In other words, we can basically flush always and forever.

Shit.

CHAPTER FOUR

Remember Where They Came From

BEST WORST LAID PLANS

At the time of my first meeting with the kids, Amelia was ten and Max was seven. Rich and I had been dating just over a year and, though we'd long since pledged our love to one another, we had intentionally kept our relationship (and me) hidden from the kids. Hidden? That sounds sneaky. It wasn't sneaky. Rich knew the kids had been through so much in the previous few years as witnesses to the implosion of their parent's marriage. I knew the kids had been through so much in the previous few years as a witness to the struggle I saw in Rich. We agreed that there was zero need to rush any meetings, as no one had yet settled into this new life. No one actually even knew what this new life was going to look like. The shifting of homes was still happening, the divorce finalities were still being signed, and I hadn't made any plans at all on where I might end up should this thing with Rich continue.

As is typical, Rich and I laid out our plans with a nod of satisfaction to each other that we were really knocking it out of the park. Does "best-laid plans" sound too cliche? I'm sure we had just congratulated ourselves again on how well we were handling the hiding when the universe laughed in the

face of our plans and provided a completely accidental intro-
duction between myself and the kids. We weren't stupid. I had
started coming to Virginia to visit with Rich on occasion.
When I did, we did not traipse around his small town. In fact,
we'd stay in a hotel thirty minutes away, essentially avoiding
any chance of paths crossing when the kids were out and
about with their mother. The very first time I did stay at Rich's
house, we planned on staying put all weekend thus avoiding
any rumor mills that included Rich being spotted with some
short blonde. The universe laughed again. The kids were delivered to my doorstep. Well, actually, it was Rich's doorstep.
The doorstep belonging to the home that had just been returned to his name twenty-four hours prior to the kids showing up in a surprise twist.

As is apparently common in divorce and separations,
Rich's ex-wife was given the family home for a year while they
waited out the allotted "apart" time to make a divorce final.
Which was stupid. Rich wasn't going back to that woman no
matter how long the state made him wait. At the end of that
twelve-month period, she was to move out and Rich would re-
claim the home as his own. During that time, Rich stayed with
his mother, and the kids alternated between staying with him
at Grandma's or staying with their (bio)mom at their home.
Rich and I would see each other when he came down to Raleigh, usually a combo work/Jyl trip, or when I came up to
Richmond, usually a chance for Rich to try to sell the area to
me. As the magic day approached when he would have his
home back, we planned a weekend of cleanup and my first
view of where he had lived with his family. He was so proud
to have the keys back. He was so excited to give me the tour.
He wanted so much for me to love it immediately.

Have I mentioned yet how naive we were?

The house was absolutely trashed. Epically. Embarrass-
ingly. His pride retreated, his excitement waned, and we stood

looking at a house full of garbage and reeking of cat urine. This was not the homecoming he had hoped for. I felt awful for him. I felt confused as to why a person would do this to any home, let alone one that they'd lived in with children. Was it spite? Vindictiveness? To prove a point? Which one? Was this how all divorces went? Was there a back door through which I could make a quick exit? What in the world was I walking into? I'm not sure how long we assessed the situation before Rich picked up his phone and called for the delivery of a dumpster. Yes, the big kind. We retreated to a hotel to regroup.

I came back up two weeks later, armed with work gloves and a positive attitude in order to help Rich dig through the mess. We spent hours tearing up carpets, scrubbing down walls, and taking load after load of garbage to the big dumpster. It seemed huge in the driveway, something we would never be able to fill. After one day of work, it was clear that we would fill it and possibly need another. Good grief. What was I getting into? As we started on the second day, Rich got a pleading phone call from his ex-wife asking for him to take the kids, as she had a headache. We looked at each other in shock. How was this going to work? Should I quickly pack my things and head back to Raleigh? Just to the hotel? This was not how we'd planned the initial meeting. We hadn't planned anything at all. I listened while Rich explained to the person on the other end of the call that he was working on the house and that he had a friend here helping. I listened as he agreed to have the kids dropped off, but that they would likely be picked up again by their grandma so we could keep working. Oh shite. I couldn't even find a closet to hide in.

Quick commercial break: That was the first conversation between the ex-spouses that I'd ever witnessed. Here are the red flags/light bulbs/previews that I missed:

- Headache. The ex-wife had a headache. This would be an ongoing pattern in our lives that often interrupted our non-custodial time as the headaches always came and often disabled her from keeping the kids during her designated visits. It meant that whenever the kids were with her, Rich had to be close enough to jump in with a phone call's notice.

- Grace. Holy grace. I never once heard Rich blurt out, *"I'm cleaning up the complete shit show condition that our house was left in!"* Which is what I wanted to say. How did he not launch into a tirade about the destruction of property or insist that she donate to the dumpster fund? Holy grace. That was my first glimpse of another theme that would camp out in our relationship.

Shortly after that phone call, a beat-down, black Mercury pulled into the driveway. I waited in the house, though peeking out the musty front window. *It's happening,* I whispered to myself, *it'll be fine. I've got so many qualifications.*

Two short people hopped out of the car and came plowing into Rich's arms as he returned their enthusiasm. There was not much conversation between parents, just a wave and a *feel better* from Rich. I watched him kneel down to the kids and start an animated conversation, his arm motioning to the house. *Oh shite,* I thought, *he's telling them about me. Yes. The friend. Act like a friend. Nothing More.* And, just like that, they came to me, hands were shaken, names were traded, and we sat down for a strategically timed round of McSomething's. Once everybody was stuffed with burgers and fries, Rich doled out tasks. Amelia and I were put on pulling carpet staples. It seemed too easy. Sitting in her old bedroom together, pliers in hand, yanking staples from the floor while we talked about, well, I have no idea what we talked about. It just seemed easy. Within five minutes, I'd gone from nervous to complete over-confidence in my ability to just jump in and be present. Even a monkey could do it!

That confidence was crushed an hour later when Max announced to the room that I wasn't his mom. Right. I can't even remember where that came from. Just a quick seven-year-old declaration of *YOU DON'T BELONG HERE.* New to (step)mom-ming? Prepare your answer to this declaration. Make it super casual. And don't get upset. You actually aren't their mom, so yeah, totally accurate. Play it like that. I did. Just a quick, *oh yeah, I know, but you can still grab us the pliers.* And, frankly, I was quite relieved by the reminder. Yes. Thank goodness. I was surely not going to sign up for that gig. No need to, right? They had a mom. I would just be a fun addition to their lives. Nothing more.

Quick commercial break #2: Here's another red flags/light bulbs/previews that I missed:

- At some point, Rich's mother did come over to pick up the kids, though they wanted to stay with us. We'd just taken out a wall and, well, it was cool! I was sitting in the back bedroom with Amelia pull-ing staples again when I heard his mom's voice echoing down the hall, *"Are you sure she should be alone with her? Don't you think that's dangerous?"* I thought it was sweet that she was worried about me until I realized that I was not the one she was worried about. Wait ... me? ... dangerous? ... what was happening?

For six months, I'd see the kids on occasion, then more often, then quite often. And then it seemed like we blinked, and I was living with them part-time while they traveled back and forth from household to household. Another blink and that ended, too, as we were thrown together into one household. These are the months that we enjoy looking back at with wizened hindsight and a pointed finger toward stupidity. This is pointless, of course. What happened, happened, but we still enjoy beating ourselves up over the many wrong turns. We had many moments of trying to put a square block in a round hole, but at the time of shoving, neither of us was able to be told why it wasn't working. We also didn't have much of a choice other than to make it work. And that is the reminder we follow up to ourselves with. We did not have a choice.

I moved into Rich's old home thinking that the kids would be with us part time.

The hindsight: I shouldn't have moved directly into the house. I should have gotten an apartment to allow for a period of integration.

The reality: I had a house in Raleigh that was on the market, yet still required a mortgage payment. To encourage its sale, my Realtor suggested that if I could go ahead and move out, I should do it. Rich had a new and whopping alimony/child support payment to make each month, a number larger than my mortgage and larger than the mortgage he also had. Together we'd quickly discovered that during the year of separation, the bulk of bills related to said house (and car and doctors and activities) were not paid by his ex-wife and, therefore, creditors were knocking.

The Outcome: Once the commitment to move my life north was made, it was made. There was no turning back. There was also no funding for an apartment on the side. And, frankly, I don't know if I'd have taken it, anyway. Feeling like a kept woman living in a one booty-call bedroom down the street was not something I was up for.

If only it ended there. Four months after I moved my life north, the predicted implosion of Rich's ex-wife did, in fact, take place. I had been warned about this. I got a lot of hints about this in the form of the kids landing at "our place" for some period each time they were to be under her care. Head-aches, feeling sick, having to work, Martians ... it never failed that each time the custody agreement fell into her lap, the kids would fall into ours. And poor Rich, dealing with an anxiety-ridden forty-something in a friendless new town AND with two kids bouncing from an apartment to a very small house. We almost immediately started searching for a bigger home, waiting for mine to sell in order to find some room to spread our wings.

Four months after I moved my life north, we loaded a U-Haul to relocate all of our lives into a much bigger house two miles away. Did I say four months again? Yes. In fact, both events, the move and the implosion, happened within days of each other. Our strategically scheduled move, planned for when the kids were at their (bio)moms, hit a major speed bump when just days before the last box was loaded, Rich was called into action as his ex-wife reported a break-in at her apartment. Included in that report was the request that he take the kids indefinitely until she could get things straight-ened out. Through some more phone calls and sleuthing, we realized that there was no break-in and nothing to straighten out. The reality was that his ex-wife had been locked out of her apartment courtesy of the sheriff due to months of non-payment of rent. She'd been squatting. With two kids. *What had I walked into?*

The kids left for school from their (bio)mom's only to re-turn after school to their dad's. Except it was also a brand-new house that hadn't even been unpacked. That is how we came to be a full-time family so much earlier than we'd planned and definitely not how we wanted. We were surrounded by boxes. I was surrounded by boxes. Rich had been called away on a business trip just minutes before the implosion and had long forgotten that commitment while standing in emergency custody meetings. I found myself full of confidence, encouraging him to go ahead. *We'll be fine!!*

I was surrounded by boxes in a new house, in a new town, with two new kids.

Just like that, I had become a full-time parent.

Just like that, the kids were thrown into the deep end with a full-time (step)mom and a whole barrel of confusion as to what had just happened to their tiny lives.

Just like that, we started down a long path of hits and misses, successes and failures, and counselors on speed dial.

Even as I write this today, I cringe at what they went through. I cringe at what I went through.

I cringe at thinking of where they came from.

A TALE OF TWO KIDS

I have very different relationships with each of my kids. With one, it is as close to a mother-child relationship as can be. With the other, it is solidly camped out on the stepmother side and, most days, an evil stepmother at that. I used to wonder what I was doing wrong. Why were my relationships with the two so very different? Eventually, and after talking to loads of other moms, I began to get a whisper of it being totally normal. It was a whisper because, as a (step)mom, you automatically jump to the "it's probably something I'm doing wrong" conclusion first. The whisper got louder over the years and more confirmation from other moms. While I can see lots of reasons why my eldest will never fully join my camp, I am fairly content with the idea that different kids equal different relationships. I suppose it mirrors the parents. My kids have a very different relationship with their father than with me or with their (bio)mom or with their grandparents.

I think the reason that it still stings is that it actually started out the exact opposite as it is now. In fact, I remember laughing with Rich about how wrong our relationship predictions were. We'd assumed that, upon meeting, Amelia would be the hard nut for me to crack and that Max, well, Max would love anyone and everyone. It's why on that first day when Max proclaimed my *not his mom*-ness while storming past the Amelia and me lovefest, I thought, *wait, is this how we said it would be or did we think it would go the other way?*

After the implosion of their (bio)mom, Amelia really took another leap into playing the role of Max's protector. We had no idea this was a role she'd been playing for years prior as their (bio)mom worked her way out of parental involvement. The discoveries that Amelia was responsible for getting her brother up for school, making sure he'd eaten, etc. came much later. When the shit hit the fan in the form of an eviction notice on her apartment, Amelia finally had enough. It was an awkward conversation when we tried to brush over why the kids were staying with us and were interrupted by an eleven-year-old saying, *I know what happened, I've seen the pink notices for months.* That fallout put a huge dent in Amelia's relationship with her (bio)mom and caused Max to pull even closer to Amelia with the worry of an eight-year-old wondering if she, too, might disappear. That's a hell of a day for an eleven-year-old.

And, while I hate to call it a benefit, the benefit was that Amelia and I became accidental allies. For nearly a year, Amelia wanted nothing to do with her mother, refusing to visit, passing on phone calls, and ignoring her if she came to say hello. My counselor's response to this was a brilliant challenge to make sure that Amelia and I didn't rely on a common interest that circled around a mutual dislike for her mother. That was not easy. I was certain that the anxiety and anger and confusion I was feeling at being thrown into the deep end was absolutely Amelia's (bio)mom's fault. Or at the very least a STRONG indirect consequence. I absolutely wanted to share that disdain with someone, anyone, just to feel less alone in my loathing. Rich was pretty much all done with the loathing. He'd done enough of that in the previous years to have filled that bucket, taken it to the dump, and gotten rid of it. My loathing was brand new, and I needed someone to confirm its appropriateness.

I understood my counselor's challenge, though. An eleven-year-old, emotionally busted-up child was not the route to go.

My job was to encourage Amelia to rebuild. My job was to tell her that her mother was doing the very best she knew how to do. My job was to tell Amelia that her mother loved her in the only way she knew how. My job was to encourage Amelia that her mother might not be the person she wanted at that moment, but that someday she might be exactly the person she needed.

The thing is, Amelia and I were both a bit lost. She was figuring out a life in which she didn't necessarily want her (bio)mom involved, while I was figuring out a life in which I didn't necessarily want two full-time kids. It created this instant *I've got a sidekick* bond for both of us. I loved sitting with her on the front porch, braiding her hair, and talking about what we'd wear if we went out to dinner somewhere fancy. I loved talking about the boy at her school whom she'd met in kindergarten and taken an instant liking to. I learned about her favorite subjects and love for reptiles (oh, dear) and why her brother drove her nuts, and what she was going to be when she grew up. I'd listen to her sing in such perfect pitch that she'd make me believe that I should also belt out a tune (oh, dear). It felt good to have someone looking up to me and wanting to share time with me. It sparked so many reminders of the close relationship I'd had with my mother. I felt like *oh, wow, yes, this is why mothers have daughters, this is the stuff.*

I began imagining shopping trips and phone calls from college and meeting boyfriends, and, and, and.

And ... then there was Max.

Max wanted very little to do with me. He had a mom, thank you very much, as mentioned seventeen times a day. There would be no allowance for me pretending in any sense of the word that I was also his mom, including in the (step)mom sense of the word. He talked back to me, refused to eat what I cooked, balked when I asked him to do anything beyond breathe, reminded me over and over who I wasn't, that I wasn't welcome, and, just in case he wasn't completely clear, would throw in an occasional bite, push, or smack for emphasis.

Have step-kids, they said, *it'll be fun ...*

Remember when I said this?:

"I have very different relationships with each of my kids. With one, it is as close to a mother-child relationship as can be. With the other, it is solidly camped out on the stepmother side and, most days, an evil stepmother at that."

It likely seems clear which is which.

Except it isn't.

In a totally unpredicted, out-of-left-field turn of events, Max is my easy one. Amelia is my challenging one. It actually all flipped on a dime. Well, two different dimes, actually.

One December night in Raleigh, at one of those infamous family fancy dinners with Amelia's hair braided and our out-fits picked out, Rich asked me to marry him. He asked with the kids right there to witness it (and my family as well). In the time it took us to go from the restaurant to the hotel, Max's entire script was tossed out the car window. We'd left for din-ner with a snarky eight-year-old fairly bothered to be there. We returned with a small, sweet boy who wanted snuggles, hugs, and kisses. It was as if hearing Rich's ask of joining their family and my jubilant response opened a space in his heart, one just big enough to squeeze in an extra mother.

What I didn't notice at the time was that, while Max was cuddling between Rich and me in our giant hotel bed (*oh ... this is why parents have king-size beds ...*), Amelia had retreated to the kids' connected room and disappeared under the covers. And by *didn't notice* I mean, until I started piecing this chapter back together. Huh. How about that?

After Rich and I got engaged, I was quite suddenly welcomed into Max's school with open arms. And I mean that. Prior to the ring application, I could not fill out the volunteer application. Naive me did not understand that—shouldn't all forms of mates be welcome in? "Now me" does get it. Imagine running a school and having to juggle your volunteers based on who is dating whom, when, and whether the moms/dads get along with the girlfriends/boyfriends. Imagine having those awkward conversations of *oh, yes, Miss Smith did volunteer for Jack Sprat's field trip, but she and Jack's father had a big fight last night and now she won't be coming and, long story short, now we cannot take the class to see how mills work.* I supposed every girlfriend that would walk through those school doors to make camp next to the copy machine would do so with the intention of always being around. The reality was that the school needed some proof of *forever* intent. Once they had it, I was able to make a fairly instant and important bond with Max as, yes, the school was thrilled to have an enthusiastic (if underqualified) volunteer. I started making appearances regularly and his face lit up each time I waved from the hall. As he grew to trust me, I started driving him to doctor's appointments, helping with schoolwork, picking out clothes, and, eventually, being granted access to a twenty-minute bedtime ritual involving songs and snuggles. We still battled on occasion (yes, still), but as time pulled us forward, Max began to rely on me for all the mom things. It was a sad substitution, but one I also felt honored with. By the end of that school year, he'd stopped offering an eight-year-old's explanation of who I was and just called me Mom around his friends. I didn't think too much of it (just kidding, I thought it was fucking awesome), but then I overheard him explaining to Rich, in a very *I'm also assuring myself of this* way, that he had two mothers. I got called into sick days (gross, hard pass) and alerted when there was an injury (seven Band-Aids usually did the trick).

Sometime in that first year, within our family, Max started calling me "Bear" rather than Jyl. An odd choice of name, the origin of which I still don't know but which his tiny-child-therapist said was a really good sign. First, his sister had made it clear that she did not approve of him calling me "Mom." Second, she explained, Max likely associated the word *"mom"* with some not-so-great stuff. "Bear" was his way of planting his flag on me with a fresh, innocent, and untarnished term.

I was enamored. It was such a cozy place to land in what seemed like such a short time.

Except that while I was being enamored, I completely missed the continuation of Amelia going the other direction.

Amelia did start rebuilding her relationship with her (bio)mom and, in doing so, started unbuilding her relationship with me. I was right. Amelia was beginning to get exactly what she needed (or wanted?) from her (bio)mom. She found someone with whom she could be worry-free. Homework? Nah. Healthy meals? Nope. Bedtime? Pass. All the things that Max was eating up (well, maybe not the healthy meals), Amelia found very unappealing. I came with access to grades, I came with a list of kid-friendly chores, I came with appropriate consequences. I came with ideas of child-rearing that did not always match her father's and if we weren't butting heads on those ideas, Rich and I were compromising between his thoughts and mine, which meant that Amelia's expectations were shifting. I say I came with all of this, but that isn't entirely true. Rich and I took most of our guidance from our counselor. However, when any of these shifts were presented to the kids, it was always received by Amelia as coming directly from the evil bag of tricks that I was hiding somewhere in the house. I became less and less appealing. A cloud started forming over us and began to grow.

I can't really pinpoint when the cloud started darkening, but it didn't take long to begin covering Rich as well. We started noticing Amelia over-dramatizing anytime she was asked to do something or landing in a devastated fetal position when told something she didn't like. She would sometimes visibly cower when we spoke to her. Admittedly, I did raise my voice at times. This was commonplace in my upbringing, but not in Rich's, so the elevated tone surprised her. She would apologize to us in a weird panicky way, speaking quickly, and looking for the nearest exit. She would stop just short of raising her hands over her face to block whatever imagined weapon was coming her way. It was hard. Rich and I felt like we were being pigeonholed into creating a consequence-free house lest we be accused outright of abuse. We often wrote it off as the collision of a sullen teenager with a get-it-done-(step)mom.

This behavior eventually lessened with Rich though never fully eliminated, but clearly, he was the one she would work with the most. For me, it mostly still continues. Even as a college freshman, she still cringes often when I speak to her. Throughout her high-school years, she'd often list me as the number one source of stress in her life. She'd follow that with a proclamation of appreciation for how much I was willing to do for her. I had a hard time keeping up. She'd say I caused her panic attacks and then bring me baked goods picked specifically for me from her job at a bakery. She'd place all the blame for escalating anger issues squarely at my feet, so much so that Rich and I began to notice how surprised her friends and teachers were upon meeting me and *not* finding a monster.

Our routine became scripted: Everything is fine. I ask Amelia to do something. It doesn't get done. I ask again. Repeat six times. I become frustrated to the point of mom-yelling and Amelia becomes hysterical, Rich comes to her rescue. Rich and I begin fighting (oh, I see it now, the splitting. Who says writing isn't therapeutic?). And down the rabbit hole we go, spiraling. We generally didn't even know how or when the spiral started. The level of Amelia's anger reached peaks and began to fill her with venom towards me. Rich and I would analyze her texts/emails/talk to counselors/poke around, all in an effort to nail down what started it each time. A week would go by, and we'd be no closer to a resolution. Instead, Amelia and I would just rotate around each other, pretending everything was fine.

After riding this merry-go-round multiple times, I knew where I was to retreat to. I'd be stripped of my parenting-Amelia duties and Rich would take the full load. It felt stupid. *Rich, can you tell Amelia to set the table? Rich, can you remind Amelia to do her chores? Rich can you tell Amelia? Rich can you ask Amelia? Rich, can you remind Amelia?* ... It was like living with a foreign exchange student and her translator. It wasn't even in person much of the time as Rich traveled, it was via text. I'm sure Rich loved sitting in meetings and feeling his phone vibrate with requests of *Rich, Amelia failed her bio test. Rich, Amelia is using grown-up language.* Oftentimes, we'd tire of this routine, and I'd revert to being the evil one doling out the responsibilities or consequences until it escalated too far and, there we were, starting the merry-go-round again.

As a (long) side note ... one of the things I was advised, as a (step)mom was to never, ever be the one doling out the bad news. *"Leave that up to the father,"* I'd hear, *"homework, punishments, and all unpleasant requests."* In today's reality, that's not today's reality. It certainly wasn't in our house, as Rich often traveled, leaving me solo with the kids. It certainly wasn't in our house, as we had full custody of the children. It certainly wasn't in our house as their (bio)mom was not interested in the difficult pieces of parenting. When the option is "Breadwinner should quit job in order to be home to tell the kids to do their chores" or "(Step)mom handles things while breadwinner is gone," it seems like a logical choice to go with the latter. I wish we'd been clearer to our counselor that her highly encouraged mode of parental operations did not work for us much of the time. If we'd been able to toss that suggestion out the window earlier, perhaps we'd have come up with a working plan in which we weren't constantly bouncing around child-rearing responsibilities with a questioning look of *are we doing it right?* Ideally, yes, that plan works. Ideally, I would have gotten to be the fun lady living at the house who never raised her voice to the level of nagging. Ideally, I could say, *"Wait until your father comes home,"* and it wouldn't have meant "Wait for four days, during which the crime will have all but been forgotten."

Eventually, we really did just retreat as far back as we could, finally acknowledging that, maybe just maybe, Amelia and I were not made out to have a normal mother/daughter relationship. Or that maybe she didn't really want any relationship with me. Maybe, with her history of weird relationships with the women in her life, adding one more weird relationship was just never going to work out. Lord knows we tried to figure it out for seven years. Maybe we'd finally reached a point of just going on a long timeout.

I didn't take that decision lightly, to put our relationship in reverse, but it did give me some sense of relief. Perhaps the optimist in me never thought it would be forever. That was actually too devastating to even ponder. The idea that this person, with whom I'd hoped to build a bond similar to my own with my mom, would never come around to loving (or even liking) me? No, that was really just too awful a thought. It was tough on Rich, living in a constant low-level panic of trying to "fix it" before Amelia headed out into the real world. As the self-proclaimed driver of the family emotional bus, he was heartbroken with thoughts of failure. How could he have one child who loved me so dearly and another who was filled with venom?

About a year after we essentially broke up, Amelia did begin popping back into my orbit. When she left for college, I privately cut the emotional cord. I told myself that the real world would be the only thing that could improve our status and worked very hard to just stay out of her new life. I didn't text, I didn't call. We were finally able to truly go to a system where Rich was the prime parent. She was gone for five months at school before the realization hit that she would be coming home for holiday break, home to where I was, this person who wasn't sure where I actually stood. She returned with enough real-world experience and the emotional space for our relationship to take some baby steps forward. I don't know if having some real-world relationships helped or if absence really did make her heart grow fonder, but we seemed to be heading in a positive direction.

We have talked minimally about it, as a family, about how the relationships within our emotional bus are not all *that* bad. We actually believe (the parents) that we were actually fairly normal in the land of families. That's one thing that has likely shocked both of our kids the most as they have matured. They are finding out that this family, with its steps and seconds and blendings, still runs very much like the majority of traditional families.

I think one of the most important lessons we've learned is that sometimes what the counselors tell you just isn't the best mode of operations. Sometimes you have to just go with your gut or your heart or that nagging voice in the back of your head and veer away from the advice of studies and scenarios. And sometimes you have to remember that the behavior of your stepchildren to you is not unlike the behavior of biological children to you. Did I say "*sometimes?*" I meant most times. That has been a tough idea to really latch onto, like it was almost easier to just think *well, they hate me because I'm not their real mom*. That thought actually provided a reason for me not to do any relational work. If the reason we weren't gelling was because I wasn't their real mom, then A = B; I'd never be their real mom, so there was no point in working too hard at it.

When I finally did find my bubble of moms to bounce life off of, I started to learn that our story mimicked those of real, live biological families. Light bulbs came on at a very low level and began to slowly brighten. There were some feelings of regret that I hadn't explored this option sooner, that my kids were behaving towards me just like "normal" kids were behaving to their "normal" moms. If I'd known that sooner, would I have been easier on myself? Would I have stopped pushing so hard for those kids to Sally Field me? What if I had been able to just let the tension roll off my back and carry on knowing that, in fact, what I was getting was typical kid attitude? What if it hadn't taken me so long to appreciate the grumbling, snarky-ness for what it was, a sign that these kids truly considered me theirs and that I was a safe person to express their moodiness to?

They embraced the idea that I was not going anywhere long before I did. And once the light bulb finally brightened, it was a big sigh of emotional relief.

They like me. They really like me.

REMEMBER WHERE THEY CAME FROM

You have to remember where your step-kids came from.

You have to remember that all that yuck of being children of divorce came along with them. The foundations of their young lives formed within strife and grief and guilt, all at an age when they could neither comprehend their own feelings nor truly understand what was happening to their family.

This baggage will stay with them for years and years before they even think of developing the courage to find the zipper to open it. What else comes with them (hopefully) is more happy memories of their past than sad ones. I felt a lot of pull toward talking about the bad memories. I suppose it was a survival technique to bring them closer to me and to a state of relief at this new setup. I felt the pull, but I didn't typically do it. I tried really hard only to engage in chatter about the bad times when the kids initiated the conversation, and then I tried really hard to let them guide the conversation to where they needed it to go. It surprised me how much their tiny brains blocked out. I had heard every gory detail from Rich, but I often found the kids were missing pretty significant parts of the story.

I was counseled not to push or pry or force open Pandora's box. This was tricky because while I was following the advice not to open the door to the bad memories, the kids felt very awkward about sharing any of the good ones. They wanted to make me happy, this new lady, so they took on unrecognized (remember, they were young) guilt at bringing up the rainbows-and-unicorns stories that were formed before I appeared. That was a really tricky place for everyone. The reality was that I *didn't* want to hear *anything* about their (bio)mom. At the start, she and I certainly didn't have much hope of building a relationship. Why would I want to know about the days when she *was* able to handle momming or wife-ing?

A piece of advice that I didn't get, but I wish I'd had? I should have asked. I should have asked the kids to tell me their stories. I should have encouraged them to catch me up on their young lives. It was okay for them to miss their (bio)mom. It was okay for them to tell me about the times they laughed or hugged or had adventures together. It was okay for them to wish for that time when life was simpler and there were no big words like separation or divorce or remarriage floating above their heads. I wish I'd been able to slow down enough in my rush to figure out what I was doing to ask them what they had done. Years into this, my husband and I started having a mantra of Tell Me Something Good. It was born when we noticed Max often launching into everything that went wrong in his day and our frustration that he was heading down a path beaten down by Eeyore. When Max would start this route, we would stop him and ask him to tell us three good things about his day before he got to the bad stuff. Typically, by the time we got done talking about those things, the bad stuff was out of his mind.

I often wonder how the kids' lives could have been improved if we'd taken that approach from the start. What if, on the nights when Amelia could not get to sleep because she was riddled with anxiety, if we'd gone into her room and asked her to share some of her favorite memories? What if, when Max blasted me for not being his mom, if I'd stopped and asked him to tell me how she might have handled the situation better? What if, instead of feeling threatened by this woman who lived miles away, if I had embraced the wins she had had with her family? It would likely not have canceled out where I was sitting at that moment, no, but it might have been a quicker route to stability if we weren't so often reminding ourselves of the bad times.

While we were still dating, Rich would pull up photos or videos of the kids when they were growing up. It didn't seem like a big deal, just a dad showing off his family, but I'd often pretend not to notice the presence of his ex-wife. Then, coinciding with "things getting serious," I started welling up with anxiety when he tried to do the same thing. I could not understand why he would want me to see him and the kids happy with his ex-wife (and their mother). All I'd been hearing about this woman, as my husband debriefed a lengthy end to their marriage, was how hellish she'd made their lives. It was easier for me to keep her in that *she's-a-bad-person* category than in one where, after witnessing all the good times, I would become even more shocked with her for throwing grenades over her shoulder while she walked away from it all. I didn't want to see those snapshots from the better times. I didn't want to see her as someone I could have liked under different circumstances.

I know (now) that I was putting Rich in a pretty strange place. He needed to both unload about the crap his ex-wife was putting him and the kids through while also sharing the memories of their past as a family with me. I couldn't reconcile both lanes of information. Either I was going to be on Team That-Lady-Fucked-Up or on Team What-A-Wonderful-Life. To summarize, I have no idea which team was the correct team to pick to this day. At least now I can understand a bit where my brain was. I can recognize that where my brain was enabled a place to be created where the kids didn't feel like they could share stories or where they felt they had permission to include that piece of their lives into mine.

We've never had any photos of their (bio)mom in our house. I'm not even sure where they would be displayed. At least in the kids' bedrooms, right? But I never asked or offered or opened that door. Perhaps I should have asked the kids, when we were putting together our new house, if pictures of their mom would help them feel less homesick for their old lives. Perhaps something that small would have given them the message that I was not trying to replace anyone, that while I was here for the long haul, I was also aware that they'd already had a long haul. Certainly, nobody told me I couldn't put up pictures from my past life.

Building a blended family is hard (I think we are blended, right? Even though I only brought myself to the table?). Coming in as an outsider and feeling like I was living in the mud easily made me forget that I was not alone in that mud. We were just in different puddles. I spent so much time learning and figuring and trying to turn myself into Mary Poppins that I often forgot that the kids were also spending so much time learning and figuring and trying to turn themselves into members of a whole new family that they didn't wish for. I shrugged off, so many times, the advice not to change anything that first year if I could help it. I came in hot, offering new menus, offering task lists, offering new school expectations, offering upgraded wardrobes, offering earlier bedtimes, etc. It must have seemed like I had no faith in how Rich had kept these kids alive for as long as he had.

In fairness, I am an information gatherer. When I realized that life was leaning heavily to the side of making me a (step)mom, I immediately Googled for books related to the topic. There were hardly any available and none that applied to my situation. The few I found were very high level, probably written by shrinks who'd never actually been through the blended family situation but had recommendations all mapped out and wrapped up in a pretty bow. As a family, we found every crack possible. *Don't disrupt the bedtime routine:* Um, pass ... kids had a pretty late bedtime that was actually past my own. *Don't change their diets:* Pass again, I couldn't stand chicken nuggets nor the idea of serving them every single meal, and, hey, how about a vegetable here or there? With very good intentions, we did upend a lot of their small people routines and were then stupidly surprised at the level of meltdown that resulted.

I was pulling most of my knowledge from my own upbringing and Rich was pulling most of his from his own upbringing. The catch was that our upbringings could not have been any more different. Growing up, my father traveled often, leaving my mom to run the household of three kids within four years of each other in a very no-nonsense way. We followed her rules, we ate what she put in front of us, we helped as instructed, and we sure as shit didn't back talk. Does it not sound warm and fuzzy? It was sometimes, but it was also how my mom survived being a single mom five days per week. Rich's parents were in their mid-teens when he was born and were married and divorced before they hit their twenties. He was shuffled between homes: mom's, dad's, grandparent's, aunt's and uncle's. He spent a lot of time alone as his mom was working and his dad was hanging with a shady crowd. I came into parenting as a drill sergeant. Rich came into it trying to make sure his kids knew he was there for them emotionally and physically.

I'm relatively sure that when each was born, the kids were taken to the top of a mountain and raised up for all the land to see. They were so *wanted* by Rich and his extended family. And it's not that I wasn't wanted by mine as a child, but we didn't live close enough to any relatives to become the permanent gems in their family crowns. When I saw the leniency Rich's tribe had in letting *all* the grandkids run the show, I was baffled. I also knew that mode would not work for me, someone with a little bit of OCD and a whole lot of anxiety. I suppose if our marriage had been the first for both, prior to children, Rich and I would have had more time to learn each other's personalities and get to know each other's families. We'd have had more of a runway to figure out how we would raise our kids together rather than slamming into each other on our first day of co-parenting.

My inability to live in total chaos made me into a bit of a ramrod as I was desperately attempting to find some stability and consistency in my upended life. And it wasn't even that chaotic, it was just normal family life. I just was not prepared, nor did I know that it would be too much. I don't think I could have approached it in any other way unless we'd had the option of *not* throwing me headfirst into overnight insta-mom. Maybe we did have that option. Maybe I should have moved out when the kids moved in, to a nearby apartment in order to get some space and a retreat back to the single life, but everything happened at warp speed at the exact time I was extremely lonely from my move. The idea of having my own place in a town where I knew absolutely no one never percolated past a point of causing complete terror. Instead, we lived in a crash, burn, and try again world.

The thing that I couldn't grasp was how to maintain that focus on *where the kids came from* and how to adjust my presentation to them with that understanding. They were broken, they were hurt, they were homesick for their old life. They'd grown up, thus far, surrounded by a lot of people who parented differently than I was parented. They'd gone through a divorce being spoiled at every turn in an effort to lessen trauma. My enthusiasm for creating or restoring boundaries was inappropriately timed for the situation that the kids were meeting me in. They had no way of defining how they were feeling, and I was too new to understand that their actions often were born of ramped-up emotions that had nothing to do with me. If they were lashing out at me, for example, they were likely just expressing emotions carried in the griefcases that they'd brought with them into this new home that they didn't even want to move into.

I have gotten so much more protective of my (step)children in the last few years. I don't question their love for me or their loyalty to me or that either would take a bullet for me (in that, they would). The irony is those feelings didn't start to percolate until I mentally threw in the towel with Amelia. It was like, by doing that, I gave away all the space that the difficulties were taking up and made room for love to move in. In the never-ending stream of subconscious hindsight, I wonder what would have been different if we'd had enough time to fall in love with each other, the kids and I, before we were sharing four walls. But then, if we had waited, if we had really eased into it over the course of years while placing me fully in the back seat to parenting, would the love we have for each other be as intense as it is now that we have that tumultuous history to share? I look at my daughter and I know she feels for me what I feel for her, that we were at war with each other for years. But we persevered. Neither of us left. We kicked each other down and then picked each other up, over and over and over. We see each other with such a high level of respect and adoration because we know that if any two people deserved to bail on a relationship, it was the both of us.

It is that commitment that is the hardest, coming into a family that was already mostly formed. The staying. There are so many times I wanted to leave, times that I didn't keep to myself, in the form of screaming, *I'm done, I'm out of here, I'll just go! You'll be better off without me!* It had nothing to do with actually doing it, though. It had everything to do with having no way to express exactly how lost I was in this new world and how unheard I felt and how I just literally did not know if I could manage it and how much that made me feel like a total failure. But that's not what the kids heard. What they heard was that I was going to leave. Over and over. Just beyond a time in their lives when somebody *did* leave and when they *were* left. And, yet I couldn't understand why they weren't getting closer to me. Of course, it's obvious now. If I could eliminate one phrase from their memories from the last decade, it would be that: *I'm leaving.* If I could remove that doubt from the past of their tiny minds, I would.

I don't know when that changed. I don't know at what moment the switch flipped, and I went from a constant, back-of-the-head nagging that I really could go if I wanted to (and that I should definitely remind everyone of that over and over). I think it coincided with my daughter's well-presented essay on her life as a child abuse victim. In a world where she was never abused, I was the source of her anguish. It was shocking to see on paper, but even more shocking to hear from her that she actually and truly believed this. It was terrifying as I wondered whom she'd told this to (other than on six college applications) and what they would think of me. It was terrifying to lay awake at night and think, *well, this is probably it, my husband is probably going to ask me to leave.* I truly felt beaten. I truly felt that this teenager had spent years concocting this narrative to destroy me, and I could not understand why. Yes, we had some massive speed bumps in our years. But we'd also had so many lovely, memorable times. Where did those pieces fit into her story? Why weren't those included? I spent a lot of time peeling back the layers of the onion in an effort to figure out just why I was so absolutely terrible at being a mom.

But the answer was that I wasn't.

The answer was that most of the behavior exhibited by both kids was typical, normal, everyday kid behavior, with a chaser of *my parents divorced and I didn't like it.* What I was learning is that children of divorce (at least the ones in my house) would stamp all bad things in their life with that badge, blame pointed squarely to their lives not turning out the way they really wanted them to. What I was learning was that I was attributing an ability to have really big, grown-up thoughts to two kids who really didn't have the capability to have really big, grown-up thoughts. While I am so grateful to have not gone through a divorce as a child, I almost think it would have been easier to have the background information that it could have lent me.

We attribute our lives to the lives of those around us. Our lives are the ones that make the most sense. The way we handled our pasts often seems like the most logical choice. It takes a certain level of maturity to truly understand that our lives mean absolutely nothing to our children. And, in my case, my life—knowing zero about divorce or trauma or being pulled between two households or well-earned feelings of abandonment—really did not deserve a dog in their fight. My best role would have been the one of sounding board or confidant or friend. My best role would have been one where the kids could have escaped a little from the melee they were working through. While that wasn't possible, if I could have tweaked enough to lean a little closer to that side, perhaps the speed bumps would not have been so gigantic.

Which Way's Up?

Just the one, then?

We've mostly successfully rounded the corner on another Mother's Day. It's an odd holiday for anyone in a "mixed" family in which a biological mother exists as well as a step-mother. Or maybe it's just odder here in our family, with our dynamics of having the kids full time, all the time, making me much more mom-ish than an every-other-weekend (step)mom person. Anyway, long story short, I want some thunder on Mother's Day. And another long story short, that's what makes it odd and sometimes incredibly frustrating. I thought we nailed it last year, actually. The kids' biological mother and I actually spoke throughout the week before Mother's Day to come up with a "We'll Share!" plan. They would spend the weekend with her and return to our house Sunday at lunchtime for my turn. I was so proud of our co-parenting that I didn't even share it with Rich ... until he texted me while I was returning, early Sunday morning, from visiting my own mother to say, "Oh, hey, their (bio)mom decided to just keep the kids through dinner."

Oh, hello ALL of the emotions.

Anyway.

While the kids were enjoying an extended Mother's Day with their actual mom, I scrolled through Facebook and *blammo* got one of those, "but look how far you've come" reminders.

Turned out that "on this day six years ago" I had participated in my very first field trip as a new (step)mother. Pictures of a tiny Max and his tiny friends poking around Henricus Park meeting Pocahontas (maybe, it looks like Disney Pocahontas in the pictures), visiting sleeping huts, whittling away at a full-size canoe flashed by and sent me *right back to that disaster of a day.*

First field trip? Sure. Also, the second documented time I lost my child.

Max's second-grade teacher was my lifeline for the entirety of that inaugural year of parenting. I came into the role hot and with zero training, other than basic babysitting and a terrible assumption (by Rich) that parenting comes naturally to everyone. This is probably accurate if you are actually present when the child makes its first out-of-womb appearance. For those who step in at, oh, let's say, age seven ... it's not quite as natural. It does seem like it should be super easy, though. Or it did. I knew people with kids. They all seemed pretty normal and unstressed and had their shit together. Granted, I mainly saw them on date nights where I performed as a third wheel while they begged for stories about the "single, no kids life." But when handed the keys to the kid-rearing kingdom ... well, it was a bit like jumping into a frozen lake.

And, having never been a little boy, Max was pretty much an alien to me.

As soon as I was granted access to the elementary school, I started a daily barrage of emails to his teacher, Ms. Farnsworth. I did not have access in the beginning, when I was still "the girlfriend." At the time, that really pissed me off. Eventually, I got it. I mean, I knew I had concrete plans to stick around forever, but the school really needed proof that I wasn't a flash in my future husband's pan(ts). Our engagement solidified my permanence and suddenly the cafeteria doors were thrown open with a scream of "Yes, we'd love for you to make copies!" or "Can you help with gingerbread houses?" or "How do you feel about Easter parties?"

I had arrived.

Ms. Farnsworth had unending patience with me and an amazing willingness to gently help me figure things out. Her reward was getting every question I had about seven-year-old boys. *He doesn't like to go to bed at night. Is that normal? Why does he put rocks in the dishwasher? Can boys do buttons, or do they just live in elastic pants? Why does he smell funny? He peed on my foot when he was trying to brush his teeth while standing on the toilet. Does that happen all the time? Will he ever eat vegetables? What's with the Crocs?*

God. Bless. This. Woman. Every question was answered with such a sweetness and a wink and a word of encouragement. She saved me at a time when I couldn't ask Rich's mom or Max's biological mom anything, as it would confirm their suspicions of my complete ineptitude.

When I made it as far as May and a field trip form came home asking for volunteers, I signed up so fast I nearly burned a hole in the paper. How hard could it be? Max was so excited at the idea of having a fun day together. I was going to take off from work and we were going to pack matching Lunchables (what was a Lunchable?). What could go wrong? As the day approached, I shopped for field trip items: bug spray, sunscreen, People magazine to read on the bus, a cute outfit so the other moms would like me, a new tote bag ... And, finally, off we went to the school with an enthusiastic "Have fun guys!" from Rich.

Oh, we will have fun, sir. This was going to be a giant piece of fun cake.

Max and I strolled into his classroom, abuzz with second-grade excitement and a few parents holding extra-large cups of coffee. Minutes later, Ms. Farnsworth quieted everyone down with a weird clapping game (was this the resurgence of tee-tiki-tie?) and started doling out children to chaperones by the fours. "Mrs. Upton ... four kids ... Mr. Strange ... four kids"... and so on ... until I was the only chaperone left. And "Oh, we're just going to let you hang out with Max, today."

"Oh," I said, "... so, just the one?"

"Yes, just the one. Let's start with that."

God. Bless. This. Woman.

Hindsight, blah, blah, blah. How did she already know field trips would not bubble up as one of my talents (perhaps the thirteen emails I'd sent her leading up to it)?

The lessons began as soon as we left the school. Parents sat together-ish. School buses are incredibly loud when you're forty-two. And bumpy. And hot. And headache-inducing. Holy shite, I was in some new level of hell. What would happen when we actually left the parking lot? When would I read my magazine?

The ride was about forty-five minutes, during which time I met the two parents closest to me, both absolutely welcoming and (well, now I see it) curious to see how this field trip virgin would fare. Riding to Henricus Park, I had no idea they'd be my saviors throughout the day, as they never batted a suspicious eye at my inadequacies. We got to the park, which sat along the James River, and shuffled the kids (or kid, in my group) to the welcoming area: a learning center where the kids answered questions about the history of Virginia and showed off their math skills while I and my two new, parent friends got side-eyed for being too giggly. In fairness, asking a child to hold a map of Africa in front of his pants basically just looks like he's holding a jockstrap.

Easy peasy!

But was it?

We were sent in groups to rotating stations (easy) and summoned back to the welcome center for lunch (so easy) which the kids sucked down faster than a dog finding cat food (still, easy). I scrapped finishing my Lunchable to start a game of "Where are we going, Max?" as he zipped around to talk to various friends and run in a field and which-one-of-those-seven-year-olds-belongs-to-me?

Like, really, I couldn't even remember what he was wearing. The groups were re-assembled to finish off the stations (easy, phew, back to easy) and, upon completion, an angel in a ranger's uniform appeared to say my four favorite words, "There's a gift shop."

I vaguely remember something else about the river and making sure you didn't lose any of your kids less they fall into it.

Max's level of excitement for the gift shop did not match mine. I explained that we needed to head straight there, get in before the rush, get in before the cool stuff was gone, and find the sales. He looked at me with his this-lady-is-nuts eyes and shuffled along. And I was right, there was cool stuff. There were things we both wanted and things we debated and, oh, dang it ... we looked so long that there was a rather long line of tiny people waiting to count their change. Max began vibrating as he could see his friends out the window darting here and there while he was stuck in line with me, clearly regretting his choices.

"Fine," I finally said, "Go ahead out. I'm sure this won't take long."

I really don't know how long it took.

What I do know is about four seconds later, I had lost him in a sea of kids outside of the building. I did not know what to do (I mean, I know now ... you put your stuff down and go find the missing child).

I had two thoughts racing around in my head: Buy this stuff vs what if he falls in the river?

What if my first field trip ended with a water rescue? But what if he's fine and I don't buy the stuff and he has a meltdown? I began to sweat, still trying to get a visual through the window, while I waited for child after child to listen intently as the volunteer told them which were pennies and which were dimes and what the correct combination of each was.

Rich was going to kill me when he found out I'd lost Max. But would that be canceled by the tiny dreamcatcher?

Wait, I finally thought, let me just text one of the other

parents. *Whose numbers I didn't have. Whose names I wasn't sure of. Who thought I was fit for this?!?*

I quickly opened Facebook and started going through Rich's friends' list with the hopes that one of the other chaperones had made contact with him at some point in his weak social media life. Scroll, scroll, scroll, BINGO. I found a chaperone who was also the father of one of Max's classmates. I sent my request (please be my friend, please be my friend, please make it snappy). I got an almost instant pingback (thank you, Lawd Jesus) and immediately sent what I hoped was a very un-worrisome message.

"Oh, hey ... just here in the gift shop ... no big deal ... so is Max out there with y'all?"

Max, in fact, did not fall into the James River that day.

As soon as I was reunited with him, I basically threw him over my shoulder, carried him onto the bus, and strapped him to the seat with my shoelaces. When the bus departed, I pretty much collapsed into a heap of "I will never, ever chaperone anything ever again."

Max was unfazed, chattering the entire way home while I nodded and tried to bring my pulse back down to a normal range. We arrived back at school, collected the car, and went home. When I'd left six hours earlier, I looked as fresh as a daisy in my First Field Trip outfit, hair nicely done, a bit of makeup. I returned looking like I'd jumped into a wind tunnel full of slime.

"Oh, hi," Rich said, "How'd it go?"

"You're going to have to do the next one."

I'd rather focus on the rocks in the dishwasher.

CHAPTER FIVE

It's Never Their Fault

TWO HOMES

Probably the most consistent outcome in a divorce is the immediate creation of a feeling of shuffling for both the parents and the kids. You take a whole family unit and you split it in half and the result, at minimum, is two households. Ideally, both parents want very much for the children to live with them. Ideally, the children aren't asked where they'd like to create a primary residence and, ideally, there is enough thought and consideration put into that decision that the transition between houses is as easy as it can be. Did I say ideally? In the same paragraph that speaks of divorce and multiple households? No, there is nothing ideal about this at all. If I could change anything about divorce and custody and how it all plays out, it's that nothing was signed until a living situation trial run was completed. Instead, those decisions play out at the exact moment when the entire family is being ripped apart, a time when no one is close to their emotional best and common sense has gone out the window.

There is no formula to this. If only there were. If only there were crystal balls available to peer into, allowing a peek into how this or that combination of custody and visitation would pan out. If only the signing of those papers didn't put at least one parent on an auto-defense keeping the schedule as dictated by the courts, regardless of the post-divorce effects it was having on all those involved. That is how it happens, typically. With divorce papers come schedules.

Ours sucked.

For some reason, our kids were asked what they would like to see in a custody schedule as if a nine- and six-year-old would have any idea what it would mean to travel with a bag of clothes and a toothbrush for the next decade. As if a nine- and a six-year-old were ever going to sit in a room with both parents present and say *oh, well, I guess I'd much rather live full time with dad.* I've heard of instances where the original house was kept, kids living in it full time, and it was the parents that came and went. I always thought that was insane until I was in the middle of the shuffle. The custody schedule in our house started out to be a modified 50/50 split. However, instead of spending the entire week at one house or the other, there was a night during the week that the kids would flip houses for twenty-four hours and another night where they would dine with the other parent. It could not have been more confusing. It was thought up by the six-year-old and some idiot judge who looked at the layout and said, *"That looks great, sweety, good luck!"*

I moved into the middle of the beginning of this agreement. I literally had no idea where the kids were going to be when or if we were picking someone up or if there was an activity we needed to attend. It became a daily question before school, *"Where am I going tonight?"* If the documents hadn't been signed and notarized and filed, I suspect Rich would have bagged that plan almost immediately. It was very obviously not healthy for anyone; however, after wrapping up a year full of lawyers and trials and accusations, the last thing anyone wanted to do was ring up the courts again to tweak a few things. Hence, why a trial period should be a must and well thought out with adult emotions put aside.

Six and Nine. No clue on where they were going to be each night. No clue in which house they should keep their favorite items. No ability to feel settled. No sense of home. Any movement, to school, to karate, to birthday parties involved carrying a bag with extra clothes and whatever was deemed that day's security blanket. We had a giant calendar at our house, color coded, indicating who would be where when, created by me as I tried to make a chaotic situation seem colorful and fun. It was not colorful and fun. It gave no more clarity to me or Rich than it did to the kids and yet we would point the kids to the coded blocks whenever they had questions, hoping they would get some use out of it and start learning their own locational pattern. We had no idea that staring at the rainbow assortment of locations only induced anxiety as they saw a jigsaw pattern where a fairly simple life had once existed.

We often hear how resilient kids are, how they will be okay in the end. We say it to make ourselves feel better about our mistakes. Yes, I suppose, in the end, most kids do end up *okay,* but is that where we really want them to land? *Okay?* The fallout from the constant relocations has now (nearly a decade later) dwindled down to neither child being comfortable throwing away anything at all. That nomadic existence induced both of them with a fear of losing their things. They obsess over keeping all important items out in the open in their bedrooms as if having a visual on the piles provides a sense of belonging in that spot.

It's an awful way to be lucky, but when their (bio)mom was evicted from her apartment (the sheriff waited for her to drive off with the kids before putting a lock on her door), we were able to insert some stability. The crushing blow was she was driving to take the kids to school. The door the sheriff padlocked belonged to their other home. They had already started laying the building blocks of feeling that they needed to keep everything they owned within reach at all times so that it could be easily transported. The eviction confirmed that for them when they learned that they wouldn't be going back to that apartment. They each started a mental inventory of the things they loved that were now beyond their reach, including a pet fish. Really, the only plus to the situation was our ability to gain full custody immediately, eliminating the insanity of the custody schedule with no more lengthy hearings. That was an awful way to get there. And it really came too late as the kids already felt that their lives would always be one step away from being shuffled again.

Our new custody agreement did not give any visitation or custodial rights to their (bio)mom at all, twice. First, at the time of the emergency change and, second, a year later when she filed for a second hearing to regain her rights. It was such a bittersweet moment as we knew we could be doing the shuffle so much better than originally laid out, but we also knew how hard it was for the kids to navigate not really knowing when they would see their (bio)mom next. The inconsistency of those years still plays out quite frequently. Rich and I often felt like we had three children as we managed time together while wondering why the kids' (bio)mom wasn't reaching out to them. We tamped down our anger and bitterness by telling ourselves (Rich and I) that she was likely embarrassed and that being distant made it easier to swallow with that lack of connection.

The problem was there was no way to make the kids understand that. What they saw and felt was that she was not placing them on her priority list. When Rich and I would encourage them to make plans for dinner or a weekend visit, we would see a look pass across their eyes that we later pinned down to both exhaustion and disappointment. The truth was they did not want to be in charge of their visits because hearing her excuses to pass hurt their hearts too much. It's that sweaty feeling of asking for permission to do something that is a total long shot and bracing yourself for the inevitable denial, except that feeling was coming on a weekly basis because we thought we were doing the right thing in encouraging them to build their relationship back up.

There is no formula.

We still have a bit of a struggle getting the kids organized for weekends at their (bio)mom's house. We went to an air-quoted every-other-weekend schedule years ago, with the caveat that she could take the kids to dinner or come for a visit whenever she wanted to. Except she hasn't. The kids still approach her weekends with an honest shrug of *yeah, I think we're going over.* Because they don't have a lot of interaction with her, the kids have always held her confirmed weekends a bit sacred, never making plans with friends, trying not to work, and saving homework for Sunday night. We basically have a loop running, encouraging them to attend birthday parties or soccer games on her weekends, that it is okay, that if she balked at driving or wasn't feeling well, that we would come collect them.

We did start to see priority shifts as each kid reached their mid-teens, preferring to spend time with friends on a Friday rather than heading straight over to her house after school. Of course, the pride of watching them make their own choices comes at the cost of the guilt from the other end. And—hindsight alert—we would remind the kids that they could see their mother *anytime they wanted* until one frustrated response popped out of Amelia's mouth: *I know, you don't have to keep reminding me that she doesn't want to see me.* Well, shit. We didn't even try to explain just how much that wasn't what we were trying to do. Instead, we went with our best poker face, a heartfelt apology, and a hug.

One of the common phrases in a two-home household is

"but, that's not what we do at mom's house!" This is yet another tricky part of the shuffle. The divorce textbook says that both homes should follow the same rules: same bedtimes, same homework schedules, same discipline structure, etc. Also, there is no divorce textbook and also, that's pretty much impossible. I imagine if we only saw the kids twice a month, we'd likely throw most rules out the window as well, just wanting them to have the best forty-eight hours of their lives each time they came to visit. It's tricky in that you can either expect the kids to memorize two sets of living guidelines or you can spend a lot of time saying *well, you're not at mom's house*. We went somewhere down the middle after years of frustration. We posted a list of house rules for our house, no memorization needed and, also, here's where we land on chores, grades, etc. ...

Ironically, once we got to the point in co-parenting where we felt able to communicate more openly, we often found that the *"But, that's not what we do at mom's house!"* instances were often quite embellished. Once we got to that point, we felt a little silly in our past thinking that it was a free-for-all down the street. We took our children's reporting of wild weekends as truth and jumped to a sometimes incorrect conclusion that common sense was thrown out the maternal window. I hate to say that the kids were playing both sets of parents, as I'm not sure at their ages that they even knew what they were doing, but that's the best explanation I can offer.

The best advice I can offer is that if things are done differently at the other house, do not make it a roadblock in co-parenting. There will be differences, but we could only control what was happening under our roof. We had to do our best not to eye roll or sigh or have a look of panic on the reports of wild weekends, for these would all have been a direct giveaway that we were not supportive of the other parent and that there are cracks in the parental armor through which the kids can slide. We became experts in the art of nodding and smiling and turning to face another direction when our real reaction came to visit. We had to choose the big stuff carefully, the items that we really wanted to buckle down and insist on consistency for in both houses. Is it really an issue if the kids stay up later at the other house? Probably not, unless the school is finding them asleep at their desks. Should the phone rules be the same everywhere? It would be nice, but it is also unlikely. Do chores matter everywhere? Again, probably not.

Choose your battles wisely as transitions are not easy, especially for children. They are also not easy for adults and especially not for the adults in the home to which the kids are arriving. Going from house to house is hard. Carrying the bulk of your life in a bag while tracking which rules belong to which structure is hard. The actual integration from one home to another is near impossible. It can turn everyone's life into a lengthy relational derailment which may finally seem settled only to have the shifts begin again. This has been the hardest part for me as a (step)mom for many reasons, none of which compare to what the children have been forced to deal with through no fault of their own. They have just spent a full weekend with their (bio)mom, whom they miss having daily interaction with. They have just spent a full weekend with little responsibility. They have just spent a full weekend visiting with the fun parent doing the fun things and essentially taking a vacation from real life. And then, with a quick ten-minute drive, they're asked to revert back to a totally different life. They did not choose this. If asked, they would choose for everything to be the way it used to be: no divorce, no split of homes, no (step)mom, no blurry lines. Each time they make that short trek back to real life, it is a reminder of a past that has been left behind by the adults they trusted.

Touchdowns in our home were difficult for many years. The kids would come home from their (bio)mom's, and their dad would be thrilled to see them with enthusiastic questions about their weekend and stories of how much he missed them. It wasn't that I wasn't happy to see them. Or maybe it was. That time off from (step)momming was also a vacation for me, a retreat back to the life I had before kids when I could come and go as I pleased. I had no responsibilities. It was simple, clean, and fresh. I did not have the same sense of missing the kids that my husband did because I hadn't spent the first decade of their lives with them at my hip. I did not have the same sense of *Oh, yay! They're back!* What I got instead was a feeling of dread and a feeling that the merry-go-round was starting again and a percolating bad attitude and a panic that I just was not ready to do this all again.

There were never-ending land mines and we would almost willingly jump on just to see if the explosion was as bad as with previous transitions. The kids and I would, sort of, orbit around each other, unsure of what we should be saying or doing. The truth was, they didn't miss me very much either. I was still this woman who just popped into their lives on whom the jury was far, far, far out. I was the person who replaced their (bio)mom in their lives and in their dad's life and in the place they called home. It was a big ask to expect the reunion to be unicorns and rainbows and none of us were ever ready for it. That feeling snowballed for years, a subconscious recollection of the stress and the stomach churns each weekend as the touchdown neared.

We would often have arguments. We would often snap at each other. Rich would try to right the ship and I would get pissed that he wasn't seeing things from my point of view, a point of view that I actually could not articulate beyond more snappy, snarky, verbal bombs. The entire house would function like a snow globe that had gotten shaken, except the glass was cracked and the water was seeping out. I had no idea that the kids were behaving the way they were behaving due to skyrocketing anxiety sparked by missing their mother the instant they closed the door of her car. They had no idea that I was behaving the way I was behaving due to skyrocketing anxiety sparked by the loop of saying goodbye to a child-free life every other week. And my husband just had no idea what to do at all. Kids come home, they are miserable. Kids come home, and the wife is miserable. I would say his biggest land mine was the assumption that I (in the end) didn't want the kids in our home. That wasn't it at all. My previous sense of normalcy was restored when they were away for the weekend. When they returned, my new normal arrived, and I had not yet gotten used to it.

Wash, rinse, repeat.

We tried many ways to alleviate the stress, most of which did not work. We planned big Sunday dinners for when the kids returned, except that put the stress of coming up with a great menu on me or it would be blown to bits as their mom decided to keep them until after dinner at the last minute. That started a rage of *"Well, when are they coming home???"* We started asking for a return time (okay, yes, that is Shuffle 101, have a schedule). That started a rage of *"Why do you need to know?"* or *"By bedtime."* or *"Why are you trying to keep the kids away from me/Us away from our mom?"*. None of which helped though we told all participants over and over that we just wanted a gauge on when the kids would arrive home on a super basic courtesy level. I did finally realize that if I were occupied at touchdown, whether watching a movie or knitting a scarf or walking the dog or painting my nails, it was easier. If there was something simple to prevent us from feeling that we all needed to run into a giant "Kumbaya" circle, we could ease back into life at each of our own paces. Let the kids come in and get settled. Let them have some solo time in their rooms. Let me remember what it felt like to have a full house again. Allow the reunions to occur more organically and less staged.

That solved 90 percent of the problem. The remaining 10 percent will likely be a wash as we have yet to nail down how to nail down a return time. Luckily, the kids are now old enough to come home to an empty home, if needed, and we have shifted to a fend-for-yourself dinner plan on those transitional nights. If they eat before they come home, great. If not, we have plenty of options available for them to make themselves. If I happen to cook a big Sunday dinner, they are certainly welcome at the table and if it is a rather quiet meal, that is fine as well.

COMMUNICATION GAMES

As I write this, our kids are eighteen and fifteen. They both have the best of the best in technology, mainly because my husband and I both work in technology. We often jump into technology things with a sense of wonder before realizing that maybe letting the kids jump in with us was a bit premature. Technology has a running theme, in our home, of us (the adults) providing all of the things only to be followed by some great and awkward hindsight later. Amelia has had a phone since about three seconds after the separation of her (bio)parents. I was not present at the time (nor would my opinion have counted or been correct that early in our lives together), but I suppose the phone was an easy way to soothe the *I'm going to miss whichever parent is not in earshot* fears. Or, more likely for my husband, *This will provide a way for me to reach out to the kids when they are not in my care.* Divorce sucks on so many levels, and communication is no exception. Divorce can cause a surge of stubbornness, which can result in an unintentional blocking of back and forth between whichever parent is currently hosting the children. There will be actual moments in which you think *"This is our day/weekend/week, why is your mother/father infringing on our time???"* The hope is that the thought remains delightfully internal and is not actually presented to the child on a silver platter for use in therapy further down the road.

I suppose prior to all this technology, the communication between kids and parents was much simpler, as the only real option was the phone hanging on the wall. If a child was with one parent, there would be few opportunities for talking with the other parent, as that phone on the wall was the only option. Today we have texting, email, and a thousand different chat applications. This is both good and bad. The good is that both parents are always equally accessible. The bad is that both parents are always equally accessible. The hiccup in that is that it creates a false acceptability to let the children handle all communication rather than leaving the bulk of it to the adults. The reality is that, because they are children, most communication should still remain on the plates of the grown-ups. That is very difficult, especially in the beginning, when all wounds are fresh and the last thing any of the relevant adults want to do is actually speak to the others.

I'd read of sending a notebook back and forth between houses with any questions, concerns, requests, or instructions needed for the other parent. We did not do that. We had two very in-tune children with a high reading ability from the get-go. I take that back. We used a notebook once, which is when we realized that a notebook being passed via the children could easily be opened. We tried many other modes over the last decade: an ongoing email trail, a group text, chat groups; none succeeded long term. The group text would often somehow magically lose someone's number, or the email trail would lose a member when a responder forgot to hit "reply all." Spoiler alert: The party who was left out of the party was 100 percent always me. My husband would not notice that I'd gone missing from the conversations. I'd realize a day or a week or a month later when we'd learn that, not only were we not on the same page anymore, but we were also not even on the same chapter. That would spark a surge of frustration within me as I felt that I was absolutely being tasked with full involvement in child-rearing yet given no opportunity for input. That frustration would spill over to the kids, as I often saw them as an extension of their mother (true, they are) and her questionable behavior (false, they had nothing to do with it).

We naively thought that handing a phone over to each of the kids would take us out of the lines of communication. We thought it would be easy for them to reach out to their (bio)mom about when she would be picking them up for her weekends. We thought they would invite her to the events they wanted her to attend, soccer games, or art shows. Or, maybe, they could just let her know that they missed her and could she please come take them to dinner. Instead, we spent years nagging, questioning, and getting not-so-nice feedback from their (bio)mom for being left out of important moments. It does make more sense now. We should not have expected children whose parents had just divorced to understand their role in keeping everyone on the same page. But at what age does that begin? And when it does, how do you handle it successfully?

Bad news. I don't know the answer to either of those questions.

Perhaps there are eight-year-olds who jump right into the game of knowing which weekends they are with which parent and start planning said weekends days before they arrive. Perhaps they track all school events and insist on multiple invites so that all parents and stepparents can attend. That did not happen in our house. In our house, if the parents didn't communicate, information did not move downstream. It was further complicated in that the kids' (bio)mom was fairly terrible at *any* kind of communication with the kids, even beyond events and schedules. We have yet to understand that, and I do hope it is not the norm.

Our kids would go days and days and days without hearing from their (bio)mom. It was (and is) very odd to us. When she lost all custodial rights, we created our own every-other-weekend schedule. We began playing a loop in our words to her, indicating that she was also welcomed to see the kids whenever she wanted to. We played a similar loop to the kids, indicating that they were welcome to see her whenever they wanted and that they could call her day or night. We had a land line (a wall phone, yes!) installed specifically for that use, dedicated with a number that was only given to their (bio)mom. It never rang. Or it never rang with any consistency. Or it only rang on a regular basis when either Rich or I was out of town and made at least a daily phone call to the kids. It was highly frustrating. Moreover, it was heartbreaking. We weren't aware just how heartbreaking until that fateful moment when we reiterated *"You can see your mom whenever you want"* and Amelia lashed back with a declaration of not needing to be reminded. Her feeling of rejection brewed without our knowledge. Ouch. While we were being frustrated, we were completely oblivious to the idea that the kids were hyperaware of what was(n't) going on.

We fell into a pattern where, most weeks, the kids would not even know it was going to end with a visit to their (bio)mom's. We would ask them to reach out to her to find out the pickup details and they would approach the task reluctantly. We'd bounce back and forth as to whether it was the right thing to do, encouraging them to reach out to her for details. We have never understood why the conversations weren't initiated on her end but, with the human brain's ability to draw conclusions, we all assumed that it was just not her priority to see the kids. If it were, she would see them, right? If it were, she would reach out to them, right? If it were...

This conversation has been repeated. We have chatted with her about how the kids sort of feel a bit left out of her life and that she really needs to be more involved. *Just ask how their day was*, we'd say. Each time the topic came up, communication would improve very briefly and then jump right back to the same (non) pattern. Which is how we have arrived here, with a fifteen- and eighteen-year-old playing whisper down the lane. There is an age when the kids should take over communication, yes, but I cannot say for sure when that is. We based our adjusted responsibilities in conjunction with communication with teachers. At about ninth grade, we stopped playing the over-involved school parents, asking about homework or grades or field trips and let the kids start advocating for themselves. Kids do not like to be uncomfortable. Talking to adults makes them uncomfortable. For some reason, the "other" parent, no matter which one of us it is at any given time, falls into that category of discomfort in our house. It's as if the kids' assumption was that no matter which parent they were relaying information to, the response was going to be ugly.

The thing is, they weren't always wrong. And if you are having your kids ride the parental pony express, you have got to do everything in your power to maintain your poker face if the memo you are receiving is not how you would do it, not what you decided, not what you wanted, not what you said should happen, etc. ... These little messengers are messengers. When you lash out at them for delivering bad news, you are encouraging them to keep any communication regarding the other house to themselves. They will quickly fall into a pattern of *silence is golden*. You'll know when you are there because you will reach out to the other parent for something with an exasperated tone and they will respond *"What? I **told** Johnny to **tell** you this already!"* And that is the moment when your red flag should rise to regroup on communication strategies. It is a moving target, probably forever.

One of our bigger challenges was the missing *répondez s'il vous plait.* We would pass along the details of an event to the kids' (bio)mom and then she would not show. While at the event we would start the questions, *"Is your mom coming? Did your mom say she was coming? What time is your mom coming?"* which was the perfect way to suck the joy out of the moment. The parental light bulb did go on, eventually. The kids were well aware when a parent was missing. They were hurt. They were pissed. They were confused. We did not need to rub salt in the wound with a backhanded self-compliment. That's really what it is, you see, when you ask the location of the other parent, what you're really saying is *See me?? I'm here!* They know you are there. They are just feeling angry because their other parent is not. This is not their fault. Let them live in that mood in a way that is encouraging and empathetic, not in a way that offers you an attendance award.

Our children have had all means of communication possible at their fingertips for years, yet we still have a constant struggle in getting them to collect information from their (bio)mom. I know, I just said *let the adults handle it* like two seconds ago. I'm getting to that. With our college-aged daughter, we simply cannot remain in the middle of her and her mother anymore as the retrievers of information. She no longer lives in our house, she has taken the space of being away from her family very seriously (as she should, it's college), and it is truly up to her to decide when and if she wants to see or speak with her (bio)mom. That mark of eighteen years old was the first super clear benchmark of *okay, now we step back.* In her prior teen years, the lines went from blurry to clear to blurry to clear over and over and over.

With her launch, we had to start another round of training, this time with her younger brother. We have now let him start handling discussions on visits and dinners and soccer games and school events. The first problem has been turning on that light switch after years of playing the parental switchboard. The second problem is that when he drops the ball (fifty percent of the time), we can feel the accusatory stare down from his (bio)mom from across town. In the past, that was totally on target, as we rightfully should have taken the heat for not passing along game times or school conferences.

As that changes, however, the kids do reach an age and responsibility level where they should not only be responsible but also be able to clarify which adults they want/need present at which events. And, for the record, you may not be the parent they want/need at some events. In which case, suck it up, thank them for being truthful, and go get a pedicure. If the retraction of attendance was not given nicely, save the Miss Manners lesson for later. While your feet are soaking, remember, your non-invite is likely more centered around your child trying to avoid an uncomfortable moment for them. They do have some agency in not feeling like they are juggling their parents. They may have picked you to sit out because they know you will be the one who will most likely carry on loving them just the same. Take it as a compliment, ask no questions, and plan your own outing later.

BLENDING FAMILIES

It's going to happen. It really will. And it should. It's the fair thing to do. But when? And how will you handle it?

At some point, you are going to be a part of a *true* blended family event.

No, not just the one where you move into a house with an already established other-half-of-a-family. Or, in my case, three-quarters-of-a-family. That will actually feel like a warm spring breeze when the first real blending event comes. That first real blending event will feel like the breeze of an incoming hurricane.

Today's children have calendars that never end: birthdays, holidays, school plays, awards ceremonies, soccer games, art shows, first dates, doctors' appointments, driver's license acquisitions, graduations, move-in-to-the-dorm-days, move-out-of-the-dorm-days, etc. ... All you really need to do is take a stroll back down the lane of your own life and recall all the singular moments where *your* parents were present and then multiply by 135 to equal today's expectations. With a family created via divorce, all of those moments become potentials for having more than the expected two bioparents involved. Which then brings up the confusion and bargaining and negotiation of which parents get to be involved in the current form of the family.

Couple facts on this one:

- The stepparent/second wife doesn't want the ex-wife/first wife to be present any more than the ex-wife/first wife wants the stepparent/second wife.

- The kids don't want anybody at all to be present because they fear the enormous bucket of awkwardness that will also arrive.
  o This is not their fault.
  o Which means all invitees must play nicely.
  o VERY NICELY.

I suppose there are two roads for resolutions. Events that are truly family related, such as birthdays and holidays, can be split in twos. There can likely be a birthday party at (bio)mom's house and a birthday party at dad's house. Holidays are typically dictated by the court with Christmas and Thanksgiving and Easter flipping houses from year to year. That all seems pretty straightforward, except it's not. When both parties are hosting birthday parties for an eight-year-old, how do the invites work? Presumably, said child will want to invite the same group of friends to both parties, but should those friends really be expected to attend a repeat performance of whichever house goes second? Are duplicate gifts required? Give the gift once and then re-wrap it to take to round two? Does this mean the hosting parents have to make a handful of weird phone calls explaining that, yes, there will be two parties, but, no, presents are not expected at both, and, yes, they may fall within the same twenty-four hours of each other, because, no, parents of young children cannot possibly make sense of why one party will take place a week or two later to make it less complicated.

Would it be easier to have the child create a list of guests and split it down the middle? Handing off one half to one household and keeping the other half for yours? Heck, yeah! But who is that actually easier for? Probably not the birthday boy or girl. Which brings us all around the bend to a combined party and a whole different set of impossible issues. Who will be the host? Will the ex-wife be welcomed into the other home? Will the stepparents be welcomed into the other home? Will everybody act fairly normal and try to hide the obvious walking-on-eggshells look? Is it possible to create an environment in which the celebrator is *not* counting down the minutes until everybody is back in their respective corners and life can be back to whatever normal is?

Does that sound stressful? Imagine how the eight-year-old feels.

We have never been comfortable having my husband's ex-wife as a regular presence within the walls of our home. I'm not sure if that was the right approach, though. Perhaps we should have just dealt with the uncomfortableness until it seemed relatively normal. I'm not saying we would have given her a key and a spare bedroom, but the times when she did appear in our living room were so infrequent that it often signaled that somebody was in trouble and a BIG TALK was about to take place. The kids referred to us as the trifecta in those instances and the trifecta always meant un-good things were about to happen.

I honestly don't know if, in our case, we would go back and change that approach. We were a bit limited (and leery) as there were enough legal issues following the ex-wife around that we established early that, if there were no adults home, then she shouldn't be in our home either. Perhaps we should have eased up on the *We are just not comfortable with her here* bit so that it wasn't so foreign to see the trifecta interacting.

I don't know what the correct target event should be to first try a combined, all-family-members shindig. For us, it didn't happen until our daughter was graduating from high school. Our first truly blended event was a graduation party, hosted by us in our home. I should probably start by saying we totally lucked out in the weirdest way possible by this occurrence landing in the middle of a pandemic. COVID restrictions sent the actual graduation ceremonies down the toilet and left us with a Class of 2020 faux diploma presentation and socially sensitive celebration afterwards. (*Yes, I'm one thousand percent imagining someone reading this book in fifty years and wondering what the hell I'm talking about. Coronavirus 2020. Look it up.*)

The stress of how graduation would look began the second Amelia walked out of her junior year, which was when I started wondering who would get the golden tickets to commencement. I'd already heard of limits and arguments and family throwdowns because this person got a ticket and that one didn't. I knew that, in our district, the magic ticket number was ten. Which meant Rich, me, bio(mom), Max, Rich's Mom and then, five tickets to spare. It was possible that my parents would attend (down to three tickets), and the kids' maternal grandparents would attend (down to one ticket). So, in the beginning, there didn't seem to be a looming issue.

Except graduation was canceled due to social-distancing limitations.

Okay. So, still, not really an issue?

I was so proud of myself for reserving a table with seating for fifteen months in advance post-graduation. Again, attendance math seemed to work, and we didn't anticipate any issues or arguments over who could come to the luncheon as we had built in extra spots.

And then the restaurant canceled due to COVID protocols.

This was 2020. Did I mention that? The year of flexibility? While I was trying to wrap my head around the idea of my family mingling with Rich's family while mingling with Rich's ex-wife's family, social-distancing restrictions were constantly jumping all over the place. The first big kicker came when the school announced individualized graduations, meaning that each senior would be allotted an appointment to come to the high school (where they'd not been in four months) to wear their cap and gown, have opportunities for photo ops, and walk across the stage to pick up their diploma (actually pick it up, off a table, six feet away from any other persons).

We were thrilled that Amelia would have some sort of closure to her school year until we heard that only five family members could attend. Rich, me, (bio)mom, Max, my mom, Rich's mom. Wait, that was six people. And by this point I was pretty determined that my mom would attend, as she was the one who held my hand through a tumultuous year of (step)momming. That's when the arguments started, in the weirdest way possible, as it was a basic throw down of people volunteering *not* to go and then everyone else insisting those same people *do* go while Amelia would occasionally pipe in with her total lack of interest in the whole thing.

We got through it, speed walking through the halls of her school, hoping no one would notice that we actually did bring six people. The accelerated pace left zero opportunities for anyone to say anything offensive or weird or rude. Not that anyone would do that on purpose—we really do try—but nerves and new people sometimes do not also mix and, also, my mother and I do not have a filter or an ability to whisper.

The luncheon was moved to our garage. This involved parking Jenga, seats spread far apart, a buffet in front of our workbench, a lot of fans pushing the ninety-degree heat, and a lot of wine (for me). On the plus side, COVID restrictions meant that we had to limit attendees, which knocked out the invites for most of the extended family. However, it would still be the first event in which this group mingled: Rich. Rich's ex-wife. Rich's mom. Rich's dad. The latter two had not spoken (in under 110 decibels) since divorcing shortly after Rich was born. My parents. Oh, yes, they had never really spoken to Rich's mom due to the many stories I had passed along to them in fits of tears and rage. The kids. Oh, yes, they hated combined events because they had no idea who to sit with or who to talk to and were petrified of one parent thinking that the other one was getting more attention.

We also invited some family friends because it seemed easier than retelling the story later.

Reaching this benchmark should come with a large billboard that screams *This is it, this is how every big event will be going forward.* As the (step)mom/second mom/newest member of the guest list/etc., that banner represents a huge question of what your role will be. Are you just the organizer? Will you be recognized as having something to do with helping your shared child reach this achievement? Will someone else who, maybe, wasn't so involved take the opportunity to swoop in for the hero shot? Will they offer all the oohs and aahs and tears of pride that were missing for the years before? Yes, the banner brings up a lot of worst-case scenarios living in awkward possibility. For me, the same question always follows: How will I handle it? Again, I go to "grace." That is always my goal. Let the entirety of the guest list look back on any cringeworthy moments and think *oh, she handled that with such grace.*

Remember, these moments are not about making you feel comfortable, they are about allowing your children to feel celebrated and, also, comfortable. If you can start these combined events off on the right foot, the chances will increase that events will continue to include invites for all parties. This is why life throws smaller events out in the beginning, like school plays, football games, and piano recitals. It gives all parties a chance to mingle, in view of the children, politely and, hopefully, like adults. There will be bigger and bigger moments as the children age: awards ceremonies, graduations, proms, engagements, weddings, the births of their own children.

Do not be the (step)parent who rains on those parades by acting like a wounded duck. Life sometimes does not feel fair but keep the snarky comments and the eye rolls to yourself. If you truly cannot attend gracefully, do not attend, lest you inadvertently cancel your own invites to future events, which is probably not what you want. What you probably want (and is probably the source of any angst) is to be included.

You want to be present.

You want to be a part of all the glory and the successes and the shining moments.

You can be. You just may have to do so with a bit more grace than anticipated.

BECAUSE IT ACTUALLY IS YOUR FAULT

One of the neat things about the many issues of a blended family *not* being the fault of your children, is that the many issues of a blended family will fall squarely on whichever parent sports the word "step" before their name. Having never been a biological mother, I have very little business weighing in on how green the grass is on that (bio)mom side of the fence but sometimes I do look over there and think, *"Oh, your kids are pissed at you ... wait, that's it?! They're just pissed?"* I'm relatively sure that somewhere in every child's rearing they will drop the *I Hate You!* bomb. (Step)moms just get a chaser of "AND *you're NOT my mom!*" And for extra points *"I Wish You'd Never Come Here"* or *"This Is All Your Fault"* or *"If It Weren't For You ..."*

Within the normal rounds of kid crankiness surrounding chores or homework or writing thank-you notes, this is not a big deal, though it does take some time to get used to. For the more intense topics, it is rough. I was not made aware of this phenomenon before I signed that dotted line on the marriage certificate. Even if I had been, I probably would have spent the next years trying to figure out why I was always the bad guy. The answer is simple: Part of being a (step)parent is being the designated person to blame.

Because our kids' (bio)mom was mostly uninvolved, I spent my days sweating and toiling and raising and coaching and organizing and cooking and planning and taxi driving and making copies and then felt like, *"Oh, hey (bio)mom! Just swoop in every other Friday on a parade float gathering all the love and forgiveness available!"* That does actually happen. It causes painful eye rolls. Our son, for example, often has communication issues with his (bio)mom. More than once, she requested that we hire him a life coach. It was perplexing, of course, as we were quite certain that that's what parents were meant to be. It was also offensive. Why were we being held responsible for a child not communicating with his (bio)mom? Full disclosure, the life coach gem came to us when this child was fifteen, not a toddler who'd yet to master full sentences or texting. What he hadn't mastered was texting *her*. After years of these blame grenades landing in our laps, we have gotten to a point where we find them more comical than offensive.

Exhibit B: Our failure to treat that same child's ADHD appropriately. When Max was younger, he was tested for ADHD because the school kept reporting that he had ants in his eight-year-old pants. What we learned was that he had tendencies toward it, yes, but that the real issue was that his level of intelligence far exceeded his grade. I spent hours with young Max, teaching him study techniques, how to organize his schoolwork, how to make to-do lists, and how to take breaks if his bored brain needed to take a break. Rich and I had several meetings with his school, waving IQ tests in front of anyone who would read them. We explained that, no, Max wouldn't be skipping grades, but that he needed to be challenged where he was, with his peers. It was actually an amazing success, this child, as he entered high school two years ahead in most classes, but still with his closest friends. Yet, that same year, I felt like I'd been slapped in the face for "not treating his ADHD appropriately." I knew all that we had done. I knew how successfully we'd navigated years of elementary and middle school. And still, it was a zinger that stabbed straight through my pride as a (step)mom. It's worse when the zingers come from the kids themselves, which is a bummer as they tend to be more frequent (but also less intentional). They strike right at the heart of an under-confident (step)mom brain, which sounds ridiculous as I was weighing the parenting advice from a grade-schooler versus the common sense in my own forty-something head.

I did develop a thicker skin slowly. I also developed an ability to see the zingers coming from all angles. I knew that if a visit with Grandma was delayed because someone had to make a bed or clean the litter, Grandma would lay that horrific task assignment at my feet. Yes, I had figured out a secret path in which I could lounge on the couch and eat popcorn while the kids cleaned out the refrigerator. We did not get bonus points for teaching responsibility, only dings for chores. Did I say "*we*"? Just me.

I knew that if one of the kids came down with a fever that their (bio)mom would go on red alert with questions about how they got sick. The questions would be vague but with a suspicious tone. *How did she get a fever?* *Why is he throwing up?* At the first sign of a sniffle, I wanted to collect and destroy all means of communication so that word wouldn't leak out that I had personally invited the black plague to enter our house.

If we passed along an incorrect time for an event, the assumption was that it was on purpose, that I had done it on purpose, and that I had done it to cause the invitee to be late. If shoes were deemed too small, it was because I refused to buy new ones. If clothing was uncomfortable, it was because I insisted on black tie all day, every day. If grades were poor, it was because I was asking too much of the kids. To this day, I have not bought my daughter underwear because it was determined early on that I refused to, creating an ongoing span in which she came home from each visit with her grandmother with new underwear. I'm still not sure how that became a thing.

If there isn't something visible to blame you for, someone will make something up just so they can show how they would have (and how you should have) handled it.

Adults passing blame is awkward and frustrating yet still much easier than when it's the kids. With adults, you can state your case. With kids and their complete lack of rational thinking, there is rarely any point in trying. With kids of a divorce, who are likely angry with one or both of their parents, there is absolutely no point. They've already lost their parents once. There will be no harsh words that will cause them to lose their parents again. The result is that any blame that should be directed to their (bio)parents will be deflected straight to the steps. In our house, another bonus. As I was the one handling all the lost mom roles, that blame came attached to feelings of abandonment and reworked into emotional blowouts.

If I had a nickel for every time, I told myself, *"They aren't mad at you, they're mad at her,"* I could probably get my own counseling degree. The entrance of a (step)mom gives kids an almost exact date to pinpoint when their lives changed for the second time. They don't mark the "changed for the better" moments, instead they memorize the "didn't like that very much" moments. I suppose that it is human nature to remember moments by what went wrong even if the majority of the moment went pretty right. With my kids, my arrival marked a clear before and after. I know that a whole lot of icky shit went down *before* I arrived, obviously. It wasn't a "hey, these unicorns and rainbows are great, but let's flip this whole family upside down for a bit" situation. There were years and years of trauma before I was even a blip on the radar, but that's not what the kids remember. They remember when I arrived and the trauma that came after. I suppose it's their minds' way of allowing both biological parents to maintain their positions on the pedestal.

The part I play is tricky. Because we have full custody, we do our best to allow *weekends with the (bio)mom* to be stress free, trouble free, just time for fun and relaxation. It is hard enough on kids to go from one house to another, why make it worse by sending along a list of *So ... you should probably know that this kid got caught cheating in Latin or that kid was turning into a bit of a mixologist* ... As their time with their (bio)mom together is measured in hours, we take a lot of hits to preserve the goodness of it. Does that sound fair? Not at all. And while I've gone back and forth as to why we do it that way, I (usually) do see the logic in it. The Catch-22 of this mode of operations is that it feeds directly into the Evil (Step)mom narrative. The kids get essentially no grief from their (bio)mom, their father spent a lot of years making up for divorce guilt by holding back on consequences and, bam! the Cinderella prophecy is fulfilled almost instantly the second a piece of broccoli is plated, a bad grade is discussed, or emptying a trash can is requested. None of those items even had to be my idea, but any expectations that were raised after my arrival were automatically slated as something I brought to the table.

In the memory of our kids, ages seven and ten, it likely went like this:

My parents had a bad night.

Blink.

I'm spending more time at my grandma's because that is where my dad is.

Blink.

My mom had to move out of our house to an apartment.

Blink.

Dad moved back into our house.

Blink.

A strange woman was there one weekend when Mom took us over unexpectedly.

Blink.

The strange woman moved in.

Blink.

Mom lost her apartment.

Blink.

Everything was fine until the strange woman showed up.

Blink.

We got a new, bigger house while Mom got a room in a rental.

Blink.

I miss Mom.

Blink.

The strange woman is becoming more involved in my life.

Blink.

The strange woman is creating schedules and chores.

Blink.

I miss Mom.

Blink.

And it goes on and on, building the narrative.

The reality is learning how to be a (step)mom is actually pretty easy in comparison to learning to be unaffected by the bucket of fault you get to carry around. I had to develop a habit of thinking, "*Sure, we can say I did that ... that this is all my fault ... but I know it doesn't all belong to me, I'm just carrying this bucket until **you (my child)** understand that.*" Admittedly, I spent a lot of time plotting and planning for the day when the kids realized that I wasn't the sole source of the drama or unhappiness in their lives. I hoped for some sort of awakening when they understood that not only were there other people at fault, but that some of those people were their own biological parents, the very people who were deemed incapable of doing anything wrong. And when they *did* finally reach that revelation? It actually sucked. When they did start fielding those thoughts in their heads, it appeared as anguish on their faces and a cracking tone in their voices.

I suddenly wanted to backtrack and just take the blame again in order to remove that gross emotional growth.

No, you cannot attribute blame to children of divorce. But how can you set them up to move into their teens and young adulthood with an attitude that doesn't start logging every misstep in their lives as something that would have been avoided if that fateful day when that strange woman showed up hadn't happened? The answer is, I don't know. I know that I eventually started feeling okay taking the blame as I realized that the bucket of fault is something I *can* carry in order to relieve the others. It's very Joan of Arc, actually. *"Sure, you can be mean and nasty and hateful to me ... but please love your dad forever, because he's really the best of the bunch."* Or the more common, *"I know you're really angry with your (bio)mom and that it is easier to take it out on me. She already left once. I know risking that again is too much for your tiny brain."* At some point, I accepted the digs because it was alleviating stress in my children's hearts. At some point, I found that doing that no longer affected me the way it used to. At some point, I understood a mother's love.

Will this be my fate forever?

No. It is already turning with our children nearing a launching age. It is difficult. As the children mature, they are beginning to reconcile where much of the blame should and does lie, and it is painful. It creates emotional chaos. It is a roller coaster of never knowing whether to stay and listen or run and hide. My daughter is quite vocal in her feelings and wears quite a bit of anger on her sleeve. My son stuffs his down and I fear an explosion. Sure, they realize now that I am not the source of all evil. My name no longer floats to the top of their most-hated list. I would even say that they love me unconditionally. All very big "real" mom wins, not relegated to the role of (step)mom at all.

Which is also how I hope they see me in the end.

Which Way's Up?

Mom Vision

If you're a female over, say, thirty ... you can probably just stop reading here. You already know where this is going, having just rolled your eyes and said, "Mom Vision, yup." I didn't even know mom vision was a real thing until I became one and was immediately able to see things in other rooms, under beds, in the back seat of a car, in the future, or in a school locker without even leaving the comfort of my mom throne. I also didn't know it was limited to those with children. It turns out it works upon the acquisition of a male partner, as well.

Recently, I was tasked with finding my husband's label maker after he searched, searched, and searched but still ... he "coooouuuuldn't fiiiiiind it." Three steps into his workshop and *bam,* spotted. It was sitting in (my) plain sight on the corner of a shelf, just begging to address the heckle out of about thirty-five Christmas cards. Rich did not respond happily.

*It annoys the piss out of him, this wondrous sense acquired upon receiving my engagement ring. I know for a fact that Rich puts off any announcements of lost items because he doesn't want to clock the land-speed record I set when finding them. Or maybe it's my very dramatic announcement of "Mom Vision, Engage!" that he doesn't like. Hard to say. Currently missing are his Air Pods. I haven't cracked the code on those yet and I have an 80 percent suspicion that they aren't even lost. I suspect he just wants to enjoy watching me **not** find something.*

And children? Good grief. Do they have any vision at all? I can sit at the dinner table, cutting a steak while holding a conversation about the Second Amendment, and throw in a quick blurb to the child staring into the open refrigerator with the latitude/longitude of the ranch dressing including its proximity to the other bottles of the same shelf without even looking up. Oftentimes, when I'm sending one of our children off to find something, I lay the location out with such specifics that I'm fairly certain Stevie Wonder could find it though he has never been to our house. Still, said child will likely return with the inevitable, "It wasn't there." Still, it was there.

"Can you grab a plunger? It's in the garage, twelve steps from the door, stuck on the right side next to driverside rear wheel of our gray 2011 Jeep Compass, between the old Ikea dresser that's been painted green and the black, plastic, folding table that Dad saws on which is stored just below the kayak paddles—the yellow ones, not the red ones. The plunger is black with ridges, twenty-four inches tall, and smells a little like something that should live in the garage."

Sometimes, I amaze myself.

Sometimes, when asked if I've seen something, I feel like I go into this weird locational trance. "No, I don't even know what the Superpower Gosh Diggity Nerf Bullets look like. No ... wait ... hang on ... something's happening ... (eyes close) ... yes, yes ... I'm seeing them ... there they are ... yes ... look in your closet, behind your laundry bin and under the stiff socks on the right ... yes ... you will find what you seek ... and please ... yes ... please, do something with those violated socks."

What I've learned is that this superpower is not limited to tangible items.

What I haven't learned is when I should actually step in and use this superpower.

What happens when you can see into the future and the mistakes that your children are directing themselves to? I suppose that's age dependent. I suppose that because I do have one child that is fourteen and whom I can look at and say "No, no, no, that is not going to happen, abort." He will *look back at me with an annoyed stare, but he will stop what he was doing. I also have one who is seventeen. We are trying to "prepare her for life in the real world," yet keep running into common sense (or lack thereof) road-blocks. Step in or not?*

Honestly, it sometimes feels like I'm standing by my own burning house with a hose at the ready and being encouraged by other parents to just "let it happen" for the sake of the lesson.

My sweet husband, whom I love dearly while also wanting to toss out the window, is all about natural consequences. I get it, buddy, really. It takes the pressure of having to think of actual consequences off the table if there are natural consequences just around the corner. Those are like a parenting utopia. I do like them (or have come to like them), these answers from Karma, when they actually happen. But what I'm finding in this whole parenting of a young adult is that the natural consequences don't stop at our station very often.

We stand there (the parents), looking down the tracks, watching the Natural Consequences Express zipping its way to our stop. We get a little gleeful and giddy ... it's happening, yes! And we didn't have to be the bad guys! Teehee!! ... and then our hair blows back, and our heads snap as it speeds right through, only to be followed by a slow-moving child with a very smug, satisfaction-filled face.

*Oh good. So, you've learned **nothing at all**.*

My least favorite part about Mom Vision is the seeing of everything that needs to be done around the house. It completely takes away my ability to relax and often makes me wonder if I've opened a home for the blind. Am I only here to note the pile of leaves in the middle of the kitchen that clearly needs to be swept up? Is my one purpose to monitor the level of the cat food bowls? No one else notices the inches of dog snot on the front window or the air intake hiding behind a quarter inch of dust or the vacuum still sitting on the upstairs landing or the sweater that's been air drying for a month or the slippery oil spot in the garage or that we used the last toothpaste or or or or ...

I never believed in "eyes in the back of my head" the 172 times that my mom indicated she had them. But, yes, mine have been installed as part of the Mom Vision. This weird bit of a stomach lurch, just enough to say "alert ... you're up." When it happened to me the first time, I had to turn all the way around to face both of my (step)children, scan them up and down to assess what was going on and what was wrong with the situation. Today, there is no stop, no scan. Today, I can feel an eye roll or a dropped wrapper, or a punched shoulder or a silent attitude change.

There is no greater victory than announcing mid(forward-facing) stride, "If you roll your eyes like that again, that phone will belong to me," and seeing another mother nod with a quick "mmm-hmm."

Yes. I see you too.

CHAPTER SIX

Remember Where You Came From

THAT GIRL FROM BEFORE

There are so many moments in parenting in which you stop for a split second and think *my goodness, I am really nailing this*. My husband and I occasionally have those moments together, trading glances of *We're doing it! We're adulting!* Those moments are a testament to the fact that none of us actually knows what it actually takes to raise good humans. And by none of us, I mean all adults in the world, not just the two in my home. I had no idea, as a child, that my parents were just older versions of their teenage selves figuring out family life one day at a blessed time. It terrifies me to think that my own kids believe that we have a better handle on everyday life than they do. It terrifies me more to think that this may be discovered in a parenting-fail-turned-revelation. Will I stand before my disappointed children one day admitting that, *Well yeah, we're all just sort of winging it*? My husband and I take those very clear winning moments quite seriously in our house. They are a nice compliment to the many very clear not-winning-at-all moments. For those, we do not give ourselves high fives. Those moments are more about wanting to throat punch my partner in lieu of patting him on the back. Those moments are more about him looking at me with a shocked glimpse of *is this the person I married?* Typically, those moments cause me to pause and reflect on how I got so ugly and angry and mean.

Where did my patience go? Wasn't I supposed to be the cool (step)mom? Where is she? Wasn't I easygoing at some point? What happened?

Marriage is hard. Add parenting and ... holy hell. I had no idea that being married would include longing looks back in time to the days when I looked longingly to a future that included marriage. I often miss my life as a single girl. I am almost ashamed to say it happens multiple times per week. Not every week, but during the weeks when that thought is popular with my brain, yes, multiple times. I feel guilty because, though I had all but convinced myself that there was nothing wrong with aiming for a life as the Crazy Cat Lady, I actually really wanted to meet the love of my life. How dare my brain take me back to those glory days of low-range responsibilities? Shouldn't I just thank my lucky stars regularly that, at forty years old, I did find the love of my life?

Being married turned me into a new version of myself. Becoming an insta-parent turned me into a new-new version. I can hardly wait to see what becoming a grandparent does (*no really, kids ... I CAN WAIT*). I have become a person I do not always recognize and that I definitely do not know very well and, occasionally, a person that I am appalled by. It did not seem funny or ironic the first time that I heard my own mother's words coming out of my mouth. I was never going to turn into my mother. But then I started zoning into her logic and, suddenly, our pantry became devoid of junk food, we created a time-out chair, and we instilled firm bedtimes. I morphed rather quickly into a much more realistic version of "mom" than the one I had planned on being. There were chores and favors and demands and lists where I thought there would be lax rules, acceptable swears, and loads of new clothes for no reason. The mom I had planned to be turned out to be so much cooler and chill and wonderful than the mom that I actually became.

There are moments when I cannot stand the words I speak to my family. There are times when I am so filled with frustration that I want to kick something (and, truthfully, we do have a dent in one of our basement walls). My fight-or-flight hackles rise quickly, pleading for an outlet or, yes, for a return to that single girl I once knew. That single girl, I loved being her so very much. That girl had such promise and ease, able to slip in and out of most situations without batting an eye. That girl was going to be the best partner ever, supportive and kind and accommodating. That girl had plans of being the wife that all of the other wives would look to, longingly, because her marriage always presented as perfect. That girl was going to be the favorite mom of the neighborhood kids, living in the friend zone of all those who congregated in her kitchen while she served fun snacks and participated in gossip from the halls of school.

And then reality kidnapped that girl.

The first time I heard a tone of venom leave my lips, it was a punch to the gut. Where did that voice come from? Was it the marriage or the parenting that had so quickly turned me? There was rage and impatience and, admittedly, a tone of hate. The tone came again. Then again. I would try to reel it in but soon learned that I was guessing as much as everyone in my household as to which version of myself was around the next emotional corner. I felt a loss of control and a loss of innocence and a grief for that single girl that I had loved being so very much. I felt as if I'd slammed into a brick wall in my quest to be an amazing wife and (step)mom. I felt shell-shocked as I realized that I might not be cut out to be either and, certainly, not a second wife or a (step)mom who could so easily be compared with the previous owner of my slot. I began to question my abilities with every task as my confidence started a slow descent towards failure.

What had happened to that girl from before? Where was that girl who was so sure of herself? She had such promise! As recently as a year ago, I thought she was lost forever. I thought I'd made a huge mistake and was destined to live in a constant state of grinding towards an end that I did not want to picture. My goals of being a cool mom and an awesome wife were thrown to the side and replaced with just getting the kids grown up enough to not have another round of divorce trauma. That was how sure I'd become that my role in this blended family would end in flames.

Marriage is hard. Parenting is hard. Being the wife who follows a first wife and being a mother who was nowhere near the delivery room stacks the deck to a level of disadvantage that is impossible to comprehend. Regular, run-of-the-mill, standard marriages often do not come with warnings from club members about the hard work it will take to maintain a healthy marriage. Marriages that involve blended families? Those should come with a warning label written in neon flashing lights. The differences between a man and a woman in this rocky boat are not helpful, either. Men feel things differently than women. Men have the ability to compartmentalize and brush things under the carpet and close their eyes to the things that have a 'big deal' rating to women. At least the man in my house does. I, on the other hand, have feelings that blur together from minute to minute and are always worn on my sleeve. There is typically a rotation of a half-dozen events rattling around in my brain that require resolution, banging into each other while I try to convince myself that none of them really matter.

Where did that fun, carefree, giggly girl go? She never would have been saddled with endless paranoia or anxiety over whether her home was going to implode around and, perhaps, because of her.

Trying to convince my husband that I got no joy out of being grumpy all the time became a mantra in our relationship. And I really didn't. I also didn't enjoy a good fight or a total breakdown or an epic tantrum. Yet, there were stretches of time when one or all of those items were regulars in our daily life. There are so many things that mothers are tasked with, an endless list of items that when crossed off for completion, auto-refill, often with four new items for every single item that finally had been removed. I liken it to getting one painful cavity filled only to find out that three more developed while you were lying in the dentist's chair (and there is no such thing as Novocain). My husband often asks when "it" will be good enough. When will I be happy? Never, I suppose, if we are measuring by man standards (mandards?). Shortly after pulling on my wife/mom boots, a ticker became implanted in my brain, listing the next five tasks at any given time. Of course, I would love to go back in time and reconnect with that girl who didn't have a Rolodex of to-do's flopping around in her head. Of course, I would love to be able to shut it all down. Unfortunately, it is all part of managing a household, which often defaults to the person sitting in the role of the wife/mom.

In our situation, where I am the (step)mom on paper but an actual mom in function, there is a certain level of *what-the-eff-ness* in managing my family. (Bio)mom lives only a few miles away yet does not participate in any of the day-to-day business of running the kids' daily lives. *What the eff?* I am plagued with the dirty work while she gets to be the fun one. *What the eff?* The kids have General Mom (me) barking out orders, assigning chores, contacting teachers, making appointments and they also have Fun Mom (her) offering concerts, dinners, road trips, movies, and no restrictions. *What the eff?* The girl I used to be was supposed to be the Fun Mom. Going into my marriage and gladly pledging to be a part of the parental trifecta, I thought my role would land firmly on the side of the favorite adult. The kids already had a mom, right? She would handle all of the icky stuff, right? I was late to the parenting game. Wouldn't my responsibilities be limited to the less serious items like back-to-school shopping or learning to drive or pool days or blurring the lines of the rules put in place by the *real* parents?

What the eff?

Life did not pan out that way. I am not the Fun Mom. I am the clean-up-the-mess mom. I am the swoop-in-at-the-last-minute mom. I am the get-screamed-at mom. I am the receiver-of-the-eye-rolls mom. I am the frustrated and tapped out and exhausted mom. I am the mom hanging on by a thread 50 percent of the time. I am the mom that sounds ugly and cranky and at my wits' end the other 50 percent of the time.

Where, oh where, is that lucky laid-back girl from before?

As my kids begin to move closer to the time when they are no longer part of our daily lives, that girl from my past has begun to make appearances again. It started when Amelia obtained her driver's license, inserting a noticeable sigh of relief in our home. For me, there was suddenly a third person who could share in the errands or be available for the many taxi runs that are the hallmark of parenting. Even with the simplicity of last-minute pickups being lifted from my plate, that girl from before began to emerge. When that same eldest child packed her bags for her freshman year of college, even more weight was lifted. It was not because she was more difficult or time consuming or energy sucking, it was because having one less child in the house freed up critical mental space in my brain. Mental space counts a lot in momming. That Rolodex (chore distribution, appointment maker, school liaison, etc.) depletes that mental space. Removing an entire file from that Rolodex made life exponentially more manageable. There was comfort and success in knowing that we had grown one whole person to fruition. We had done enough to enable one bird to leave the nest. If we were able to grow one person, then surely we could grow two, right? Added bonus? We now had a blueprint of things that worked versus things that didn't.

That girl from before, the one who was living the single-gal life in her Barbie townhouse, was an ace at keeping herself happy. It was simple! There was only one of me to appease! And I could do that any which way I wanted! Adding three other people to the mix put me in instant overload as my female genetics whispered *Keep Everyone Happy* while my logical side was screaming *What Did I Just Get Into!!??* I didn't know how far away I'd gotten from that girl I used to know until I was finally able to slow down and find some breathing room. I started enjoying the day-to-day-ness of life again. I started laughing more. I started finding time to be creative again. I started surprising myself with a lessening response time to house issues. *"MY GOD THERE IS JUICE ON THE CAR-PET!!!!"* turned into *"Juice on the carpet? What color? Should I get a towel?"*

Because my kids are only four years apart, it was easy to start thinking about our (the parents) next steps. A finish line appeared announcing a future in which my husband and I would be back to life as a duo, just two folks enjoying growing old together. That is much more appealing to me than going all the way back to that single girl from before. Yes, to being carefree. Yes, to being laid back. Yes, to being flexible.

Much like that girl from before.

But now with a partner and a gold stamp for surviving the muddy waters of parenting.

IF YOU DIDN'T YEARN FOR CHILDREN

Not every woman yearns for children. I know this because I am one who didn't. For that matter, not every woman plans out her wedding at age six and then spends the next two decades searching for the appropriate groom. I know this because I am one who didn't. I (hardly) remember the first wedding I attended when my mom took me along to the nuptials of a friend of hers. I couldn't have been more than seven. I was not impressed or impacted or filled with thoughts of being a princess someday. That may have had more to do with my strong lean to the tomboy side at that age, but no, the event did not spark a vision board for my own wedding. Years later, I spent the end of my college years going from wedding to wedding as friends got engaged, got graduated, and got married. Again, nary a spark was born. I did enjoy the open bars, though. I did not enjoy the near dozen bridesmaid dresses I had to buy. I was quite relieved after a minor falling-out with my closest group of friends to be taken *out* of the bridal party lineup. At that time, I *was* in a fully committed relationship that included the occasional *we'll get married someday* chatter. We even went as far as ring shopping. Still no sparks. No urge to run to the altar, a relief in the end, as we definitely would not have lasted.

Having children was even lower on my list than getting married. I think now of how that must have confused my mother, as I spent the bulk of my teen years as the neighborhood babysitter. I loved playing with other people's children. I loved kid toys. I still love kid toys. I loved kid television and kid books and the ease of socializing with someone under the age of five. I also loved leaving when it was over. I never thought much about my maternal side (or the fact that it was well hidden) until I met my would-be stepchildren. Then I thought about how much it was missing and wondered when it would kick in and if I should take some sort of hormone to develop it. I did eventually find that maternal side buried in the depths of my personality, though it wasn't until I was nearing fifty.

I played with all kinds of dolls as a kid: Barbies, Muppets, one named Chrissy who could grow her hair, and about a dozen Cabbage Patch Kids. I would line them up and dress them and create stories about their relationships. I would change their diapers and send them into the CPK hospital for repairs. I never renamed them, they just stayed whomever they were out of the box. I did not have a mental list of names that I would use for my own children someday that I felt compelled to test out. It never crossed my mind. I never imagined that my own little girl would have thick, blonde hair or that my boy would have brown curls like the ones assigned to them by Xavier Roberts. I just liked losing myself in the make-believe and then being able to put them away when I wanted to return to regular life.

I recently came across a note that I had jotted down a few months after meeting my now husband. We were still at the *we're just having fun* point, but there were still questions presented by him that I now know were part of the (step)mom tryouts. Not that he was leading the witness. I don't even think it was intentional, but he was definitely putting the feelers out there. One of the conversations we had a few times in our early dating span was whether or not I would be okay **not** having my own children. He found it incredibly odd that it didn't faze me, and I found it incredibly odd that what I was saying didn't sound totally logical. It forced me to take note that I was possibly unusual in my non-desire to have my own children. It wasn't new to me, though. I don't really know why, but I had always assumed that any children that I would raise would come to me via a different-than-the-norm path. I loved the idea of a blended family from my first viewing of *The Brady Bunch* or my first reading of *Cheaper by the Dozen* (I've since learned that all twelve kids belonged to the same parents). When my husband and I met, we were both in our forties. On our very first date, he let it slip that he'd had a vasectomy years prior. It did seem like an odd first date fact, but I know now that we were both immediately taken by each other, and he was instantly thrown into setting expectations. He was a decade away from sending his youngest child to college. While a decade may seem like a long time, in child-raising years, it's like a thousand years. His parental finish line had become visible, and he wasn't highly interested in tacking on another decade (at least) for another child.

Still, he asked the question often. Would I be okay not having my own children? He asked the question more frequently as we built our relationship towards marriage. I look back now at that repetitive question with such love as his level of concern that I would have eventual regrets in being with him was so extraordinary. He went so far, at one point, to offer a reversal on his vasectomy. This was not a test. He really would have done it if it meant fulfilling a need in my soul. By that time, we were in the throes of the difficulties of (step)momming and this offering served as a lifeline. He had so much joy in raising his children that watching me struggle broke his heart. This option he offered gave me a chance with "my own" children and, perhaps, a repeat of the joy he had experienced.

I declined. I was exhausted. I did not want to start fresh with the hopes of a better experience.

I did not want to start fresh at all. I didn't want to start, period. I knew he wasn't being pushy, but I still felt pushed. I had thoughts of *Is this so hard because I am just doing it wrong? Shouldn't I want kids? Shouldn't I want a representation of our marriage? What was wrong with me? Why was I indifferent towards the idea?* And it wasn't only my husband asking. It wasn't only me asking. A common theme in our early marriage, when I still explained my kids as actually being his, was people asking if we were going to have our own children. I'd answer no and then, often, be volleyed with an almost demanding *but why don't you want your own?* I just didn't. I felt compelled, at times, to throw back an *Oh, I can't have children* just to stop a conversation that would only leave me feeling, again, like there was something very wrong with me.

Not everyone dreams of their future children. That doesn't make us bad people. It actually makes us very in touch with what we are willing to do (or not).

The note.

Yes, I recently came across a note that I had jotted down a few months after meeting my now husband. I found this note nearly ten years after it was written. I wrote it as I was trying to find some way to explain to this wonderful man that I was dating why not having my own children had always been exactly how I predicted my life would pan out.

April 7, 2012

I don't know how to explain the not needing my own kids thing without sounding like a nut job.

But I've always known.

I don't know why.

I think it's why my aging uterus doesn't affect me like it would other women.

It's why there's a bit of relief that as I grow older, the pressure recedes.

For a long time, I thought it was impossible, anyway.

What with the depression and anxiety destroying me (I used to be broken).

The thought of coming off the drugs for nine months was inconceivable.

And that hasn't really been a risk I wanted to take.

Not really something you can just test out. See if it happens. See if I survive.

I've been at the bottom of the well. It's not a place you take a chance on.

And even now that the anxiety and depression are in

check, the reality is postpartum lurks.

Am I going to look back one day and wish? I already have.
But it's never been about wishing there were kids.
It's been about wishing I'd had a more solid option to choose.
And I don't know which I would have picked.
And it's not something I spend much time thinking about.
Because I have yet to figure out how to change my history.

I just always knew.

I realized a few years into our marriage that this absence of a desire to have my own children may have been the root of many dodged relationships in my past. Things would start getting serious and I would find a list of things wrong enough about that boyfriend to toss him out the door. It never felt acceptable to shy away from the ring aisle or skip the *What will our children look like?* game. Meeting parents? No thank you, that would just involve the inevitable questions of *Do you want kids? How many? How old will you be when they start shooting out of your vagina?* I am a little bit jealous of my own daughter. I think society has come far enough along now to know that those questions are not actually appropriate. When I speak to those just getting started on their own lives, I rarely ask anything about children (or even marriage) unless they bring it up first. It's really none of my business. On the flip side, I often throw in a brief summary of my path to parenting if it comes up. I'm not trying to start a club of women with no womb service, but I do feel that there is not enough said about the acceptableness of not wanting to have one's own children.

My husband was shocked to learn that my maternal instincts did not grow in the second we said, "I do." His experience in having children was that as they were born, his wife/mother/aunts all started circling with coos, snuggles, and swaddling abilities. I'm not sure why he thought that would happen to me. He admits it outright, though. He honestly did think that the acquisition of children would kick off some hormone cycle that had been hibernating and I would instantly start making homemade birthday cakes or become the third-grade room mom. For me, I remained more on the acquisition side than the Mary Poppins side.

It has taken me nearly a decade to start feeling truly maternal. It makes absolute sense to both of us, now, that this is by design. If I'd had actual infants, they'd never know that I had no idea what I was doing for the first ten years. Or, at least, they wouldn't remember it. Stepchildren are a different case. They witness every misstep and they remember it, writing it down in their mental bank with a thick, black Sharpie. That is both the best and the worst scenario. They have heard my tears of frustration; they have seen my tantrums. They have also watched as I have grown into a person whom they love and trust. They know that I would jump in front of a car to save them, but not because I'm programmed by biology to do so.

I would do it because I've chosen that role.

Not every woman yearns for children. And that's okay.

You may get them anyway. And that will be okay, too.

FORGET THE RESOURCES

Finding realistic resources for (step)momming is nearly impossible. Or, at least, it was when I became a (step)mom. It wasn't that there weren't resources, it was that they all said essentially the same thing. *Let the biological parent do the parenting.* I suppose that's why accepting the position did not seem like it would be, at all, the big deal that it actually turned out to be. My future husband warned me that I would likely be heavily involved in parenting, but the few books I found indicated otherwise. I am a researcher. When I got the first inklings of this potential future life, I ran to the library for guidance. I like to be the best at everything I do. Preparation would point me in that direction and books were the slim source. Everything I read indicated that I would be able to swoop in and hang out while my husband did the hard stuff. Even the counselor I was seeing in my hometown leaned me towards that side of the operational coin.

That narrative, in which the biological parents handle the brunt of the child-raising, never worked in our home at all. I suspect that that narrative is no longer realistic in most blended households. That narrative was probably developed decades ago when the divorce formula always equated to the biological mom having full custody of the children with the biological father seeing them every other weekend. That narrative was developed during a time when the female parent typically did not work either, so the solution was quite obvious. When I think back to my own childhood, I can't remember many children of divorce in my orbit, and I definitely didn't have any friends who lived primarily with their father or flip-flopped from house to house. Today's equation is much different. Custody has become blurrier and more equal between parents.

When I moved in with my pre-made family, I found a local counselor. She also leaned heavily towards the side of letting my husband do the hard work and to leave my mental space available for supporting him. It did not take long for me to push back that directive as unrealistic in our world. While we did have 50/50 custody, there were weeks when my husband had no choice but to travel during our week with the kids. His ex-wife was also extremely unreliable, which meant that it was not uncommon for the kids to land in our home during her custodial weeks. Our split quickly became closer to 75/25, with a need for one of us to be available during that 25 portion. That meant me. It never crossed our minds (or would have been possible) for my husband to quit his job so that he could be home full time with the kids. It's not that he wouldn't have, but, in addition to split custody, he had to split his paycheck between his home and his ex-wife's.

I often wonder if the universe was intentional in hiding any honest resources from me in those months leading up to my move north. I often wonder, if I had known everything that I know now about (step)momming (oh heck, let's throw marriage into that bucket as well), if I wouldn't have run screaming for the woods. I often wonder if running screaming into the woods is still an option. I definitely would have had very serious reservations about what I was agreeing to when saying *I do.* For sure, we would have slowed our track down with the acquisition of an apartment for my move rather than a jump directly into the deep end of living full time with Rich. I certainly would have carried on in my single-girl townhouse for much longer, allowing Rich and the kids to have a longer settling-in time as they adjusted to their new life.

If I'd been able to miss a few years of their transition, we could have skipped a thousand arguments that ended with threats from me to pack my bags. We could have cut down our stress and ever-present tension headaches. We could have missed juggling multiple therapy appointments each week. Me? I could have missed the constant stare downs from the ex-wife. Or the near-constant stare downs from the kids. Or from my mother-in-law. I'd have missed the chance for other moms to give me the side-eye as the newest girlfriend in town. I could have missed the guilt that comes with wondering if it was my arrival or the trauma of a divorce that gave the kids feelings of anxiety and mistrust and instability. Heck, I'd have missed the chance to have the blame for just about every misstep during our first five years together put squarely at my feet.

But there are other misses that I often and should not forget. The misses that I really should focus on rather than the negatives. I would have missed Max's second-grade field trip, my first as a chaperone (it was terrifying). I would have missed Amelia's sixth-grade musical (she was amazing). I would have missed years of solo dates with each kid (something we did each Sunday in order to get to know each other). I would have missed coaching Max's first soccer team. I would have missed taking Amelia shopping for her first bra. I would have missed what ended up being the last Christmas during which we still had a reindeer believer in the house. I would have missed a chance to dry sticky tears born from the loss of a favorite toy or being the one someone called when they weren't feeling well at school. I would have missed the giggles at failed meals (except those still happen). I would have missed the moments when I realized I was latching onto these people, like that first time I did throw myself in front of a driver who had ignored a crosswalk or preparing to launch a war when I heard that another child was making fun of mine.

Had we slowed down our trajectory, I would have missed days or months or years of being here, present, with these people that I would come to love so very much. I would have missed feeling so proud of my husband and, as a couple, because we made a conscious decision to buckle down, dig in, and work harder than we've ever worked at anything to ensure that our marriage would remain whole.

I would have missed so much.

MOVING FORWARD, MOVING IN

We never had a proper housewarming party when we moved into our new home. I still debate having one and then keep putting it off until we finish renovating. We're not actually renovating, but each time I hang a new curtain or buy a new throw rug, I think maybe that counts. Our circus of moving in included a speed trip through Ollie's to grab the cheapest of everything: curtains, towels, throw rugs, plates, etc. Each time I replace an item, I think *Maybe now is the time to have a housewarming party.* It's been nearly a decade. Perhaps time to let that idea go.

When I made the move from North Carolina to Virginia, my landing pad was the house in which my husband (and family) lived in when they were a different family. There was a different wife and a different mom and a different past and a different future. It made sense for me to slide into the open position for so many reasons that now make no sense at all. The kids had already been through so much, moving them would add unnecessary trauma. I had a house on the market in North Carolina; putting a second house on the market would be silly. Moving into the existing house would give us all time to figure out our next steps.

If we could repeat that move, we would absolutely do it completely differently. As it turns out, any buffer available that you can grab between an old life and a new one should be grabbed with two hands and nailed down. I went from living in a 1600-square-foot townhouse by myself (with two-and-a-half bathrooms) to a 1300-square-foot, stand-alone home (one bathroom) with another adult and two children (who'd all just wrapped up a divorce). This was a huge mistake. There is not a person on earth who can make that pivot without fallout.

My anxiety spiked the second I piled my suitcases in the bedroom as I realized that I had just given up any "alone" space indefinitely. My husband's anxiety spiked as he realized that moving a woman into a home with children did *not* kick off a hormone rush that would turn her instantly into a housewife and mom. It did not go well. One of my first requests was that our bedroom be a kid-free zone. I understand now why my husband looked at me funny, but man, he sure did look at me funny. I needed "me" space. There had been a great shift in bedrooms, as my husband did not want to sleep in the former master bedroom. That room was given to the ten-year-old and her previous bedroom was given to the seven-year-old and his previous bedroom was turned into my husband's office. The new master bedroom was planted in his former office, a dark wood-paneled room with green carpet and a washer/dryer in the closet. Delightful.

There were so many things that I instantly hated about the house. It sat on a busy road, and I knew that I'd never not hear the cars whizzing by. It was old and musty with unlevel hardwood floors. There was no garage, so my car was constantly covered in frost and debris from the trees surrounding it. The yard was patchy and muddy. One bathroom for four people was not enough and I often had to mop up urine off the floor surrounding the toilet as one of those four people preferred to brush his teeth while peeing, sending his stream all over the place. My clothes were scattered in five different closets as there wasn't one in the new master. Of course, right? Because that was where the washer/dryer lived. I hated going to sleep with the constant hum of clothes washing next to the bed.

The thing I hated the most was living with all of the memories of the former family. This is where the mom and dad had a huge fight. That's the couch that Dad slept on for three years straight. Over here was the room that housed an argument. That door is crooked from when it got slammed. The path on the side of the house was the runaway route that Amelia took in an effort to escape the deconstruction of a marriage. This refrigerator was where the dad found a note from the sheriff asking for a return call about an unjustified restraining order. I felt like I'd moved into the remnants of a war zone.

I didn't want to be there.

I knew that for each bad memory that lurked, there were probably a dozen good ones, but I didn't want to hear those either. I didn't want to know where the Christmas tree always went. I didn't want to stand in the same spot that the mom stood to wait for the bus. I didn't want to learn, mid-jump, that the former family used to all use the trampoline together too. I had no urge to make eggs in the same pan that the dad used to make breakfast each Saturday morning. I wasn't drawn to sit on the stool next to the tub to hear stories of the bath toys.

I didn't want to be there either.

I had moved away from a wonderful life to start a wonderful new life, yet I found myself knee-deep in the fallout of someone else's. My husband, oh goodness, he tried so hard. He would pull out photo albums or videos to connect the dots that I'd missed. Neither of us understood why it stung so much. As we grew further into our own life together, it became clearer. What I was seeing was something I thought I'd never longed for, the creation of a family from its inception. What he was trying to show me was how I could just step right into the good parts of its past, but I wasn't able to hear the stories or look at the pictures without a wince for years. With each wince, I felt immense guilt as I could see the joy in his eyes brought by sharing begin to dull. I already felt like I was losing myself; was I also going to take his joy away at the same time?

It did not take long for us to realize that this could not be our permanent arrangement. It took us much longer to realize that it shouldn't have been our arrangement at all. Hindsight told us that we should have waited until my house had sold to move and then to move into my own space, whether an apartment or purchased home. That would have given Rich and the kids the time they needed to sort out this new version of their lives while acclimating more slowly to my presence. We try not to live with regrets about our path to building a family (especially when hindsight is involved), but that is one that we readily admit to.

Realizing that we needed to make a physical change brought a great sense of relief, as I felt there would be an end to living among the ghosts of marriage past. It also brought a feeling of impatience as I started willing the phone to ring with news of an offer on my North Carolina home, which would enable us to put an offer on a new home here. The impatience translated to importance as we began putting a lot (too much, as it turned out) of weight on how that new home would instantly settle all of our emotions and represent the starting line for our new family.

When the pieces finally fell into place, we were full of excitement and promise and hope. Check that, the adults were full of excitement and promise and hope. The kids were full of nerves and fear. There was excitement, sure, but there was also a finality. We saw a start; they saw a finish. We saw a new family forming; they saw the old one officially ending. The old house was the only one they'd ever known. Moving was foreign to them. Moving into a home where a new woman would take the "other parent" role was beyond comprehension.

We tried so hard to make it easy. So hard. We love to play chicken with fate. It never works.

Our move took place in February of 2014. We had a race going between our "Days until the move" clock and the "Days until the road opens" clock owned by the Department of Transportation. The exact bottom of our new driveway marked the starting point of a bridge under construction that seemed to have no end. The stink of it was, we would not be able to make the turn into our driveway, with a U-Haul, if coming from the opposite direction. We pushed and pushed and finally got word that the road would be opened on the eleventh. Our move was scheduled for the twelfth. Which was the day the first snowstorm of the year arrived.

We scheduled the move to coincide with a week that the kids would be with their (bio)mom. This would give us time to prioritize setting up their rooms and make the new house extra exciting. Then their (bio)mom imploded. We set aside boxes and collected the kids from school as we started learning about an eviction that kicked off a need to file for emergency custody. Unpacking was halted for visits to a lawyer and a judge, all on icy roads. Our plans for a move-in ready home went out the window. My plans for easing into the role of stepmother went out the window. Less than ten weeks from saying "so long" to the single-girl life where my dog, cat, and I lived peacefully on our own, I was in a shocked daze as we moved everyone into the new house at once.

Because we hadn't planned on having the kids at home that week, my husband had also scheduled a business trip. He tried to travel during the non-custody weeks as we, by then, knew that I was not ready to be a full-time parent. But there I was, in a brand new, strange home with two tiny people who were not only very leery of me, but also very confused (and angry) about why their (bio)mom's apartment was no longer an option.

Living in chaos is not my thing. I do not perform well in chaos. I am not chipper in chaos. Moving is chaos. Moving with children suffering from abandonment issues in the middle of a snowstorm with no help is chaos with superpowers. There would be no leaving the house as my North Carolina car was not equipped for more than a whisper of snow. I did put on my best happy face as we opened endless boxes together, the kids and me. I could see worry on their faces but had not yet developed a talent for nurture.

The best thing I could come up with was sledding. We did lots of sledding. I found muscles I didn't even know existed. I also found out that I couldn't actually leave kids outside in freezing temperatures for indefinite amounts of time. I found out which box the hot chocolate lived in and was guided in how to add mini marshmallows to warm up two tiny, frozen icicles.

Terrified doesn't begin to describe those first days. It was likely by design (fate ...) that I couldn't get my car out. If I'd been mobile, I'd have mobile-d myself right back down to North Carolina, changed my phone number, and never looked back.

Instead (or in spite of it all), we managed to form the first of our family's memories.

Which Way's Up?

Battles of the Sexes

Since Amelia went off to college, I have absolutely noticed what it's like being the only girl in the room. Prior to her departure, we had a nice, equal combination of estrogen and testosterone that went back for years. When I brought this to his attention, my husband spit out his water. Amelia and I do not nail the "girly" mold in the prissy sense, but we do still rate. Rich and Max aren't edging anywhere near the jock-ish land of man-land, but still. With Amelia out of the house and our numbers now two (males) to one (female), there is a huge increase in burping and farting with no warning or apologies. Hello?

Please note, Amelia was not our primary source for manners. Why, then, did her departure open a free pass to remaining at the dinner table while blowing some butt wind.

When we were four, we had a nice balance. What Rich and Max strive for in competitive eating, Amelia and I would counter with a conversational speed between bites. Now, I've got to be more cognizant of the rate at which the boys empty their plates, in case I might want to get in there for a second serving. What's the stinking rush? Do our meals now have deadlines?

And why the uptick in sounds made while eating? Why do I feel like I'm surrounded by aardvarks? Is it the stress of having a child in college that engages a sucking action for each serving? Why hasn't mine engaged? Is that a male thing as well?

Yes, I have always been sensitive to loud chewing. It's ridiculous. In fairness, Amelia was hyperaware of this and, God bless her, served as my shield, alerting others when they were reaching an auditory danger zone that would result in two eye-sized holes being bored into their souls.

Since she was not available for vacation this year, I lost my mind and let Max bring a friend. A male friend. Male. Three against one. Why am I an idiot?

I haven't decided what kind of trophies I'll be passing out to the moms of **only** boys, but it will be large and topped with a wine bottle. Do years of living as the lone female in a household create some sort of sensory blindness? Is that why nobody warned me?

Fourteen-year-old boys plus inconsistent deodorant plus sporadic showering practices plus bike riding plus swimming plus seawater plus mini-golf plus greasy vacation meals plus a husband in the glory of male bonding ... and my gawd.

Why am I an idiot?

My husband has decided to make this vacation week the moment of his farting opus, leading an operatic performance with two teenage participants.

I'm starting to believe that the three of them write out instrumental melody goals at breakfast, then spend the day eating agreed upon combinations of gummy bears, Funyuns, and ice cream to produce The Song of the Sphincter as I'm drifting off to sleep with Q-tips stuck up my nose. And I absolutely don't blame the smell on our guest child. I'm just not sure if I should be proud or mortified at the fumes my child is letting out, but I **am** shocked that we've not been evicted. Our beds were at opposite ends of a rental, yet I've mistaken the odor for elephant droppings directly outside my bedroom window multiple times.

I miss the days when the ratio of smelly people to not smelly people was 50/50 and not 75/25.

I miss the days when nightly showers evoked a barely there scent of Irish Spring and a much stronger scent of "Is that Bath & Body Works?"

And the shoes. Good grief, the shoes. Each night, as size

canoe sneakers were peeled off six male feet and distributed into various corners, I'd nonchalantly put my COVID mask back on. I now understand the purpose of those scented sneaker balls, though I was confused as to why they were so much bigger than the nostrils I was trying to shove them up.

I am at the crossroads of "a little bit fraternity," and "still sweet."

I have aged well, keeping one foot firmly planted in the camp of "that's what she said" while still loving to host a formal tea. I do think farting is funny, just not necessarily 473 times a day. No, I am not overly prissy or sensitive but, left as the only female in a crowd, I have definitely noticed a desire for more feminine camaraderie.

Rich has entered his glory.

Not one, but two boys willing to spend time with him chatting about books and wars and science words that I don't care to understand. I hide behind a People magazine while hoping not to be asked to weigh in. That's fine, right?

We all have our things.

I just think I might like mine with a little more chatter about why celebrities are just like us and a little less about the size of one's poops.

Which, apparently, are very impressive.

CHAPTER SEVEN

These Are Your Kids

MINE? WHAT? HOW?

The chances that you walk into a marriage involving existing kids and have an instantly perfect, long-lasting bond are slim. Like, *impossibly* slim. And if you are thinking, *Oh, that hasn't been my experience at all*, then you may want to keep that seat belt handy because, eventually, you are going to need to buckle up. When you walk into that marriage involving existing kids, you will want a simple mantra. Something that really speaks to you and reminds you of your place in their lives. Something quick and easy with the verbal ability to put you back where you belong. Here it is.

They did not ask for you.

These existing kids did not ask for you to come into their lives. The younger they are, the less they have the ability to understand even *why* you came into their lives. What they asked for, without actually having the words/maturity/thought to form the question, was to have the two people that are their parents to be together and happy and their primary source of love and stability. Your arrival turned that snow globe containing their ideal life onto its head. Your arrival gives permanence to the splitting of their first known parents. Your arrival signals that the band is not, in fact, going to get back together.

Your arrival means the separation of their team. Something that didn't seem so serious before has now become serious. Your arrival has given their lives a "before."

They did not ask for you.

But that doesn't mean that you cannot be an important part of their lives. And that certainly doesn't mean that these children cannot become an important part of yours. It just takes more time, energy, and tears than you likely thought possible. The chances that you walk into a marriage involving existing kids and have an instantly perfect, long-lasting bond are slim. The more common pattern is waves of simplicity alternating with waves of emotional chaos. In the beginning, the children will be intrigued by you as they soak up your shininess, much like the start of each school year when they show model behavior for a new teacher. You will know when they are becoming more comfortable with you when they begin to show normal, age-appropriate misbehavior. You will know when they are feeling overwhelmed with anxiety brought on by the realization of your permanence when that misbehavior amps up, potentially to a level of demonic possession.

They did not ask for you.

They are still adjusting to the letdown provided by their parents via the separation. They probably don't even know what that word means or what divorce or custody or alimony mean, either. What they know is that someone they love left, and it hurt and now there is a new someone else who, in their tiny brains, will probably leave as well. That's a lot to carry without being asked.

Patience. Time. Silence. Commitment.

Patience because the road to a relationship is so long.

Time because it takes so much of it: time together, time apart donated to the other parent, time to allow your differences to bare themselves, and time to build those differences into a connection.

Silence because you will often stand by, biting your tongue, keeping the peace, hanging on.

Commitment. The commitment is yours. It is a willingness to give that time and have that patience and be a partner through your silence. It is a commitment to giving your energy and your tears and your love and still remaining though none may be returned.

Is there joy? Yes. Success? Of course. Wins? Yes! It would be so easy to write about all of those happy moments of bliss (and also really sell the whole idea of (step)momming). But if that were all (step)momming was about, it would not be a position typically portrayed as evil in shows and movies and cartoons. It is all the other moments that will become the most important to building that relationship with your (step)children. It is the moments in which you would rather throw in the towel and go back to your old life that will become the foundation that builds your relationship with your (step)children. It's the awful, heartbreaking, frustrating, and mind-numbing moments in which you *stay* that will matter most.

The longer you can avoid those moments, the better, yes. The most common advice given to (step)moms is to work your way into the relationship slowly. Start off by *not* meeting the kids, something else to put off as long as possible. Not indefinitely, but definitely until there is a well-formed future in the brains of your significant other and you. If you aren't there, if you are just casually dating, sure, you can still meet the kids. As a friend. As someone their father hangs out with for company. As someone who isn't going to make breakfast in the morning. Once you place that stamp of permanency in their tiny minds, extraction is (and should be) next to impossible.

In my case, starting slowly worked for an entire year. Then I was thrown headfirst into the deep end of a pool I thought I was only testing with my big toe. The instant I came up for air,

I started chipping away at my high level of anxiety by implementing schedules and chores and bedtimes. I should have leaned into my role as the newcomer and stayed there until the kids were ready to promote me to a more important character. My commitment to becoming a parent should have come silently. I should have walked the walk without talking the talk. I had two young people who had just witnessed the splitting of their first two parents. Still, it never crossed my mind that they would not want a third parental option or that, in their minds, a third option who would eventually leave as well. I should have lived more peripherally. I should have done all the "things," taking all the leads from my husband, and not expecting any of the grateful returns. The returns did come, yes, but they came in my (step)children's time, not mine.

If you feel a rush to experience that feeling of "Oh, these are my children too" there is an easy way. Or rather, an easy way that is also quite difficult. Your husband will have the ability to spend hours and hours telling you more than you thought you ever wanted to know about his children. If you can, **listen**. If you can. It can be quite trying to hear all about a previous life that involved another woman. It can tap into one's jealous side to hear about all the wonderful things that woman shared with the person you have fallen in love with. You will feel a gut punch with each picture you see that includes an (ex)wife and (bio)mom, even if she is the most perfect woman in the world. The reality will always be that she was there from the start. The reality will be that she was theirs from the start, your partner and his kids. It took me years to feel comfortable opening a photo album from that first family, but I wish I could have done it sooner. I wish I could have compartmentalized that history into a learning exercise rather than allowing it to drive me to averting my eyes. How much simpler it might have been if I knew something about their stories from the beginning? I could have been a much more active participant in the recalling of those stories. Rather than hoping I didn't look disinterested, I could have perked up with an "*Oh, yes, your dad told me all about how much you loved your beach vacations. Tell me more!*"

The work of building an intimate, important relationship with my (step)children was ultimately my responsibility, though I often needed an assist from their dad. One of the greatest wins in the forming of our family was Kid Swap. Every other weekend, my husband would take one child on a date while I took the other. It gave him a chance to reconnect and remind his date that he would always be with them. It gave me a chance to connect and start *having* moments with mine. It was important that I begin to build moments that we didn't share with anybody else. It was also terrifying. I had no idea where to take an eight-year-old boy or an eleven-year-old girl. I had no idea what to talk about or how much time was enough time or where to take them or, oh yeah, what to talk about. I was forty-two. Most of my interaction with the younger set was during my days as a gymnastics coach where our hours were guided by provided lesson plans. This new date-a-grade-schooler seemed so smart in theory, but my initial execution was fumbly.

I did seek guidance on the "where," as I found that asking a tiny stranger what they wanted for dinner always ended in "*I don't know,*" or "*I don't care*" or "*I'm not really hungry.*" What they were really saying was, "*I really don't want to do this.*" When we did finally land on a place that one or the other liked, we would repeat it often. I had no idea that, unlike adults (or at least this one), kids didn't mind repeating restaurants or activities. I'd say that they even liked it after a while as those Groundhog Day Swap Nights grew into, "oh, that's where **we** like to go" places. It didn't take long to form a few very predictable evenings, which provided a comfort to all of us. I learned that restaurants with activities worked best, such as those with arcades or bowling or playgrounds. I learned not to be offended by their missing attention spans, a true case of *it's not you ... it's them ... and they are not going to have a long, deep, mind-blowing conversation with you over french fries and a Frosty.* It was much easier to stand side-by-side at a Skee-Ball machine and see who could get the most tickets to trade in for plastic prizes than to take a stab at resolving issues from a childhood that they were still experiencing. There was less stress in sliding down a bowling lane following an eight-pound ball than explaining why I didn't have any of my own kids.

I learned to always be surprised, be interested, and be involved when they were speaking to me. I found Chatterboxes (found online or in craft stores)— tiny boxes filled with tiny cards with tiny questions. These were lifesavers. I started taking the boxes everywhere with me, tucked away in an upgraded, mom-sized purse. The pre-written, simple, get-to-know-me questions often started with one-word answers and often ended with car-ride-long debates about why chocolate was the superior ice cream flavor. I learned to follow most of their opinions with the words, *"Tell me why."* Tell me why. Three simple words that gave them a green light to let me in just a little further.

As terrifying as it was for me to have alone time with these people I hardly knew, I'd also feel jealous when they wanted to spend time alone with their dad or (bio)mom instead of me. That has morphed over time from being their "but I don't know you" preference to a "Dad (or (bio)mom) are more fun" preference. This is accurate. I now sit on the side of the task-master and the list keeper. It is a bummer sometimes, but it is also the place in which I thrive at parenting. I am the most stable person in their lives when it comes to the doing of the things. That is not because their dad isn't interested, it is because this is my forte and where I have found my greatest gift in offering them the ability to depend on me. It took a long time to get here. It required forcing myself to be involved in a very public world that I had missed in the first decade of their lives. When I was able to, I began volunteering at the schools and signing up as the soccer team manager. I didn't do the "front and center" things at first. My time at the school was behind a copier and not within the classroom, a calculated move that allowed me to share a story of *being at your school today* without interrupting the rhythm of their day in a place where not many knew yet that there was a new lady in their lives. Ten years later, I could pretty much walk directly into one of their classrooms and drop off deodorant and nobody would bat an eye.

But it is a waiting game. There will be invitations, but they will come way down a road whose length varies. You may first be invited to come to the holiday pageant "with my dad" and you must say, "yes," knowing that there will be an awkward moment in figuring out who is sitting next to whom. You will be asked to chaperone a field trip out of the blue and you *cannot* decline, no matter how loud and chaotic you suspect it will be (and lawd, it will be). You will be summoned to chaperone a friend group to a movie, "but don't sit near us," and you *must* go, and you *must* not sit near them.

This is when you will know you matter. These are the first cracks in the shield that children of divorce hold firmly in front of their hearts. They submit these requests with a fear of rejection that they are likely not even aware of. They are simple invitations that are tied to big feelings.

You must say yes.

ON MY WATCH

Things I never thought I'd say:
"Max, please don't get on that treadmill with that cast on

your foot."
Followed by:
"At least, PLEASE, stop trying to run!"

There are beacons that appear as a latecomer to (step)momming that have stopped me in my tracks, momentarily, while my brain dropped a gear into place with a signal of, "You're Doing It!" There were moments when I would hear what I was saying to my (step)child and give myself a mental high five for being so stinking good at this major project that I walked into halfway through its completion. There were also moments when I would hear what I was saying and hope that they weren't smart enough to realize that I was absolutely and very leerily faking it.

And then there was the moment when my teen tried to use the treadmill with a new cast on his leg just to see if he could.

We made it nearly seventeen years with all the bones of both kids still intact. That's something, right? A late-night run-in with a railroad tie ended that, though the actual story still holds a lot of secrets. Something along the lines of *"We were playing tag in the dark"*, or *"We were running around in the dark"*, or *"It was dark so I didn't see the wooden thing"*. This was while Max was at a church retreat. A church retreat. The kind of event where parents can take a break from worry. The kind of event where parents don't have to ask, "What could go wrong?" because, well, it's a church retreat. For those with him, the incident was deemed minor as the wounded mostly carried on, with an assist from ice and ibuprofen. This was such a relief for us as a four-hour drive to pick him up wasn't what we wanted to do during an awaited childless weekend.

Both of my (step)children had a flair for dramatics long before they came into my life. One, the younger, would demand no less than thirty-five Band-Aids after a stumble that never actually landed him on the ground. The other, the elder, often filled our heads with stories so unbelievable that she was often applauded for her creativity. We paid very little attention to either child when they ran off into the emotional woods of the wounded. This approach to parenting has not always been met with approval from their (bio)mom (or their grandmother now that I think of it).

Exhibit A: We paid very little attention to the text from the church retreat delivering the message of an injured foot. We did ask for a comparison shot of his two feet, though, a cyber-diagnosis sent back that everything looked fine (or would after a good night's sleep). The lack of a peep the following day confirmed our ability to doctor from afar. The silence, an indication that Max had recovered enough to spend the day in a backwoods orchard picking something like 17,000 pounds of apples.

(We're doing it!!)

Mid-afternoon the second following day, we collected a very dirty, very disheveled, and very tired child with a predicted spike in dramatics as he sprung a heavy limp while approaching our car. All signs of an excellent weekend, nothing to worry about. By the time he was within hugging range, he was dragging his leg behind him as if the entire thing was sliding out from his hip. Have I mentioned his flair for dramatics? The church retreat chaperone began to stammer, explaining that this level of limp was brand new. I did my usual cut-it-off-at-the-pass (step)momming by lobbing a question to the wounded on whether he was going for the sympathy vote. I told him he would get it, of course, he'd spent the weekend picking apples for local food banks. Of course, we would offer all kinds of sympathy!

As he assured me that he was not being dramatic, he slipped off his shoe and sock, which was when the eyes of all surrounding parents bugged out. It appeared that his foot was drawn by the same artist who did Fred Flintstone's feet. Which was a real bummer, as right before I saw it, I had had another one of those passing "I'm Doing It!" moments, believing that Max's dramatics peaked because he'd been holding the misery threshold down all weekend. He wanted to hoard it until he saw me, his beloved (step)mom. It is a warm feeling when you realize your children aren't afraid to let those tears flow around you. That feeling went out the window with words of *uuuhhhh* ... and *hmmm* ... and *that's not great* ... . Here I was, the newest parent and also the one who had insisted on a permanent pass on anything medical, faced with playing it cool while staring at a grossly deformed foot.

I did pull myself together enough to diagnose the injury as a broken metatarsal via a trick I'd learned as a gymnastics coach called, "*Does it hurt here?*" We headed home to scrub off forty-eight hours of dirt before heading to the emergency orthopedic office where that broken metatarsal lit up the x-ray. *I'm doing it!* The prelude to the x-ray was a very panicked child with no history to tell him exactly what an x-ray entailed. Weeks prior, I'd had a live MRI, involving needles and dye. This child, phobic to this day of needles, rode silently to his fate, too brave to ask how many needles an x-ray required. It is so easy to forget that your kids don't come with the same database as you. We were discharged with his foot firmly wrapped in bandages and instructions for rest/ice/ibuprofen until his foot began looking more human and less hobbit, at which point a cast would be installed.

My request to be on the bench for all things medical came honestly and early in my parenting relationships. I have never had a super-warm-fuzzy-it-will-be-okay side, nor have I ever had a useful adrenal rush for times when there was either sickness or injury around me. Rich told me often, early on, that it comes naturally to mothers. Once I started settling in, some sort of magic dust would be sprinkled on me while I slept, forcing my hormones into a formidable force against vomit or blood. He'd seen it happen to his (ex)wife when the kids were born, so I suppose it was not a big stretch to think it would happen to some random lady he met at a high-end lounge.

This was not the case.

The foot incident was not my first round of dealing with the sick and the poor. The first was shortly after my installation as a third parent, while Rich was traveling. I got a call from the school about a child with a fever. I really had no idea what I was supposed to do, a tone that was picked up quickly by the school nurse as she explained that I needed to come get him. *What? And then what?* We laugh about these moments now but, at the time, Rich was absolutely stymied by my lack of knowledge in a kid crisis, firmly perplexed that my hormones were not delivering magic answers or tactics.

That is not the case.

Going from zero kids to any kids at any age is difficult. It involves a constant stream of second-guessing and wondering and assuming that you will make the wrong choice. It involves others jumping in immediately to tell you if you made the wrong choice, often with a tone of disapproval so strong that your inclination is to turn all parenting over to the next person who crosses into your field of vision. There may be nothing harder than feeling like a complete and total moron at age forty-four (in my case) because you didn't know that you should have Children's Tylenol in the medicine cabinet at all times. I'd worked in the corporate world for two decades. I'd project managed the shit out of difficult assignments over and over yet I couldn't seem to nail caring for children in this maternal *"Oh, it just came naturally"* way that others did.

I actually suspect there are many pieces in mothering that do not come naturally to any of us, biological or not. I suspect that this is one of those topics that all mothers feel, but none want to admit to lest we are labeled as a failure or as incapable. I've found the support system in mothering has a major break between the bios and the steps. I suppose it comes from wariness or jealousy or an inability to let someone new handle the lives of the kids that once belonged primarily to someone else. The tale of the broken foot was no different. I was the one who scheduled the weekend away, therefore the injury happened on my watch, right? Not really. This child had gone on a similar mission trip for years and my only involvement was finding out the dates and signing a form while the nitty-gritty details were left up to the sponsoring church. I was thrown back on my heels when the retelling of the story to his (bio)mom and (bio)grandma was met with a verbal side-eye from both.

How could this have happened?

Who was in charge?

Why wasn't he immediately picked up?

How could you have let this happen?

This was not the first time I was sent to the jury after a totally normal "kids are kids" incident, nor would it be the last. It seemed that whenever a child became sick/injured/sad/unshowered while I was living anywhere on the same planet, I was immediately shuffled to the bottom of the Parentally Qualified Totem Pole. I've never understood it, nor have I had a similar reaction when the situation was reversed. I suppose because in the beginning, I often assigned myself to the bottom of that totem pole willingly. That was my place, after all, right? Rich's attendance during these events was often discounted. It didn't matter if Rich was the one driving the actual bus, if I was seated anywhere on it, then my *involvement* outweighed his presence. It baffled me. It still baffles me. I still seek a world with unicorns and rainbows where the women treat each other like the gifts that they are by supporting each other and lifting each other up and offering great advice and endless leniency.

As the incoming parent, I was almost always assigned a

lack of trust. I would think that it would be less for those incoming parents who already have children of their own, but my guess is not. My guess is those children of their own serve as an example to those poised to jump on any parental hiccups. At least in my case, there were no other children to point to with a knowing, *"Well, look how she did with her actual kids."* It might have been easier to simply accept that I would never make the right decision or have the correct reaction than to play emotional whack-a-mole. It is almost comical to think in terms of *"Yes, I did do that. I did send this child on a church retreat knowing perfectly well that there would be a midnight round of flashlight tag in a field where there was one random railroad tie placed."*

But this was my life. It was annoying that if my husband made a child-rearing mistake, it was quickly put in the past. If I did, it was marked as a tragedy.

After a minor knee injury at soccer. *"Oh, I wish Max had never started playing soccer. I just think it's ridiculous."* This happened in my child's fourth soccer season. Four years. Yes, I was the one to introduce him to soccer. Yes, his father and I had a blast coaching his tiny little recreation level teams. But if it weren't for me ... that knee ...

After a sleepover that ended in tears. *"I don't really know why you even let Amelia go over to Jane's house. I never liked her at all."*

After either child leaves for the bathroom during dinner. *"This is your fault. Ever since you put your foot down on not being a short-order cook."* Um, no, children poop at dinner. Look it up. It's been happening for years.

Rest. Ice. Ibuprofen. Emotional Shield. Wine.

We figured we'd get two mastered fairly easily.

Rest: By relinquishing any limits on video game time (a dream come true in our home). Ibuprofen: Self-solving. Max was old enough to decide if the pain was worth the pill.

Ice: Okay, we really had no shot here.

The emotional shield and wine were for me as I prepared to hear, for the next four to six weeks, about my involvement in the breaking of this child's metatarsal.

I'm doing it!

And then I heard the treadmill.

Surely, no.

Then, pat, clunk, pat, clunk, pat, clunk in cadence with the digital beeps of a belt being driven to the next level.

Me: *"Max, please don't do the treadmill with that cast on your foot."*

Me, again: *"Okay, well. At least, PLEASE, stop trying to run!"*

To which a response came, *"But I need to see how much speed I can get with this thing on!"*

How could this have happened?

I guess because I was the (step)mom of a regular, run-of-the-mill, very busy boy.

And because I was just a regular, run-of-the-mill, very naive (step)mom who had no chance of slowing him down.

THE LESSER PARENT

"Oh ... so you're their (step)mom."

"So, they aren't your kids ..."

"Yeah, but they aren't your real kids ..."

And my all-time favorite, *"Oh, so you're not their real mom."*

Or, for an even more dramatic lurch to the gut, any of the above statements routed from the mouth of your actual (step)child.

"She's just my (step)mom ... she's not my real mom ... you're not my mom ..."

These statements, true or not in the world of hairsplitting, offer such a jolt. They offer an unrequested combination of a stab to the heart and a stab in the back. They flare up feelings of anger, failure, injustice, offense, and despair. When it comes from the (step)kids? That's a fairly simple thing to talk one off the ledge from. After all, having more than one equal parent of the same sex is a lot for a child to comprehend. But when regular, everyday people (read: morons or busybodies or know-it-alls) feel the need to make that clarification, I often wonder if they would do the same in the other (technically) hazy instances. One of my closest friends has a second child who came to their family via an orphanage in China. Do people look at her and say, "*Oh, so **that's** why he doesn't look like the rest of you ...*" Or, for those who do adopt a cosmetically matching child, does the paperwork come with an asterisk referencing a line deep into the document that reads, "Thank you for doing this but remember, this is not this child's *real* mother."

I have yet to figure out why people really think that it is acceptable to throw out that verbal reminder. Are they just so naive that it would seem perfectly appropriate and not just plain hurtful?

These children that I live with are very, very much my very, very own, real children. We (step)parents, through whichever portal we arrived, are very, very real parents. I've heard that the journey to having children often involves endless hurdles and headaches and heartache. I've witnessed the same, from a front row seat, in the journey to adoption. (Step)momming? Yes. Hurdles, headaches, and heartache. The journey is not the walk in the park that some believe it to be. Ignorant comments like those above are a large part of the reason I abhor the word "step" in relation to any parent. The decades of negative connotation (thank you, Disney) have not helped either, other than to give our children a benchmark of why their stepmonster is flipping out over abandoned socks or collections of half-filled water glasses. When I hear my children refer to me as their mom, my heart swells. I doubt that will ever get old. I often wonder if "real" moms have that same feeling or if it is reserved especially for those of us who collected our children via hurdles and headaches and heartache that we hadn't necessarily planned for. Typically, having a child involves planning. Typically, adopting a child involves planning. Typically, becoming a (step)mom involves a quick blindside.

What people often hear when you announce your position of (**step**)mom is that you are, actually, the lesser parent. You are the parent who does not have to make difficult decisions. You are the parent who only sees the kids when they are scheduled to be in your life. You are the parent who does not have to have deep discussions about kid futures. You are the parent who gets time off. You are the mother who can legitimately say, "*Go ask your mother.*" When a woman says she has kids, she gives an unintentional road map of her life. Whomever she shares this detail with goes through an unrecognized mental hula hoop as they categorize her as someone who met someone with whom she wanted to start a family, was able to get pregnant and give birth at least once and has endured all the highs and lows of motherhood from the moment her precious child came out of her womb. When a woman says she has (step)children, the unintentional road map is much more vague and the mental hula hoop often lands on, "*Oh, that sounds so easy.*" I know this because I used to think the same thing. I never knew any (step)moms who had their kids full time. I only knew women who had married men with an every-other-weekend custody schedule. What's so hard about that?

Everything.

There is no rhythm to building any kind of relationship

with the (step)children. There is a father who feels a piece of his heart leaving every other Sunday night. There is an awkward transition between homes that bleeds into the spousal relationship before and after each visit with the kids. I used to think that an every-other-weekend schedule would be bliss. Then I realized that it actually caused more emotional instability than the schedule we have with our children, which is a full-time flexible kind of schedule. Full-time (step)children are hard, yes, but at least I get the chance at full-time involvement and full-time relationships and full-time presence without a constant side-eye lingering over the custody calendar.

The lesser parent. I am the lesser parent. That is me. The one who started this gig with a sign over my head announcing that I definitely didn't know anything about my insta-kids. *Does she even know where the schools are? What about the Band-Aids? Does she have any idea how they lost their first tooth? Does she know about the time Santa brought a bicycle? Or that her child will eat raw broccoli but not cooked broccoli? What happens if there are decisions to be made? She doesn't get invited to that part of the parental table, right? Her two cents are not really worth two cents, are they? If she has any thoughts, she takes them to the actual parents for vetting and workshopping before they go into production, right?* I went through all of these scenarios for years, slowly chipping away to find my place at that parental table. And now that I am here, and I have been here for a few years now, I can still see the passing look when I tell someone I have (step)kids. So no, that is not how I describe my children anymore. Now, I call them my children, the very real children of this very real mom.

I am the designated taxi driver, signer of the forms, keeper of the ibuprofen, planner of meals, liaison with the schools, the shoulder to cry on, vacation planner, appointment maker, and the clothes buyer. It's a real mom's resume straight through. I feel like a very real mom when I'm driving one kid to practice before speeding in the other direction to take the second kid to work. I feel very real when I'm consoling a child who has been wronged. I feel very real when I'm behind the stove hoping for dinner success while simultaneously noting who needs new sneakers while mentally composing an email to a teacher and visualizing what gifts we have for a coming birthday. I feel especially real when I get a random hug. I feel real by the amount of need my kids have for me, even if they are slow to admit it. I feel real by their acceptance of my very real nagging, which they know is the cost of my very real organizational momager skills. I feel especially real when I'm told "*I love you*" by one and the other follows it with a grumbly "*Yeah, me too.*" And when I was slapped with my first, "*I hate you!!*" after counting to ten multiple times, I felt the most real of all. Those words, after all, are the highest form of (real) parental flattery.

But what's it like? What's it like being a (step)mom?

It's an impossible answer to nail down and one that orbits around any feelings of reward. Being a (step)mom is always doing my best for my kids, giving 150 percent, while knowing that it's never going to count or put me anywhere near the level of love they have for their biological mom. And yes, I know it's not a competition, but it will always feel like one. The biological relationship between a mother and child is something that can never be broken, no matter what that biological parent does (or doesn't). I am endlessly grateful (and sometimes endlessly frustrated) to have a live example of this in my husband whose parents were fifteen and seventeen when he was born. My husband's upbringing was the definition of unstable as neither parent was ready for the responsibility of a child. While his extended family did jump in as they were able, his father spent much of his time rotating through gangs, meth houses, and jail. His mother's family housed them both for much of his childhood, which did enable her to work toward a GED and, eventually, a nursing degree, but that was in conjunction with a second marriage and divorce and many, many moves. The output, for my husband, was shuffling between two homes that rarely had a consistently positive parental vibe. This is not to say that Rich wasn't well loved by his parents, but they were hardly more than children themselves. Despite the fear, instability, and never-ending disappointments he experienced as a child, my husband grew up adamantly defending both parents at all times to anyone who might have disparaged them.

Biology is real. There have been many times when I've wished my own children's mother would just drop off all of our radars, especially my (step)children's. That is typically followed by a rush of guilt for thinking that they would really be better off with only me in that maternal seat. After that, I move on to feeling thankful that she hasn't dropped off the radar because I can't imagine the devastation that would cause my (step)children. I remind myself, and occasionally my (step)kids, that I made a *choice* to be with my husband and that that *choice* included another *choice*, which was to also be with **them**. It was a decision I thought through carefully (though quite naively). It was a decision with a difficulty level that I underestimated horribly in my single-gal world of unicorns and rainbows.

The competitiveness of momming never ceases, despite a hit-or-miss understanding that comparisons are pointless. It is something that every (step)mom does and evolves through many forms. On a very basic level, females are programmed to want to be the most popular (and the prettiest and the tiniest and have the best shoes and, and, and ...). Of course, we want the blue ribbon for momming as well. The problem is that a green ribbon for regular momming will always outweigh a blue ribbon for stepmomming. The blue ribbon is an unattainable goal for the (step)mom. If I ever meet a (step)mom who can say, in a very believable tone, that she does not feel competitive with a (bio)mom, I will probably offer to check her pulse.

My husband likes to use flowery statements like, "*The more people that love the kids the better.*" I did understand the statement, and I did offer an eye roll every time I heard it. There is a catty girl still living inside of me. It was easier in the beginning. I could swoop in, take the kids to ice cream or Starbucks, sit on the sidelines at sporting events (in full glam), and praise their achievements. I would make mental notes of anything their (bio)mom had done for them so that I could replicate it while also silently reminding myself that I did *not* have to outdo her. It became more difficult as I grew closer to my (step)kids. At the exact moment when they began to take up more space within my heart, there began a noticeable "pulling away" from their (bio)mom, creating a distance that none of us were anticipating. The competition took on less of a blue-ribbon-mom vibe and more of a sensitivity as to how various actions were making the kids feel. I no longer counted the events that their (bio)mom was doing. I began counting the ones that she was *not* doing. Instead of feeling blissful that my (step)kids were relying more on me for those magical moments, I began to feel angry that she was no longer providing them. The competitiveness was replaced with sadness for both me and the kids. I wanted their (bio)mom to recognize them as just as special and important as I did. I wanted to feel elated that I'd gone further up the totem pole than she, but with that growing love, what I felt was, well, awful.

That's what being the lesser parent is like. That's who people are referring to when they say, "*Oh, but you're not their real mom.*"

SOMETIMES BEING GOOD ISN'T GOOD ENOUGH

This is a tough one as writing it seems to border on defeat. As I was working on the first draft of this excerpt, I was sitting in a room waiting for my (step)daughter to finish four hours of psychological testing thinking, "*Yes, just wave whatever color flag you can.*" The question that has come up the most in my years of (step)momming her is, "*How did we get here?*" I have spent more time thinking of ways I could have handled countless interactions and how those tweaks might have driven our relationship to a field of daisies under rainbow skies. But that does not seem to be our path. It has not been our path for most of our time together.

I'm not sure where biological mothers sit on this topic, but I know for stepmothers, it is devastating. Or at least it feels that way to me. Coming into an unexpected family as someone who leans towards being the best at everything has not always meshed. As with most of my accomplishments in life, big or small, my initial prediction for this new life was (*Step)mom, check, got it, will most likely be amazing.* I was not amazing. I wasn't terrible, children weren't a totally foreign object to me, but I definitely was not amazing. It clicked in my head just recently that there is a reason that infants are the traditional first phase in motherhood. Nature's design is to offer new mothers years of trial and error before their children have the capacity to start making mental notes for future therapists about how their parents performed. Ideally, by the time a child reaches that age of awareness, their mothers will have graduated from trial and error to trial and reached occasional success. Or, at the very least, they will have gained the ability to hide the truth, which is that most mothers really have zero idea at all as to what they are doing.

(Step)moms don't have that luxury.

Even those (step)moms who already have their own biological children find themselves completely stymied by their stepchildren. The road map to feeling like a qualified mother is unique to each child. The only real guarantee is that if something worked perfectly with the first child, then it will fail miserably with the next. For me, it feels like one step forward, two (or seven) steps backwards even now, nearly a decade in. (Step)momming is a position that requires constant *trying* with very little return on investment. The most consistent ROI, for me, has been a finger of accusation pointed directly at me as the source of all things horrible in my children's lives. That finger has been at the end of my children's arms, of course, but also at the ends of the arms of my husband's relatives who (still) do not trust his choice in spouses (first or second) and, by extension, in his choice in moms.

This was the first assignment in my life where I went from feeling completely confident to completely incompetent with no chance of recovery almost as soon as my suitcase was unpacked. It didn't take much longer to begin agreeing (silently at first) with any criticisms of my performance. All those criticisms came without pause, even as I was actively begging for help or advice. I felt like I was sinking further into the ocean while a handful of people stood watching, holding life preservers, while telling me how my way of treading water was only hurting the fish below me.

One of the challenges in (step)momming is that most people don't talk about (step)momming. I thought I was in this small, secret club. My line of reasoning was that as I didn't know any other (step)moms, there must not have been any around me. I knew loads of regular moms, but with my confidence in parenting destroyed so quickly, I was leery to bring up my feelings of failure with any of them. These regular moms all sounded like women who really had their child-rearing shit together. I was certainly not going to be the lone floundering member of the clique. I had moved to a new town in conjunction with gaining my grade-school sidekicks. I was attempting to make a whole new life, including friends and hobbies, while wondering why I couldn't figure out the pieces of my life that lived in that new house with me. It took years for me to feel comfortable enough to expose my shortcomings about parenting to other moms, especially after the sting of poor reception from my husband's mother. I spent those years hiding all the emotion and tears and anxiety from this new public except when I was taking it out on my new husband (God bless him). He'd made a very male brain leap when inviting me to his hometown, assuming that women just automagically find friend groups and support systems. Maybe I thought that too, that the mothers would welcome me to their fold. Perhaps that is how it works for biological mothers, but for those of us who come to mothering a different way, it doesn't seem to be true.

When I did find my person, the friend with whom I could finally be vulnerable to without fear of a speed dial to protective services, the floodgates opened. She probably didn't even know that she was chipping away at the coat of deficiency that I had taken to wearing. She had a son in my (step)son's class. She had a daughter in my (step)daughter's class. She had a daughter ahead of those kids. And she also had *two stepchildren*. Talk about someone who had their shit together. Except she almost immediately told me she didn't. I couldn't fathom it. Small statements like *oh, that's typical boy behavior* or *yes, my daughter hates me as well* became beacons to finding my confidence. Was she implying that the long list of failures that I'd been carrying around in my emotional (step)mom suitcase really were really just examples of *kids being kids*? Because she straddled both worlds, (step)momming and (bio)momming, I knew that if she said something was totally normal, it really was totally normal. And I knew that if she said that not every argument or misstep or desire to pack my bags should not sit in my column of fault, she was probably right. I still think she is the perfect mother. I think this while she pulls her hair out almost daily at the misbehaviors of her youngest (bio) and the poor decisions of her eldest (step). She would tell me not to place her on a pedestal, but because she was the first woman to acknowledge my anguish, I will leave her up there.

She is proof that sometimes being a perfect mother just isn't enough. Sometimes it doesn't matter if you've made all the right moves, said all the right things, signed all the right forms, or showed up at all the right times. Sometimes you can do all of those things and, still, your kids will turn their back on you. And then they will do it again. And again. The discontent will be palpable but explained away by adjustment periods and by hormones and by finding themselves and by reaching adulthood and by finding themselves again and ... yes, it will always be explained away. It is easier to explain this resentment away, after all, than admitting that *this just isn't working out*. I think back to the day when I told my (future) husband that I would not be the cause of any more emotional damage to the kids. I knew what they'd gone through via the end of their parents' marriage. At the time, I was relatively sure he and I would get married, but I promised both him and me that if there came a time when we thought that our relationship was not going to be beneficial to the kids, we would acknowledge it and that I would move on. The idea that I would be a source of any more strife for them was something I could not do. It sounded very Joan of Arc, at the time.

There were times when we did almost pull out that playbook, where I could slowly back myself out of our relationship, perhaps move to a local apartment, and allow calm into their home. But the further along we got into our merging, the more "their" home became "our" home, and we knew that getting (and staying) married was exactly what we would do. WE. The whole family. Our wedding was a WE event, pledging ourselves to each other (him and me) and pledging ourselves to our kids. It was the most moving five minutes of my life, watching these two children crumble to tears as they realized that they, too, were being provided vows to agree with in solidifying our bond and promise to fight for our family forever.

Yet today, I am sitting in a waiting room waiting for my (step)daughter to finish four hours of psychological testing.

How did we get here?

I know now that this path was not created with my shovel alone. I know now that I am not my (step)daughter's proclaimed biggest problem. I know now that I am not the source of all her angst and anxiety. I know now that she would disagree with all of that and that with each new therapist, it will be my name that comes out of her mouth first. It is devastating. But I also know that there is more to her unhappiness than just me. Only recently, my husband and I were able to reroute the direction that her struggles would send our relationship, committing to a halt when we felt her wedging herself between the two of us. Mostly. It is still quite difficult (understatement of the year) and has required him to accept that she has played a part in her own history. That was also devastating. I actually thought that if and when that day arrived when his eyes opened a crack into what I'd been seeing and dealing with, that I would feel some sort of vindication as he had his aha moment. Instead, I wanted to cry. The anguish washing over his face was visible. I wanted to turn back time and go back to the days when it was just her and me butting heads and me being saddled with a directive of, *"You're the adult, work it out!"* I wanted to go back to pulling explanations out of a hat in order to make her behavior fine and my reaction overblown. I wanted to take away that loss of hope and the questioning of his own parenting abilities. I wanted to go back to pulling her aside to tell her that she needed to *just stop*. I wanted to go back to blaming it all on having parents who divorced and a father who remarried the most evil person to walk the planet.

We got here when our daughter quietly dropped out of her second semester of college and then spent months pretending to us that she was happily attending. Living in an apartment, rather than the dorm (thank-you again, pandemic), made the facade easy. Upon the discovery that there would be no second semester transcript, we went into red-alert mode, digging and digging to find out what had happened. The answers that came back were not great. *"I just stopped. For two months, I didn't get out of bed. Lying about it was easy. Maybe it was three months. Lying about it was easy because it's what I've been doing for my whole life. I think it was four months. I've told so many lies that I don't even know who I am, what is real, or to whom I've told what."*

Suddenly, a red alert did not seem like a high enough measure of our feelings of panic. We'd actually made a lot of progress, she and I, in the year that she was away at school. We'd found a rhythm to our relationship, and the space seemed to hold the softening edge that we both needed. And none of it was true? While she was living downtown, next to campus, I'd finally been able to recognize the successes in how I'd handled myself in that first decade of being her (step)mother. Without the consistent barrage of insults, I was finally able to see that I'd actually done pretty well. With no dented teenager to insert herself between her father and me, we were able to discover our successes as a team, and there were many. Those feelings of success ramped up as it came time to think about her return home for summer break as we had had time to view our perceived failures differently. We were able to see the hidden wins, once overshadowed by our struggling child's unhappiness. I had started to peel off that coat of deficiency and re-place it with one of reconfigured memories. The shadow that had rested over us for years had begun to lift.

And then the rug was pulled out from under us.

We brought her back home almost immediately out of con-cern for both her mental health and our inability to get sleep due to worrying minds. She came home packed with anger and tears and annoyance. This was not going to be the sum-mer of happy memories that we had planned.

I felt different, though, having had the time to beef up my parenting confidence. I approached her with less fear and stomped right over the eggshells that I had taken to walking on in her presence. I was able to see myself for what I knew I was, *good*. I was sad that she was unable to set aside all that she continued to carry with her as she might have been able to see me as well.

I knew, finally, that I was a good parent. I was a good mother.

And I also knew that, sometimes, not even that was enough.

IN SUMMARY

For me, being a (step)mom meant spending our family vaca-tion watching my children's anxiety spike as they worried about finding **the perfect gift** to bring home for their (bio)mom, all the while knowing that when they went on va-cation with her, there would be no gift shopping at all for me.

Being a (step)mom meant that I had to be the heavy one sometimes, knowing that the story would be adjusted when told to their (bio)mom in order to affirm to her that, yes, it was I who was an evil one. It means ignoring the pull to ring her up or text her to say, *"No, that's not what happened"* be-cause I learned to let their relationship be their relationship.

Being a (step)mom meant watching something unfold between my kids and their (bio)mom, knowing that it would likely hurt our children in the end, yet remaining silent while simultaneously preparing to clean up the mess.

Being a (step)mom meant standing aside after games or award nights or graduations and allowing my child to hug their (bio)mom first, alleviating the stress of having to choose who to reach out to first after such events.

Being a (step)mom meant biting my tongue nearly always and opening my arms twice as much.

Being a (step)mom meant keeping my face neutral if my children needed to unload about their (bio)mom, instead staring at a spot on the ceiling so as not to give my actual emotions away.

Being a (step)mom meant having an ally one day and an enemy the next yet knowing that I could only project the positive side of that to seesaw to my children.

Being a (step)mom meant feeling like I lived in a competition where there were only two participants and only one who had to deal with all of these feelings.

Being a (step)mom meant realizing how hard verbalizing that competition would be on the kids.

Being a (step)mom also meant not freaking out at the first unexpected handhold. Even if that tiny hand was a little bit sticky, a little bit wet, and definitely dirty.

Being a (step)mom meant acting cool when I was the *first* one called when a child needed help in leaving an uncomfortable situation.

Being a (step)mom meant hiding my feelings of pride when it was *my* email a child asked a teacher to type in to relay a story (and the consequence) of getting caught cheating.

Being a (step)mom meant being part of a unique team— one thrown together by happenstance—and feeling relieved upon realizing everything was going to work out.

Being a (step)mom meant telling my children that they were (and are) my children because I chose them. I thought long and hard and took it all more seriously than anything I'd ever done in my life prior. I made a choice to have a life that included *them* no matter what and forever.

Being a (step)mom meant learning to be okay with the idea that, across town, there was another mother who could repeat back most of the above blurbs, verbatim.

Being a (step)mom means being a **mom**.

Which Way's Up?

Poopocalypse

As we were sitting in our third therapy appointment in three days Wednesday (well, four if you count physical therapy to alleviate the neck pain from banging my head into the wall), I was thinking, "Oh my god...who has three therapists?!" Not us. Three would just be a start. We're now up to four— eight if you count the ones we didn't like or graduated from. It's not nearly as hip as saying something like, "We have three nannies: Daytime, Nighttime, and a Floater" or "We have three cars: A going-out car, an around-town car, and a beater."

Right now, for instance, I can feel some of your jaws dropping, some of you getting more comfortable, and some of you sticking popcorn in the microwave as you get the butterflies of "oh yes, this family is messy."

We are messy. Messy for us, at this moment, is making sure we only schedule one therapist per family member per day so we can keep ahead of our mental health insurance. And, as a toast to those therapists, the reason there are four is that they all understand the importance of advocating. For instance, when we realized over the summer that we needed some group family counseling, we were steered away from Amelia's counselor (who was at the heart of this need—Amelia, not the counselor) so that she (the counselor) wouldn't be put into a situation where she'd end up breaking five years of trust with Amelia if she (the counselor) happened to agree with us (the parents) here or there.

I have my own counselor, Rachel. It was one of my demands upon moving here (along with a Kohl's, a Target, that my husband gets hearing aids, and that I wouldn't handle barf or blood). Rachel has been essential in my entrance to wifehood and motherhood and kept me from running naked through the streets of our small town. Rich and I have used her for couple's tune-ups on occasion, but we have known that if it ever got weird for Rachel (like if she ever accidentally mentioned to Rich that I was usually the most correct), we would add yet another counselor into the mix.

Out of the blue a few months ago, Rich decided maybe he'd like a counselor of his very own. And by "out of the blue" I mean I've been suggesting this for years. Hello, horse, here's the water. While I won't go into too many details because that's really up to him, I will say that he's already come back with great advice and epiphanies after just a few sessions.

So yeah, that makes four counselors.

There is a bit of a feeling of a rush to the finish line with Amelia right now. She is less than a year from leaving us and, in the past six months, has really had a lot of residual junk bubble to the surface. It's been pretty, well, shitty. Both for her (I imagine) and for her target (hi, table for one, please). It's a tricky tightrope to walk as we want to get everything "fixed" before she heads off to college, but we also know that going away will likely be the thing that helps "fix" things the most.

It's as tricky as digging through what are actual, real-life issues versus just regular issues that every parent of a seventeen-year-old child deals with.

I must have really hated Rich this week, as he ended up in three therapist appointments in a row. Monday's session was supposed to be Amelia and her counselor, but when we (the parents) got an inkling that what was being translated in and out of those sessions was not necessarily accurate, Rich and I invited ourselves. I'm not sure if anything was cleared up. There were three people in the room on one page and a fourth (Amelia) who was clearly not.

Instead, she wore the face of a person who planned to simply carry on with her own versions of this life's story.

Parents, I will say this—and I am going to look like a complete moron, I know that, so please understand that I'm laying this out there for you—if your child is in therapy and there is zero feedback for, I don't know, let's say three years ... get your ass in there. I'm really not sure why Rich and I didn't register this as strange sooner. That, though Amelia was in the chair every other week for years, she'd never come home with any sort of homework, talking points, or agenda items. Though we dutifully paid the counseling center for each session, we were never asked for input or given any update for our (minor) child. I suppose we just chalk it up to our own parenting-the-first-kid, but by the time we were active participants, it was fairly clear that we'd likely missed the bus.

The second counseling appointment of the week was for Rich. I would actually love to be Rich's paid therapist. The nice (and also annoying) thing about Rich is he basically chats and cures himself each time he goes in, with very little input from his counselor. It happens when we go together as well, within ten minutes of talking there is a clear shift to "oh, Rich, you are so insightful," "oh, you have such a good perspective," "do you know any saints?" I'm left to sit there thinking about why I'm cranky and whether it's because I skipped breakfast or because something is actually wrong. I think he goes to counseling just to hear someone tell him he's right. And I know I should try that now and then, telling him he's right, but we haven't reached that chapter in our book yet.

The third counseling appointment was for family therapy. This is the newest addition to our docket and one that both Max and I drag our feet to. Max, because he's fourteen and still unable to see the value in it (nothing gets fixed by talking, he says). Me, because I just don't feel like it. The whole point of this regimen is to help resolve Amelia's issues with us (Rich, myself, etc.) but as the one sporting the sighting dot on her forehead, I'm just kind of like "meh."

The kid has worn me out. For sure a combination of being seventeen and having a lot of repressed anger that is not so repressed anymore. I know I should be relieved that she is finally letting it all out. It's just that she is letting it all out directly onto my head.

Our sessions are a bit like sparring matches where neither she nor I actually say anything, both content just to sit there being angry with each other. Amelia and I are experts at orbiting around each other. Minimal eye contact and minimal communication, although there are also times when we really go for it with feigned interest in each other's days. As the grown-up, of course, I know this is (hopefully) not forever. As the grown-up, of course, I know that a seventeen-year-old wouldn't and maybe can't understand that this is (hopefully) not forever.

So, we carry on, approaching each interaction with apprehension while attempting to be perfectly normal. It's fine, everything's fine.

Jumping into the holidays has been nerve-racking this year. Would we be able to survive two weeks of "together time?" Would I find coal in my stocking? Cyanide? Would I be able to swallow my pride enough to pick out some thoughtful gifts? Yes, actually ... that's been covered with some help from Rich ... currently the most patient husband on the planet. Still, until last week, I thought the only thing that would fast-track me through this holiday season was a miracle.

And then, God bless, the good lort, provided one ...

We added a new "won't this be great" family activity to the holidays this year. Rather than our usual drive through the event park's holiday light show, we went to walk through the city garden's holiday lights show. We piled the teens into the car, took (dragged) them to dinner, and toured the Garden Fest of Lights. This place was crawling with decorations surrounding a beautiful arboretum. Lights, lights, and more lights with only two glitches: It was freezing and, oddly, played no holiday music. Amelia and I did our usual dance around each other in pictures, lest we find out that a simple human touch melted away any of the emotional ice.

As we wrapped up our tour, glitch number three arrived in the form of my own gurgling stomach. Alert. At that exact moment, Amelia announced her need to go to the bathroom, **stat**, and began jogging for what may have been the first time in her life. My stomach gurgled again. Oh, dear. I picked up my pace and, by the time we both entered the building, we were peeling off gloves, coats, and scarves.

Rich and Max stood by, oblivious, tapping away on their phones.

"Babe, can I get some help!?" Panic. I'd had wrist surgery a month prior, leaving me a temporary lefty. The undressing was slower than required, and it was very much required as puffy jacket sleeves could not accompany a new lefty on this bathroom bonanza. I finally bolted into the bathroom, quickly scanned the stalls (relieved to see that only one was taken, presumably by Amelia), and launched myself ass first onto the toilet, praying my pants would be down before I hit the porcelain.

Have you heard of Pompeii? Because what exited me was very similar.

Which began the following string of texts in the family chat:

Rich: I'm sitting outside the gift shop.

Amelia: I'm pooping my brains out.

Rich: Woohoo!!! Ride 'em, cowboy!

Jyl: (post explosion) I'm assuming you just heard my arrival ....

Amelia: ☺ JESUS. **KABOOM**. WE ARE BOTH DYING

Jyl: We're basically in here dying. Like I want to send out the audio. (And we were, the effort was incredible.)

Amelia: Is this what the therapist was talking about? With our good memories?

Yes, Amelia, I said aloud ... this is exactly what Dad was talking about when he said he wanted to put us both in a room together to duke it out. I just didn't think he meant this particular scenario. Please end this, she whispered back.

Rich: Hahahaha.

Jyl: We can never leave. (At this point I was googling drugstores for some Imodium.)

Amelia: I feel so bad for whoever enters. This is awful, one of us said, like hazmat-able.

Rich: I'm sitting out here cackling. The people around me are looking at me like I'm insane.

Amelia: I KEEP HAVING TO SNIFF MY BOOGEES IN AND I KEEP GETTING NOSEFULLS OF OUR POOP.

Jyl: I'm in a lull ... but there will be more. I can feel it. What time do they close this place?

Rich: That's just perfect. I'll check that off my "torments my children endured before college" list.

At this point, we could hear knocking next door and "Housekeeping ... anybody in here?"

Jyl: If anyone walks in, I'm lifting my feet so they don't see me.

Rich: This is the best night of my entire life.

Jyl: Now I'm playing Christmas music (it was John Lennon ... and so this is Christmas ...) No really, what time do they close?

Here, Amelia began begging me to stop ... indicating that now she was laughing/crying too hard. Good timing, actually, as I did slip out and past the eyes of a mortified attendant, quickly taking the trash and vacating.

Amelia: OH MY GOD THERE IS SOMEONE ELSE IN HERE. OH MY GOD I JUST SPOKE I THOUGHT IT WAS

ONLY JYL. MY SOUL WILL PERMANENTLY BE TRAPPED IN THIS STALL HARRY POTTER STYLE.

Jyl: No!!! I did in fact just leave...

When Amelia did reappear, we quickly agreed to never, ever, **ever** look at each other again for the rest of our lives. We did, eventually, make eye contact again, and it was nice to start with the knowing grin of a shared humorous/mortifying moment, the result of going through an intestinal war together.

I thought about having T-shirts made to commemorate this day (Battle of the Butts? Poopocalypse 2019? The family that s**** together ...?) but never took the plunge. No, it does not cancel out the still lengthy road of issues we have to deal with, but could this be an odd start back down the path? Maybe. And all without a co-pay.

After months of basically ignoring each other, that is good news, right?

You bet your ass it is.

CHAPTER EIGHT

For God's Sake, Get a Counselor. Or Twelve.

GET A COUNSELOR. THE END.

FIND A COUNSELOR. FIND A COUNSELOR. FIND A COUNSE-
LOR. FIND A COUNSELOR. FIND A COUNSELOR. FIND A
COUNSELOR. FIND A COUNSELOR. FIND A COUNSELOR.
FIND A COUNSELOR. FIND A COUNSELOR. FIND A COUNSE-
LOR. FIND A COUNSELOR.

Better yet, find a dozen. Really. The more the merrier.

Am I slightly obsessed with this suggestion? Yes. Why?

Because it's not a suggestion. More of a demand. More of
a "Don't make me say '*I told you so*'" kind of thing.

And also, because even **with** a counselor (or twelve ...) we
have teetered on the edge of fucking this entire thing up. Yes,
I just used a swear in lieu of my real words.

That's how serious I am about this.

But in case I've offended anyone ...

Even **with** a counselor (or twelve), we have teetered on
the edge of screwing this entire thing up.

How?

Because marriage is hard. Kids are hard. When you put a
"second" or "step" in front of either of those items, it becomes
exponentially more difficult. I say this as one who has just

passed the glorious five-year mark of a second marriage involving kids. This benchmark is huge, as noted by author Wednesday Martin in her book, *Stepmonster*. Martin's book is full of affirming (step)momming is hard moments, but one statistic literally made my (step)jaw hit the floor. *Second marriages involving kids that make it to the five-year mark have a **higher** rate of success than regular, run-of-the-mill, standard, marriages.* Did I just wait until Chapter Eight to throw in a quoted author? Yes. That is how vital I believe this piece of information is. I read that statistic well prior to our five-year mark. I latched onto it like a beacon lighting the entry to (second)marriage utopia. I approached that five-year mark with apprehension. Would I really feel a rush of ease or relief or stability once we hit it?

Yes, actually. We did.

When we hit that five-year mark, it truly was as if the universe had lifted piles of weights from our shoulders. We have no good reason why. Nothing really changed in our home, but it was like a gloomy cloud evaporated and left us with a bucket of confidence. Maybe in the end, we will still implode. But as we passed that benchmark, for the first time ever, I finally felt that we were really going to make it.

Of course, it wasn't just having the guidance of a single, jaw-dropping quote that got us this far. It was work, work, work. Marriage is hard. Kids are hard. Our marriage was the first for me and the second for my husband. That has been hard, as he often references mistakes he made in his first marriage and not wanting to make them again. This often feels a bit like someone blurting out the spoiler to the end of a movie, especially if the statement comes out mid-argument. As I am new to this life, there are so many things, relationally, that I really do have to figure out on my own. He has been right more times than I care to admit in predicting how arguments or situations or plans were going to end (usually in an attempt to steer me in another direction). He does give me the space, sometimes, to carry on to my own demise. One of the many reasons I love him is because, as he waits for me to reach his level of relationshipping, he never (okay, well, rarely) greets me with, "*Yeah, I told you that would happen.*" He has been kind enough to dry my tears and never tell me they could have been saved if only I'd listened to him.

Perhaps a bonus in my late entry to marriage was having enough self-awareness to know that I had zero knowledge about how marriage actually worked. When I was still living the single life with my single friends (though some had drifted off to the other side), my toolbox was fairly limited. With those of my friends who did get married, we never chatted over margaritas about just how hard it was. I would join them for dinner (I was an amazing third wheel) and we'd all laugh and share stories and I'd almost always head home longing to have a relationship *just like theirs*. When it appeared that that was exactly what I was going to get, I knew I had to do it right. Forty-somethings do not get endless chances at turning a few fun dates into a lifelong commitment. I knew my knowledge bank on relationships was seriously low. I did not go into it totally blind to what I was lacking.

I also knew that the man I was hoping for a lifelong commitment from had been through the wringer in his previous marriage. We met just as his former life was imploding. A divorce doesn't just happen in one day with the signing of some papers, it takes months and years to decline to an end. During that time, there are wounds that form into scars that become sensitive spots.

I knew that if we were going to proceed, I needed to do everything I could to not put him through the wringer again. This was a promise I made to myself and, later, to this man who would become my husband. I knew his anguish; if I felt that we were heading in the wrong direction, we would end things quickly and amicably. I did not want him to ever worry about going through another messy end. And it wasn't just him that I was terrified of hurting, it was his kids. They had also been through the wringer. They had also been through the months and years that lead up to the divorce. They had had a front-row seat to the long end of their parents' marriage. They had their own wounds and scars and sensitive spots. I extended my promise to include the kids. If it seemed like creating another family was not going to be feasible, we would end things quickly and amicably.

All of this is why I was so adamant that we have a counselor from the moment we started having all the feel of a lifelong commitment. At that point, we knew that we would have to tread softly as we moved forward. He had an ex-wife. He had two young children. He had a mother who was taking the divorce much harder than he was. I had zero experience in parenting. I was not sure I wanted more than zero experience in parenting. I had zero experience in being a wife or, really, thinking about being a wife. We knew that if we were going to make a go at a permanent relationship, that we'd have to map it out very intentionally. There would be specific steps to be taken, information to be collected, advice to be digested.

Find a counselor.

We started seeing our first counselor during that sweet spot between realizing our relationship was getting serious and realizing our relationship was getting serious enough that I would be getting seriously involved with the kids. We found someone who was new to both of us rather than a pre-existing counselor who already knew that I was perfect. We needed our histories to be seen with fresh eyes. We needed someone who was willing to start this path with us but without a backload of stories that might skew their vision. It was difficult to review the downfall of the marriage, but it was important. I needed to know all of the pieces. I needed my husband to trust me enough to share all of the pieces. I also needed to know many things that I never would have thought to ask, questions that the counselor used as talking points but that helped him, and I began to understand what our different parenting and marriage-ing styles might be.

Which, in my case, was generally answered with a *Wait, now, what?*

I suppose we were putting ourselves through the Catholic Church's equivalent of Pre-Cana. It would have been really easy to skip it, we were both in our forties, after all. Surely, we had enough life experience between the two of us to create some sort of working home. Except that our life experience basically sat on two ends of the spectrum, starting from how we were raised as children. My upbringing was much stricter, more with a raised hand than a hug. His was the complete opposite, raised as a latchkey kid. He was raising his kids with a constant effort to avoid any of the mistakes his parents had made. I was ready to jump in and project all the successes that I felt my parents had onto his household. Ten years later, we still clash over basic decisions, on occasion. I cannot imagine how quickly one of us would have given up on our future together without the aid of a counselor from (before we even got to) the get-go.

We took equal hits in the "reel it in" categories: the "you're being too anal" category, the "have more patience" category, the "is that the hill you want to die on?" category, and the "don't sweat it, everyone will live" category. Sometimes those hits were aimed at how one of us was interacting with the kids, sometimes they were aimed at how we were interacting with each other. We still go to counseling now. You can know the status of our marriage based on how many appointments are on the calendar for the given month. One? We just need an oil change, mostly only there to gossip and maintain our existing patient status. Two? Maybe low on fuel and hearing the brakes squeak a bit. Three? We probably wanted four appointments, but our counselor needed a break. Four? All systems down. Those months when we are at once-a-week appointment status are exhausting. The counseling is time consuming. It also gives us an out in most of our arguments. There is something very relieving in being able to say *let's save that for Dr. Thom* and knowing that we won't have to wait much longer to have a referee.

What about other counselors?

Yes, please.

Really, if you can manage and afford it, get as many on your payroll as possible. There was a span of time during which we had our couple's counselor, a family counselor, a counselor for our daughter, and a counselor for me. I'd love to say that that span was at the beginning of our marriage. It was not. It was during the enjoyable time of a hormonal teenage girl and a perimenopausal (step)mom trying to occupy the same space.

It didn't take me long, in our couple's sessions, to realize that I wanted my very own counselor. I had a hard time being too vulnerable in our paired sessions, feeling quite shy at really laying out how terrified I was to sign up for the roles of (second/[best])wife and (step)mom. I knew, logically, that I wasn't *trying out* for these positions, but I still had a little voice telling me that if I said the wrong thing, this guy was going to rescind his invitation to join him as a life partner. It didn't take me long to realize how little I really knew about being married and that it was only slightly more than I really knew about raising kids of any sort, let alone two that were inherited. I also needed a space to blast my husband without wondering how long it would take him to be able to look at me again. And, as it turns out, I needed a space where my counselor could tell me I was completely wrong or off base without my husband hearing it. Having my own counselor gave me time to dive into topics heavy on the (step)momming side rather than heavy on the parenting side.

I cannot stress this enough: Do **not** wait to "see how it's going" until you opt to get a counselor. Merging into a pre-built family that has already been through the trauma of a divorce is absolutely going to "not go well" at some point. Guaranteed. It's guaranteed because things in regular families "don't go well." There is no way to avoid it. This pre-built family has also been through the trauma of a separation and the trauma of a marriage falling apart and the trauma of a family falling apart. They will have been through enough trauma to last a lifetime and if you really, truly love this pre-built family, setting your entrance up for success should be high on your list of priorities.

When seasoned adults come together under one roof, they bring with them two different histories on *How to Adult.* Both histories are likely adequate. Both. But only one will prevail in the household. Learning to compromise on whose history will take precedence is incredibly difficult without a neutral referee. It is essentially impossible to figure out on the fly. When your new family has multiple members on *one side* while you sit on the *other,* you will feel outnumbered in creating a road map to the future. You will immediately tire of hearing, *"Well, that's not how we do it."* Your counselor will help you work out your response to that cringe-worthy statement (evidently, it's not *"Well, eff that!"*). You will feel like an outsider. You will feel like you will never shake the *Us versus the New Lady* mentality.

Counseling for the kids?

Absolutely.

Consider obtaining a counselor for them to be a symbol of commitment to building the family. It does not mean anyone is blowing the children off onto another party; it means that everyone cares enough about them (and what they have already been through) to invest the time/money/energy into helping them work through the next phase(s). Yes, the kids may only need a monthly maintenance appointment, but allowing them to build a relationship with someone they are comfortable talking to during the simpler times will make the more difficult times much more feasible. My son spent two years playing Uno once a month with his counselor. These were not deep sessions. But when he did eventually need his counselor for something significant, he already knew her. He had no hesitation in bringing a few of his stuffed animals to his appointment so that they could "talk" to her about something that he thought might be bothering them. It was amazing.

Dad? Husband? Referee? Link between the past and future?

Yes, if anybody deserves a safe space, it's that guy. He will carry guilt of every color: dad guilt, divorce guilt, separation guilt, waiting-too-long-to-end-the-marriage guilt, bringing a new woman into his kids' lives guilt. Realistically? I've found that the best way to get my husband to a counselor is to go with him. He has bounced in and quickly out of individual therapy. Being perfect has its perks. When I do believe he has something weighing on him, I try to sit quietly in our couple's sessions. Or I offer cues from the week or our lives that I know will get him talking about how he is feeling.

We still get caught up in the spiderweb provided by the parenting learning curve (and the being married learning curve), but we have enough tools in our belt now to make it through. For those times when we can't, we have a Rolodex, in the form of counselors, available to help. We have some of the same counselors and we have some new counselors. Sometimes, you get all you can get from a counselor and it's time to move on to a new one. Sometimes one person will love a counselor and the other won't. There is no rule that says if you don't love your first (or second or fifth or twelfth) counselor that you can't jump to a greener pasture.

Remember that bit about finding a counselor?

I'm going to repeat it now.

Find a counselor.

OR AT LEAST GET AN AMAZING FRIEND

I actually do get it. Not everybody can or will get a counselor. We have a very odd health-care system in America, one in which mental health is not necessarily at the top of the priority list and, for many, requires enough disposable income in order **not** to create more stress in utilizing it. Counseling can be expensive. Counseling is time consuming. Counseling is easy to throw on the back burner because it doesn't relate to a visible problem. If it's all in our heads, then why is it so difficult to brush off? I have had many days when I've looked at the list of upcoming appointments with various counselors and thought, *"Dear Lord, if we could knock that number down, I could afford my own apartment away from this melee and thus eliminate the need."*

Not having access to a counselor is not ideal (ever), especially during the roller coaster of building any type of family. During the building of a blended family? Ugh. But if the reality of counseling is not possible, what then? There could be a myriad of reasons that counseling isn't an option, financial/time/willingness, etc. It doesn't feel right for me to drop in an entire chapter demanding that one get a counselor without dropping in an entire rebuttal for those who cannot. In our family, yes, counselors have been our saviors. I don't believe, however, that not having one (or twelve) means the ultimate demise of a blended family. I've looked around my life more closely to find the other resources in which I did find support. Those areas, I suppose, were taken for granted as they didn't require an appointment or a co-pay.

The three areas that popped up the most were friends, schools, and support groups.

- **If** you can find a support group, use it. I write that with a bold "**if**" as I was never able to find one in my tiny town of perfect people. I've found that the status quo among moms is to never willingly share their feelings of failure lest they look like they are not succeeding at something they are expected to appear perfect at doing. We live in an age where perfection is praised, and hard times are hidden. We live in an age where our peers think nothing of a quick mom-shame. Support groups offer, typically, a no-cost (or low-cost) alternative to praying that your mom groups do not kick you out if you are struggling. Reach out to your local mental health facilities about support groups if you cannot buckle down to private sessions. If that doesn't work, ask the school counselors what they can come up with. If that doesn't work, look for online groups. Social media groups are a great place to tag in for answers or reassurance. If you continue striking out, create your own. You may not be comfortable rounding up a group of struggling moms immediately, but once you've settled in a bit, start a small lunch group or an email chain. The more struggling minds you can surround yourself with, the better.

- Speaking of schools ... be known. Again, sometimes easier said than done, especially at the beginning of your entrance into this new family. Schools limit the number of adults interacting with their students, and rightfully so. I didn't understand that when I was first rejected as a volunteer. I knew my intentions were to be in my (step)kids' lives forever, but the school took a more leery approach. It wasn't until we were engaged and wedding planning that the school opened its doors to me, and then I was welcomed with enthusiasm. I understand that now. There are many, many children living in rocky relationship situations at home. Therefore, there are probably many, many *dad's friend or mom's boyfriend* situations. The schools don't have time for people who may only be temporary to immerse themselves in their students' lives or to take away a feeling of safe space for those children. In other words, you may have to be patient on this one, but schools are an amazing resource for parents beyond teaching, tests, and recess. The buildings are full of people dedicated to spending hours and hours with children of all personalities and moods. If you can find a teacher or a guidance counselor or an administrator that you sync with, hold on to their contact details forever. You will find their advice useful for years after your child is no longer a part of their daily lives. The year during which I finally arrived on my youngest's school scene, he was in second grade. He is now concluding his sophomore year of high school and yet I still have chats with his second-grade teacher. She and I now laugh at the endless emails I sent to her, often several times per week, as I really, really did not understand anything about eight-year-old boys. She was kind and patient and talked me off many ledges, including the one that involved rocks in the dishwasher. One of my first real friends in my new town was my daughter's sixth-grade math teacher. We met during my first-ever round of parent-teacher conferences and I knew in an instant that she would be important to me. I think I even blurted out, *"You're going to be my friend!"* Again, we still reach out to each other when one of us needs an ear. I have learned that educators are interested in our children far beyond the classroom. They want to hear updates, they want to be helpful, they want to be a part of your success.

- Phone a friend. With any luck, you will stumble upon someone who has taken your path. With any luck, they will be a bit further ahead of you on this path and will be able to tell you, from solid experience, whether your challenges are typical or not. Find someone who can help decipher which of your struggles are (step)mom related and which are just regular mom related. I always feel so relieved when relating a story to a regular mom, to be met with *"Oh, right, that happens in our house all the time."* It is so easy and natural as a (step)mom to blame everything icky in your child-rearing life on the lack of blood relation. The reality is kids are kids and sometimes kids are jerks, biology or not. I absolutely scored in the friend category. I found a friend who has toes dipped in both pools, that of a (step)mom (at the start of her marriage) and, later, that of a (bio)mom. Her advice is critically important to me as she really has the best bird's-eye view of whether or not I am a lost cause in the life I've chosen (she says I'm not). There have been very few times when she's given me the side-eye after I've said some wacky things. She is not afraid to gently call me out if I am driving in the wrong direction, and I appreciate that. She also offers endless cheers and praise—things I find I need more of due to lack of parenting confidence. She has moments as well. We have grown close enough to where she is not afraid to show her lack of parenting confidence to me. Our relationship resembles a seesaw where one of us is always lifting the other. She is my safe space. She doesn't mind my droning or repetitiveness. She is encouraging while also empathetic. She has agreed to hide the bodies while also discouraging the need to make that plan. She doesn't mind phone calls that only include sobs on my end. She knows when I really just want support and when I am ready to hear solutions. She, the wife of an Episcopalian priest, must often feel the need to present a perfect family to the world. I feel the same need in order to prove my worth at being given my children. But when we are sitting in front of a bowl of chips and salsa, we can let those pressures slip away and just expose the frustrated, nervous, *am I doing this right?* sides of ourselves. I can say things to her that I wouldn't necessarily say to my husband. Or things that I will say to my husband that need to be reworked with less of a crazy-person tone. This didn't happen immediately. Our sons have been in the same classes since kindergarten, but she and I didn't really start approaching closeness until they were approaching middle school. I think we actually met when I signed up to chair a Reading Olympics team and I was paired with her. We started with baby steps— our relationship was not built with the flip of a light switch. It is a relationship that I will be forever grateful to have been given.

But maybe you cannot find a counselor at the moment. And maybe you are so overwhelmed with putting together a blended family that you've had to draw inward. I suspect that's part of the reason new parents go off the grid for quite some time (and I extend that to new parents via marriage). It is natural to become immersed in building the foundation that will carry your family forward.

During the time that we first came together, I became completely focused on creating a (mostly) happy home for the kids to come home to each day (or every other weekend). That involved a lot of trial and error and retail therapy and tears and, on occasion, cheers. While I did start out on this path with a counselor, it wasn't until years later that I latched onto my trusted friend. If I could send a message back in time to myself, I would demand that I post an ad in the local paper that read something like "New to the Area: *Stepmother: Super Unqualified.* **HELP**." Even today, my mom friends and I get so completely wrapped up in the happenings within our homes that we can go weeks or months or years before we realize that we are all dealing with similar challenges.

There is a village for every type of mom. It just takes time to find it.

Which Way's Up?

Stress-relieving lists

Words I've made up:
Vaginacologist: It just makes more sense, right?

Procrasturbation: Why my husband (and now my teenage son) is late for nearly everything

Dethaw: I don't think it's a word, but I like to say made-up words until my family starts incorporating them into their language.

This also works with mispronunciations:

Eye-mergency: Really, why do we need to waste time with "Eye Emergency"?

Jokes at my husband's expense:
Nice eyebrows! Can't wait to see the butterflies emerge!

Let me know when you find the pea, princess. (He tends to flip and flop)

Ways I've scared the shite out of my family:
Bill-eye: the frog statue that I'd convinced them held a spy camera behind its giant eyes

Castiel: a giant cut-out of Amelia's favorite TV character hidden around our home

Inflatable Dinosaur (followed by inflatable Unicorn): worn while prancing outside windows

Froggles: a sleep mask that looks like frog eyes

CHAPTER NINE

Remember Where You Are Going. All of You.

NAP WHEN THEY NAP?
VACATION WHEN THEY VACATION.

Three years ago, my husband's ex-wife took the kids on a big summer vacation. This seems like a perfectly normal happening but, for us, it was a first. In the years since their divorce and her loss of custody, the longest time his ex-wife had spent with our kids was the four days surrounding Thanksgiving, and that tradition hadn't even started until three years prior to this inaugural big summer vacation. Those Thanksgiving trips also included the buffer/assistance of spending the holiday at her parents' home, which gave us some strange sense of a built-in safety net if anything went sideways. When the big summer trip was first brought to the table, we panicked a bit at the involvement of planes and hotels and rental cars. Couldn't she just rent a house at the beach? On our coast? The coast only hours away from us where we could swoop in as needed? Rather than the other coast, which would involve, well, very little ability to swoop in at a moment's notice?

The first suggestion of a big summer trip was actually a year prior though it did not come to fruition once it was determined that we would not be funding the bulk of it. We finally did offer to pay for airfare out of a dwindling divorce account that was earmarked (though not used) for her continued education. We acquiesced in an effort to offer the kids a chance at some great memories, though not without many heated arguments between my husband and me on whether it was the right thing to do. We landed on erring on the side of adventures while hoping that we wouldn't find ourselves on the side of regrets later. Therefore, three years ago, the big summer trip finally happened.

It was terrifying.

We waved not-so-confident goodbyes as we watched two of our favorite people head off with a woman who was historically irresponsible while trying not to think about how she was taking them three thousand miles away for ten days. We wished them good times and amazing stories while leaving them in the care of a woman who was often tired of being in charge after forty-eight hours. We had tried to sound super casual as we struggled to get a schedule of any sort —in stone or sand. We attempted to project a *we're not begging* tone each time we asked, *"Can you (at least) tell us which hotel you will be staying in?"* If we had no details, how were we going to swoop in and save the day? Perhaps that was the intent, to show that there was really no more need for swooping when one sent their charges across the country with handheld computers and accessible bank accounts. We hoped the itinerary had presumably been announced to the kids; it was just we, the worried parents, who were left in the awkward position of being completely left out. Our options were to keep pressing to the point of being the bad guys or to continue waving "so long!" while masking the fact that we were really, really, really nervous.

We chose the latter and off they went.

This is going to sound awful.

Really.

Once the kids were away for a few days, all that worry

drifted away. Kids? What kids? I began to ooze into a type of relaxation that I didn't even know possible. I had no one to deliver to this activity or that friend's home. I had only two people to cook for, one of whom was my husband and who would not only eat whatever I put in front of him, he would wash the dishes after. Chores were done by us, on our time, no nagging needed. Bedtimes? Out the window, we did what we wanted. My only real concern was whether or not I should have felt guilty for enjoying myself so much. Was it odd that I went from terrified to hopeful that there might be a *big summer vacation* the following year as well? And how about the one after that?

Yes. There has been a "big summer vacation" for three years running.

They are amazing.

We hardly even ask where the kids are going after slapping the dates on the calendar in bold letters. Instead, we follow the slapping with concurrent requests for leave from our own jobs so that we can fully enjoy the respite. We dive into the breaks headfirst, filling our pantries with snacks once reserved for snow days or hurricanes. We go on date nights over and over often pretending we don't even have kids by banning them from our candlelit conversations. We walk around in T-shirts and underwear, not because we are doing anything marital but because **we can walk around in T-shirts and underwear!** Try that in the presence of your children. The returns are not good. We go to Lowe's as many times as we want and look at our phones while at the table and leave the dishwasher unemptied as we pick out cups or silverware as needed. It's like the fifty-year-old equivalent of a frat house, I suppose.

It's bliss.

We have learned that time together, sans kids, is probably the most important thing in maintaining a well-balanced family with kids. Their time away from us was marked in the every-other-weekend column for so long that until we were able to experience a larger block of break time, we had no idea that that break time should be used to recharge our own batteries. Before that first big summer vacation, we would handle the non-kid weekends completely differently. We would try to get as many errands done that the kids wouldn't like or do work around the house that might take us away from time with them on their home weekends. We would stress about when they would be returning and what the transition would be like from their mom's house back to ours. We were doing it completely wrong. We just didn't know that until we had the ten-day-er.

I really do love my kids.

I promise.

Maybe I was late to the party on this one, but as my husband had a similar reaction to their extended departure, I suspect this is a parental mental misstep. I'd heard this saying over and over and over at the approximately four thousand and seventy baby showers I'd attended in my fifty years: "Nap when they nap." It always seems to be at the top of the advice column when it comes to raising kids. In my mind, however, it was really only relevant to those with newborns, or maybe toddlers. Though I didn't have my (step)kids at those infantile ages, I could only imagine how exhausting it would be running the show for a new person who only slept in hourly increments. I was still exhausted most of the time, though my mostly grown (step)children had reached an age where sleep lasted until noon if allowed. I've never napped when they napped because I wasn't part of their lives during the nappy years. Or rather their nappy years. I very much still have nappy years. In my single-girl days, my naps were dedicated to the couch while listening to the first ten minutes of *The Young and the Restless*. I had trained myself to fall asleep at that point and wake up forty minutes later to catch the last ten minutes. When I moved in with my make-a-family, it took actual years for me to feel comfortable napping again. It seemed so odd to just cut out of life for an hour while the house was still bustling so that I could rest my eyes.

As we went further into our marriage, my husband started insisting that I nap on those occasions when I was walking through the house with a zombie gaze. I tried unsuccessfully on the couch, stories on the television, and then finally gave in to taking naps in our actual bed in the middle of the day. I felt like I was cheating. In an OCD effort to train my body to understand that it was nap time and not bedtime, I would never switch into jammies. My permanent nap outfit is mostly nude, undies only. It is both comfortable, a signal to my body that it is naptime, and keeps the kids well clear of the bedroom lest they catch sight of my naked shoulders. I am back to being an expert napper who doesn't care if the house is actively burning down. Nap when they nap. Or not. Just nap.

As I became more acclimated to parenting, I started seeing where that directive could be relevant in other areas. I spent my first few years at the(step)mom helm feeling torn between two places nearly all of the time. I loved playing tennis in my old life. In my new one, I felt guilty being on the courts while the kids were at home. I loved perusing the stores lazily on the weekends (old life). Having to take the kids with me canceled out any perusal or lazy (new life). Coffee shops? Do moms even sit in coffee shops anymore? Cup of caffeine and a book? I let that one go due to feelings of not being productive and nagging thoughts of I should, at least, bring something back for the gang that I was attempting a break from. Coffee shops, gone.

It took until the second or third school year for me to realize that school days were my time to shine. I started using my lunch hours to poke through the sales at Target or Kohl's. With no (step)kids fighting over who got to drive the cart, I was really able to take my time debating if a wool sweater in July was worth 70 percent off (clearly, yes). It was heaven! It also meant that my toes were no longer victims to (step)kids driving the shopping cart. In a moment of bravery on a random morning, I packed up my work laptop and plugged it in at Panera. I treated myself to a quiet breakfast out with a chaser of several **silent** cups of coffee as I clicked away at spreadsheets and emails. As I got further into the groove of the (step)kids being out of the house from September to June, I suggested to my manager that a morning off each week would help me relieve some of my (new life) anxiety by tapping back into (old life) tennis again. I could finally meet the local moms without the feeling of guilt that came when spending time on the court after work or on weekends (while the kids were home, probably (not) devastated that I was gone). As I got to know those local moms, we started forming lunch groups. To this day, our favorite celebratory lunch bunch meets the day school starts, as it means kicking off the kids-are-in-school cadence again.

It isn't just about napping when they nap.

It was about using any time away from the kids to rediscover who I was when I wasn't (step)momming. That doesn't make me a bad person. That made me smart in the days before self-care was a hot word. Creating space between mom-me and friend-me and tennis-me and volunteer-me made me better at all of the above. Creating that space when the (step)kids were not sitting in the living room made me feel like I wasn't shortchanging them in the process.

When I was growing up, my parents would take a vacation once per year sans kids. It was awful. How could they? How could they just leave us in the care of a perfectly good friend and have fun without us? Even worse, my mother would take a *separate* week at a different time to visit with her parents, again no kids (or husband, brilliant). As a child, I felt bad for them. Surely, they were sad without their sidekicks, right? Surely, they would spend the whole time searching for the perfect gifts for us. Every time they returned with T-shirts from the airport gift shop, that was all but confirmed. At the very least, they missed their favorite child. Clearly, why else would they spend so much time finding the perfect globe with an airplane tucked into the floating snow?

Yes, I'm realizing as I'm writing this that those are very standard and very last-minute gifts that parents pick up at the airport probably just before they grab their luggage. Gifts that read *they love me, they really love me!* to a five-year-old but read *oh crap, quick, grab something for the kids* to the adults.

My husband and I decided to jump on this wagon a few years after getting married. No, we did not take the kids on our honeymoon. That would be weird. As it was our honeymoon and I hadn't really gotten too far into the meat of (step)momming, I had no idea exactly how much I should have relished those weeks alone. Our vacation schedule became predictable very quickly in our marriage, as there were three extended families to visit. We were fortunate that the biggest of those families lived within an hour of us as we could reserve the lengthier vacations for the rest. June and August were camping weeks with my family (with the occasional addition of my mother-in-law). Thanksgiving was for the kids to visit their (bio)mom's parents in West Virginia. December was spent traversing Virginia visiting Rich's family. March was for the four of us, typically on a cruise or to Florida. We continued on that cadence for six years. They were all enjoyable trips, but they all included all of the people. It never really crossed our minds to do something for just the two of us.

Until it did.

We started fairly small, with an overnight stay at a hotel thirty minutes away. Just one night. No plans other than holing up in a room with a giant bed, reading books, and watching terrible television. We'd walk to a restaurant for dinner and breakfast and be home before anyone missed us. It was fantastic. Something about being outside of our home base canceled out any thoughts of that nagging to-do list. Yes, we could have thrown a rock and hit our house from the hotel balcony, but we were not there getting stared down by the dust bunnies. We'd tried do-nothing weekends before at home, but they would always morph into catching-up weekends with loads of laundry or painting a door or cleaning out the pantry or signing school forms. At the hotel, none of that was possible.

We booked several more of those weekends throughout the next few years. We'd typically book the next one before checking out from the hotel just to make sure we had an adults-only weekend on the planner. We then went for broke, taking a long weekend away during the time that the kids were off on vacation with their (bio)mom. I don't know why we'd hesitated (well, beyond the obvious need to be available for swoop-ins) for so long. It was, again, amazing. We'd left a friend in charge of the animals at home, the kids were off with their (bio)mom, and we, officially, had zero responsibilities other than to relax and enjoy each other's company. We returned home refreshed and reconnected.

And, so, this became our thing, "vacation when they vacation."

We enjoyed the time off so much that we took parental breaks even when the kids weren't officially off on a trip. They may have been on dual sleepovers, or one may have been at camp while the other was visiting a relative. The critical piece was giving ourselves time to be the people we were before kids. Or the people we would eventually be when the kids were gone. It takes practice, actually. We struggled, at first, to go to dinner with a pact to keep the kids' names off the menu. It took practice. We made a concerted effort to play First Date night, as if we were just meeting and knew nothing about each other. If "Amelia" or "Max" crossed one of our lips, the other often responded with a *"Who? Never heard of them."* It takes practice.

It also takes practice to transition back to real life.

It is hard to have time off and then have it come to an end. It wasn't that hard in the beginning, but once we figured out how to flip the switch quickly and really lean into non-parenting, it was hard to return to reality.

Typically, as we round the corner to our return to parenting, my ooze of relaxation turns into an ooze of funk. I don't often have feelings of *Oh, I've missed them so much ... when will they return to my loving arms?* My feelings are closer to *Oh shoot ... this again? Already?* I know life is about to start being hard again and I am never mentally prepared. I typically don't even feel bad about feeling that funk about their return. Instead, I imagine what I feel is exactly what teachers across America feel every mid-August.

I love my kids. Really, I do.

But those vacations while they are off on their "big summer vacation" are amazing. Ten days of living (most) of my old life as a single gal with minimal responsibilities. Ten days of being Fun Me. Ten days of being Carefree Me. Ten days of flying by the seat of my pants. Ten days of going with the flow and sharing that flow with someone I love very much. No appointments for which to provide shuttle service. No forms to be filled out in a panic while trying to drift off to sleep at night. No bodies to poke awake and reprimand for yet another forgotten alarm. No schedules to organize. No schedules around other schedules to organize. No dinners to figure out that would meet all needs at the table, yet also not send the food pyramid screaming. No reminding, no pick-it-ups, no sticky blobs of peanut butter errantly discovered on the countertop when putting down the mail, no need for mom eyes to locate something **sitting right there** in plain sight.

There is just...nothing.

A beautiful silence moves into my mom-taxed brain.

Sometimes, I will even daydream the days away about how nice it will be when both kids are off to college. And then I think *Oh my Gawd!!! Did I really just think that??? What's wrong with me??*

My husband refused to join me in the traditional relaxation turned funk. He is too busy staring out the front door, dogs by his side, eyeing every passing car for signs of his well-traveled offspring. When he wasn't busy making a vision board of all the fun things we'd do when the kids returned from their trip, he was journaling activity ideas for our own family vacation later that summer. He will likely always be Santa Claus to my Mrs. Grinch.

The most recent *big summer vacation* summer had already been marked by change. It happened midway through the first summer that **both** of the children were suddenly void of wanting to spend every day doing something (anything!) with me. That number had been cut in half in previous years as the elder child disappeared to her room, taking her teenage hormones with her. I'd still had the younger to act as my sidekick, until I didn't. That summer, both kids completed the *Holed up in my room* section of growing up with extra credits for *Lack of Follow Through, Forgetfulness,* and *Presenting Oneself as Entitled.* They did appear on occasion, always polite and able to be nudged into a quick errand. But the shift from our norm was quite obvious. Perhaps their *big summer vacation* finally gave me the space to confirm that I could absolutely thrive without them.

Perhaps it gave me a minute to remember that there was more to me than my maternal role.

Perhaps I just needed a vacation while they vacationed.

"*Great chapter,*" my husband just said, "*But how does it relate to being a stepmother ...?*"

Thank you, typical male.

It's about self-care, I suppose. And probably more about being a mother of any sort. Or maybe even about being a woman. We are driven to succeed. We are driven to please all of those around us. We are driven to keep going and going and going at the cost of our own sanity. I learned this in my first real corporate job, back when I worked at IBM. It was a huge campus, and I had employees in multiple buildings. I spent my days trekking from building to building in rain, snow, sun, humidity, all while trapped in thick nylons and heels. By lunchtime, I was exhausted and counting the newest blisters. The pay was terrible, there were no rewards, and my team was constantly berated. We worked for a staffing agency that provided us with unqualified individuals and then hung us out to dry with our customers. Yet, each day I went back and tried to make everyone happy all the time while simultaneously being abused in every doorway.

I finally realized that my manager did not care about me or my customers or my team or any issues that I percolated to her plate. My teammate, Kathy, confirmed this with a shrug and the famous, "*Well, it's a paycheck, right?*" I was pissed, but yes, I did have rent to pay. I have no idea why, but I decided to start slowly dropping in a new name to my customer load. This guy was a top-level executive, super sensitive, ultra-demanding, had ridiculous expectations, and was also totally made up. It took me no time at all to realize that my manager was never going to sit in on any meetings with this pretend person or offer her support in meeting his requirements. It took me no time at all to start integrating daily meetings with him on the calendar that I shared with my team. It took me no time at all to start pushing those daily meetings to the end of each day and, finally, to create a standing 4:00 p.m. daily round-up with this made-up monster. I even made up a pretend building, 2401, where this tyrant, Victor, held court. There were so many buildings on the IBM campus, and I had gauged correctly that my manager would never vet the information in the directory.

And she didn't.

I'm not saying it was the right thing to do, but I am saying I was years ahead of the self-care movement. This was before flex time or work from home or laptops that could bring the office to the dining room table. When I pulled out of the parking lot, I was leaving it all behind. In return for my made-up customer (Victor Newman) and building (which was actually my home address number), I got to be on my couch in time to catch *The Young and the Restless* each afternoon.

Moms need breaks. (Step)moms need breaks. There is never anything wrong with taking time away from your minions to refresh yourself. Because I came into (step)momming with no children of my own, I did not understand that I was not required to attach myself to my family 24/7 until the end of time. I did not understand that I was not expected to be available as a helpline and problem solver at all hours. I felt guilty if I did not drop everything instantly, as if I was neglecting what I had signed up for by saying "I do."

Until I had that first long span without the kids, when their (bio)mom took them on vacation. It was then that I really understood the need for extended alone time with my husband and extended alone time with **myself**.

Guilt-free.

THE AFTER IN HAPPILY EVER

There are times when I think the biggest red flag in my ability to (step)mom are those times when the only thing that keeps me going is imagining what my life will be like *after* the kids are gone. Or what my relationship with my husband will be like when it is just the two of us again. That may sound crass, but I did marry my husband until "death do us part." There was nothing in the wedding ceremony that indicated the gig would only last until our nest was empty. Thinking about that empty nest just brings me peace at times. I also married my husband with a promise to stand by him "in good times and bad." There are many days during which those "bad times" rotate around our children. If I'm being honest, it is actually *most* of those "bad times" that rotate around our children or, on the periphery, their (bio)mom. I often have to remind myself that these are just stones on the path to the rest of the "in good times." Or at least the "in good times" that do not involve children or ex-wives. I am not naive. I know that the children will forever be a part of our lives, but I also enjoy a good pipedream of life getting easier at some point.

We do talk about the "after," my husband and I, especially as our kids reach the ages in which their permanent move out of our home is nearly visible. It wasn't a discussion we could have had a few years ago, as my husband's assumption was that I was looking forward to the kids leaving *only* because I didn't have the same biological bond with them that he did. The "looking forward to it" thoughts made me feel guilty and as if something was wrong with me, so I kept them fairly hidden. Verbalizing those thoughts would surely confirm that my rising level of joy at having the house to ourselves was yet another signal that I was never cut out for (step)motherhood. *What mother would gather excitement in imagining a future in which her home was empty of children?* In truth, that future is just easier for me to see because I have a much closer link to a past in which I did *not* live with children underfoot. The timing of me finally being used to having children in my home just happened to coincide with the moment of those same children starting to leave. My maternal light switch flipped on and, almost immediately, was forced to flip towards off again. The emotions were fairly fluid, making it easy to wander back and forth between seeing our home full of kids forever and looking forward to it being empty. My husband's light switch had been flipped on for nearly two decades. There was no fluidity between the life stages of his emotions.

It actually took Amelia heading off to college for my husband to start visualizing life as a kidless couple without being racked with "I shouldn't be happy about this" guilt. When the nest was half empty, we saw how minuscule our time with our kids actually represented in our lives. **Eighteen years.** That's it. A blip. A blink. With any luck, just a whisper in our time on this planet. That realization made it more acceptable for both of us to imagine a life with no kids under our roof. After all, the whole goal of raising humans is to send them out into the world, right? In the lives of (step)moms, that bit in which the kids are home takes up much less time in the big picture, often the result of a first date that ended up turning into a relationship that turned into a marriage that turned into *oh, hey, that guy came with kids.* No, the kids are not a complete surprise (or at least they shouldn't be, that seems like pretty important first-date information), but the challenges of jumping into a pre-built family are so much more difficult than most could ever imagine. There is nothing wrong with using the dangling carrot of a future in which you are simply *the two of us (again)* as motivation to continue digging through the "we are a family" muck.

We have found that as we get closer to that day of freedom from children, the motivation for my husband and me to maintain a united front often falls in answer to this question: What will our life be like when the kids are gone? Of course, the answer changes as often as the moods of our teens. *We will miss them desperately. We will finally be able to breathe. We will continue worrying about them. We will trust that we've raised them well enough to survive. They will always be welcome back. They will be welcome as long as they have a job, pay rent, and respect our new empty-nesting space.* We are currently six months into a very trying season with Amelia. It would not have surprised either of us if the stress of this trying time put a permanent dent into our marriage. But we took to whispering to each other, "Preserve the marriage, preserve the marriage, preserve the marriage." Other times we scream it very loudly in an attempt to convince ourselves that this marriage is still the most important foundational piece of our family.

What will our life be like when the kids are gone?

We do get a preview of this regularly and we know that that makes us lucky among the parenting circuit. Each time the kids spend extended time with their (bio)mom, we get to play "House: Empty Nest Edition." There are no carpools, no curfews, no nagging. The two-week break that comes with each big summer (bio)mom trip gives us a glimpse of how stressless our lives become when the kids are not the most prominent part of every conversation. We sleep in on Thanksgiving. We have Christmas afternoons and nights off. We know that "normal" families do not get these sneak peeks into their future. When there is no ex-something living across town, there is also no every-other-weekend cadence of freedom. There are no breaks at all. My mom-friends often roll their eyes at me when hearing that we'll be having yet another kidless weekend. I do understand the bitterness. But I also chalk these parenting breaks up as the universe's reward to me for stepping into someone else's parenting job, no questions asked.

I also realize that I sound dramatic to the "normal" moms when I tell them that if it weren't for those breaks, I wouldn't have made it this far into (step)momming. I mean it. I have no idea how the "normal" moms do it. Our lives recently took yet another turn when the kids' (bio)mom moved out of state to care for an ailing parent. We were encouraging and supportive of her decision but also shocked to realize that this was it. We were going to be full-time parents for the first time in our marriage. I suppose that's why so many families live close to their extended families. Their parenting breaks come in the form of weekends at Grandma's or dinners with aunts and uncles.

Those windows of freedom are essential for my husband and me. We know that forty-eight hours alone can refresh our admiration and love for each other because we have the opportunity to go back to the very basics. We can pretend we are dating again and set conversational boundaries on any hot (child) topics that would send us into a tailspin. Those windows tell us what our life will be like in a few short years. Sometimes, we just stare at each other while trying to figure out what it is that we *should* talk about, if not the kids' grades, the kids' schedules, the kids' lists of complaints. Other times, the windows fly by as we travel to a new place or try out a new activity, causing our excitement for the empty nest to build.

Our kids have only ever known a life living in our full house. The idea that we will, at some point, live here without them has been foreign and frightening. They take it very personally when they hear chatter about life after they have moved on. They don't want to hear about retirement or about our plans to have, well, non-kid plans. I hated it, too, when I was their age. I remember when my own parents started doing things without me and how much that hurt my feelings. I was the youngest, so I had their nest to myself for a few years. I had no interest in hearing of my parents' plans for weekends away (*without me?!?!*) or dinners out on a date night (*without me?!?!*). I was completely blown away when they moved to

another state in my junior year at college (*How dare they!?
How dare they get a life that did not include me?!?!*). My husband and I are quite intentional in speaking about our kidless future within earshot of those kids. No surprises here, we will have a life when they've moved on to one of their own.

Intel has told us that our son is adamantly (and angrily) opposed to the idea of us moving out of this home that we currently live in. He doesn't care that thirty-five hundred square feet will be far too much for two people and that two flights of stairs will be far too many for those same two people as they age. He doesn't care that we will have way too much unused space and that the need for that space will be much different from when four people were trying to find a quiet corner. He becomes visibly offended at the suggestion that he will always have a home to come home to, but that it just might not be the current one. Our hope is that by the time he is out of college and settled into his first career and thinking about adding a partner to his own life, he will be more accepting of us moving on with ours.

Our daughter sits on the opposite side of the fence, so much so that as she approached her twenties, she flipped the script on us. We became the ones with hackles up when hearing about *her* future plans. She insisted that she would *not* remain local. We tried to tell ourselves that this was just brilliantly served reverse psychology until we realized that her blurbs of moving three thousand miles away were not some strategic way to make us stay put. She really was planning to go. She really was planning to go far. Her suitcases were loaded from age fifteen on. We had a mild panic, as we weren't quite clear on how we would continue earning parenting hero badges. Her response to that? She wouldn't want our help anymore. *What?!!?*

Wasn't this the idea, though? To raise them and encourage them to find their very own place in this world? Mostly. But in our road map, she was finding her own space under our terms and because she was doing what we wanted her to do. We weren't being left with a chest of empty drawers because that eldest bird had packed up her stuff and had it shipped to another coast.

It has been a struggle, but we have finally (both) lost the guilt that often comes with being "just the two of us," though there are four of us. It helped in finally admitting that, yes, one of the biggest stressors in any marriage is children. We were not struck by lightning. We did not get dinged for being bad parents; we were praised for being honest ones. We learned that having mental limits was acceptable and that needing a timeout was something that could also apply to the grown-ups. We stopped feeling guilty for longing for the day when we would finally wipe the dirt off our child-rearing hands and move back to where we started, with couplehood. We saw the importance of test driving our future, empty nest days and we recognized a necessity to step out of our daily lives in order to maintain a healthy partnership *while* raising our children.

These revelations were not delivered on a silver platter or with the brightening of an idea bulb over our heads. We were encouraged to step out of our comfort zones, and after several failed attempts, we leaned into it. It took practice, at first, to be able to place the kids on the back burner of our minds for an extended period. But once we learned to check out by checking in somewhere away from home, what was left was a preview of what our life might be like when we do reach the After in Happily Ever.

BE GENEROUS WITH YOUR APOLOGIES

Strife.
There is always strife.

It doesn't matter how good the plans look or how bright the sun is shining, there will be strife. It is worse for the (step)mom because the strife is often attributed to the very basic fact of her existence. It is similar to the blame that normal moms are assigned, except with four gallons of steroids thrown in. I felt joyous when I only had one child upset with me at a given time. I consider myself lucky, in that sense, as my (step)kids often took turns placing any and all ugliness at my feet. Typically, it was Amelia that did the heavy blame lifting. On occasion, Max would jump in with a show of sibling solidarity. As one who had (and has) an incredibly strong relationship with her own brother, I understand that ingrained impulse to back a sibling's cause, regardless of the validity of their plight. I love that my son is (almost) always willing to jump on his sister's bandwagon and vice versa.

Maybe "love" is a strong word. I respect it.

I spent the bulk of four years being incapable of doing anything right by my (step)daughter. For the first quarter of that time, I really did try to dig in and be the bigger person and try to peel back the layers of her angry onion. As we moved into year two, I started feeling the pull of exhaustion. I spent the following years trying to convince myself that I didn't really care if she ever decided I was worthy of her approval. Of course, I really did care. I still do. There are just times in parenting during which engaging modes of protecting one's own heart are necessary, sometimes engaged without realization.

Hearing my own voice started to make me cringe. I grew tired of asking for help in understanding what I had done wrong (this time). I grew tired of offering new ideas for how I could try to do better next time. I grew tired of hearing from my daughter the same infractions over and over. I grew tired of hearing my own voice apologizing over and over.

Does that sound crass? That I was tired of apologizing? Maybe. I eventually learned that I could, in fact, level up in the game of apologies. This came in a shocking moment when I was informed, by both (step)kids, that I wasn't apologizing properly. Um, **what!!??** I did levitate from my chair with a feeling of, *"That's it, I'm throwing in the damn towel"* the first time the topic came up. Except the first time it came up wasn't the only time that it came up. The topic came up in quite a few of our family visits to the Relationships Issues/How Was Your Childhood/How Is It Affecting You Now/Can't We All Just Get Along Doctor. It was foreign to me that we would put so much effort into a conversation about apologies. It wasn't that I didn't think they held merit. I'd just always believed that apologies count and should or should not be accepted by the receiver (their choice really, right?) and should then be followed by some sort of moving-on plan, either acknowledged aloud or not, whatever.

Backing up a little, prior to the meat of our apologizing strife, I realized years before that my husband is a huge, frequent, sincere apologizer when it comes to our kids. I actually thought it was overdone and strange, like, *"Okay, already, do I really need to keep apologizing and in such a formal, scripted, and deliberate manner?"* Sometime, between then and now, I understood that those apologies were something my husband carried along as he drove the Emotional History Bus. I realized that those apologies were often the product of buckets of guilt. In my complete and total ignorance of how divorce affects whom, I had no idea that my husband's "go-to" feeling anytime the kids were cranky or tired or acting out was *guilt*.

When I realized that he carried endless feelings of fault, I was quite heartbroken for him. Realizing that also helped me to slow down my typical "I'm just going to be the just-the-facts yin to his apologetic yang" response.

The kids, in the meantime and over their short lifetimes, became quite accustomed to a certain standard when it came to apologies. When the topic of how my apologies were lacking arose, so much that the kids weren't even sure they were genuine, my hackles raised. I was defensive and hurt and prepped for a storm out with a solid door slam. When one of our family counseling sessions came to a grinding halt because I could not get on the same page as the three of them when it came to being sorry, I really felt like that might be the end of any hope of a positive future with my (step)daughter. It was terrifying. If I couldn't convince her that my words were true, how was the rest of my life going to play out? I spent the following weeks (between sessions with our counselor) all over the Map of Reactions.

It looked something like this:

~~Disbelief~~ Anger. Um, what the eff? My apology didn't count because it didn't meet our *children's* requirements? So, a fourteen- and seventeen-year-old were now dictating which elements my apologies should include going forward in order to meet those needs and, therefore, *count?* Maybe disbelief isn't the right label for that reaction. Maybe that's got a hint of anger.

~~Disbelief~~ Sadness. I felt bad for literally everyone involved, including our counselor. Or maybe sad, not bad. I was sad that the kids were prepared to hold onto years of anger because they felt my multiple apologies weren't sincere because they (the apologies) didn't fit the apology requirements they were now filling me in on. I felt sad for me because it felt a lot like we were canceling all the good talks and moments that we had had over the previous years, especially if those talks and moments had included apologies. I felt sad for my husband because he was getting caught in the middle. I felt sad for the counselor because I was pretty sure he knew one of the four of us was going to crack and yet he couldn't pinpoint who.

~~Disbelief~~ Determination. I really wanted to try banging my head against a very solid wall just to see if that helped. Maybe if I was mildly concussed, this spiderweb would make sense to me.

~~Disbelief~~ Open-Mindedness. In my mind, I was always up for learning new things, especially when it came to parenting. Because I still felt a varied level of confidence in my parenting skills, anyone on the entire planet could drop a hint that I was doing something wrong and put me in a total mental tailspin of *oh, man ... you can't do that ...?!?!* Sometimes, they are correct. For instance, the time I nearly dropped eight-year-old Max off at Hair Cuttery when eleven-year-old Amelia indicated that we should actually stay. Other times, I would swear they were playing on my insecurities like I'm the limping gazelle at the back of the pack.

I felt like the four of us were sitting in different lands. Or, rather, I was on one planet and the three of them were on another. I typically fashioned my apologies with words like, "*I'm so sorry,*" and a follow-up explanation of what I was thinking/doing/saying when I insulted/pissed off/hurt the recipient. There was no intention of offering an excuse, it was an offering of an explanation in which I wanted to be very clear that I had thought through my wrong turn, analyzed why I took that wrong turn, and made plans on how to avoid that wrong turn going forward. This "figuring out of turns" was not a quick process. It often took several days to go from Point A to Point B.

On the flip side, Amelia, I've since learned, only wanted to hear that I was sorry and what for, specifically. For example, "*I'm sorry I was being difficult on you.*" Hard stop. No Mas. Pound Twenty. In our therapeutic bliss, I quickly and mentally Rolodexed through our previous years and the numerous apologies that I'd offered which *had* included explanations of why (step)parenting was so difficult for me (like being brand new at the gig or because I was handed an instant family or because I'd packed up my whole life or because I was wedding planning or because I was exhausted, because, because, because). Over our years together, there had been multiple deliveries of apologies and multiple versions of the same apologies. I had, at about that very moment in our relationship, reached the point of, *"Okay, enough, the apology train has stopped; either accept my apology or don't, but we need to move forward."* Amelia had, at about that very moment in our relationship, reached an exploding point in hearing those apologies because she felt they all included an asterisk of *Here is why this happened* that canceled out my actual apology.

Have I mentioned yet how fun being a (step)mom is?

We were going in circles on this topic until the pieces started clicking. The summary? That sometimes one must tweak their apologies a touch in order for the important bits to really, *really* be heard by the receiver. I will not make a declaration on whether this theory is right or wrong. I'm also not going to declare whether or not my way of apologizing is correct or whether the kids' preferred way of hearing apologies is correct.

I will say that following that never-ending counseling session, I had the opportunity to deliver the most customized "type" of apology ever. And it was received with a clear (teen-aged) attitude of, *"I don't know if you are being sincere."* I was.

Did I throw my hands in the air? In secret, yes. But I also gave myself permission to move on. I had, at that point, apologized in every possible form known to mankind (well, I have not tried skywriting) including the laid-out method of both children under the witness of a counselor. It was now up to them to make a decision on whether or not they would accept (or not) my perfect apology and move on (or not) with me.

I have never been amazing at apologizing. I know that. I admit that. Apologizing, for me, has always been tied to an admission of personal failure or marked a lack of key character traits. I suppose that's why mine often included far too many details. I began to understand that my apologies did not necessitate a back story (unless specifically asked), especially when applied to my (step)children. I learned that if my remorse truly was genuine yet was not well-received, it was worth the effort to dig in and ask why. Of course, kids are always happy to tell their parents what they are doing wrong, but when I was finally willing to meet mine on their emotional playing field, we were able to make sense, together, of what we needed from each other in this back and forth of relationship building.

Do I love it? Nope. But when I brought myself back down to earth and looked around the therapist's office, I was able to really see who in that room had reason to be picky and who didn't. Annoyingly, it was not me. I began to understand the massive screwing that divorce presented to my kids and how their tolerance of adults had been bruised. They did not ask for any of what they had gone through. They were innocent bystanders in the path of a relational tornado. Their brains would not reconcile any of their childhood traumas for years. Asking for an apology here or there that did not include my life story suddenly seemed like a very small thing.

Do I love it? Nope. It wasn't comfortable as I often felt that a simple *"I'm sorry"* highlighted my lack of parenting knowledge. But I have now seen that offering that moment of vulnerability on my end has actually strengthened our relationship, which, I suppose, was the real goal all along. As an added bonus, I have become much better at falling on my sword with my husband and friends. The lack of reasons or *A equaled B* or *here's what happened* when it came to my slip-ups actually added sincerity to my remorse. And not just for the kids (or my husband or my friends). Because I had stopped focusing on all the excuses that made my faults acceptable, I was able to focus on those around me and why they were feeling the way they were feeling.

Why was this all important?

I suppose because it benchmarks a moment in my own emotional growth during which I finally understood how tricky it is to navigate the muddy waters that encapsulate relationships within a marriage, a marriage involving children, and especially a marriage involving stepchildren. Humans, of all ages, are moving targets. Children will always be happy to provide you with clear guidelines on their relationship preferences one day and then follow those up the next with a meltdown because you followed the previous day's instructions. This is life. People, of all ages, who have already had enough trauma to last a lifetime, pass out those instructions with zero knowledge that they will be invalid before the ink is dry. There will be apologies and more apologies and endless apologies. They are not marks of failure; they are marks of growth.

Which brings me back to the strife.

There will always be strife.

When I stopped pontificating on why I wasn't really behind the strife, I could finally see the baggage that my kids were carrying with them and how that baggage affected us as a family. My apologies? Still genuine. But now they carry a touch of sorrow unrelated to anything I've done. Instead, my apologies now include a silent nod to the past that *they* had to endure, how it affects who they are today, and how *our* relationship has panned out because of it.

525,600 MINUTES

There will come a moment when you know you have done something right. It may only be one moment or one thing, but it will be a marker in the struggle of parenting.

For me, with Amelia, it was a simple, unsolicited two-word text.

Love you!

When I saw it pop onto my phone screen, I stopped in my tracks. *Amelia told me that she loved me?* I thought it was probably a mistake, but then I realized that it was sent in a format in which she actually had to *think* and use her thumbs. She would have had time to backspace nine times rather than pushing send. She might have added a *lol* or a wink or well, anything, to make it less **right there** in digital black and white. Sure, I got a mumbled, half-hearted bedtime exchange of *goodnight, love you, see you in the morning* daily. But it always involved a very uncomfortable hug where an audience would plainly see that neither of us really wanted to be there. And the *love you* piece generally only percolated if there was another family member in earshot which gave it a vibe of, *I'm totally faking this right now.* There were many times when I didn't even return the sentiment, proving that, even in her teens, my child was sometimes more mature than I was. What was the point, though? Throwing out words that should only be used when you really, really mean them at a time when you weren't sure you really, really meant them?

Hearing your child tell you they love you probably should not seem like a big deal. In the tumultuous world that Amelia and I lived in? It was an epic deal. I fumbled with my phone in order to send my husband a screenshot to confirm it had happened. I sent the picture and a note of *Did this really just happen?* His response came back ... *Yes, it was in the family group chat.* I was stopped again. I exited from our message and reopened the one that Amelia had sent to confirm what I was sure he got wrong. No, he was right. She had written those two words in view of the entire family where there was nothing to hide behind and no chance of denial down the road when we reached our next relational roadblock.

Hearing your child tell you they love you probably should not seem like a big deal. Except it was. It was huge. It was a milestone that followed a years-long roller coaster between her and me that rarely included any genuine anything, let alone *love yous,* in either direction. The year immediately preceding this moment was filled with faux conversations most often acted out in my solo car rides. Some of those conversations were laced with anger. Some were full of resignation. Most were sad. None of them ever ended well. And none of them included the words *I love you.* I suspect she practiced similar conversations in her head. I spent months tiptoeing around her and seeking support from anyone I could. I suspect she did the same. I realized how ugly our situation had become when I blurted out the story of our failed relationship to a perfect stranger in the grocery line in a desperate attempt to hear someone say, *"You sound like an amazing mom, and she sounds like a hot mess."* Oh, okay, perfect stranger, thank you. Would you like to use my Savings Card?

I'm not even sure when the downward spiral of our stepmother/daughter relationship started its plummet. I know that it came to a head in the spring of 2019 when we could not get this child to show any interest in the college hunt. On my end, I was getting thoroughly annoyed at doing most of the work while she was the one who was going to get to go away to college and away from the stress that our family was dealing with on a daily basis. *Those grades aren't going to cut it. Have you picked any schools? Have you set up any visits? We need to get moving on this. Are you going to do **anything**?!?* I repeated these words over and over (as did my husband) and we eventually ended up on two college tours that we set up and dragged her to in an effort to spark *something.*

And, truthfully, I could have cared less where she went to college, just as long as she went somewhere. I was desperate for a date in the future on which I could write *Start Breathing Again.* I learned to keep that thought to myself after one too many wishes for a plan that brought a frustrated response from my husband of *You do know that some of us are going to miss having our family together, right?* Right. Bring it down. Be cool.

Our parental-panic turned into parental-oh-maybe-we-weren't-giving-her-enough-credit when a few weeks after application season opened, Amelia got an almost instant acceptance to a nearby school. *Oh! That was easy! With money offered? Oh boy!* We had not seen her application—forbidden to look when, out of nowhere, she suddenly wanted to do everything by herself. *Oh, great,* we said, *that's what we want too—for you to do something by yourself!!* Being of a certain age, we had no idea that in today's cyber world a college application is a college application. The data is input into one website where the applicant only has to click on which schools should receive the information. Gone were the days of papers spread across the kitchen table while an erasable Bic pen determined one's future. Gone were the days of measuring interest in a school by how much interest one had in rewriting, by hand, yet another essay. Gone were the days of parents having an easy clue as to where a child might be applying.

Our parental ignorance was met with reassurance from her high school counselors that they held the kids' hands throughout the entire application process. We had nothing to worry about.

When we could stand it no longer, we very innocently opened up the application website. We only wanted to answer one question, *where else had she applied?* The rest of the schools were out of state, at least a day's drive away from home. I was elated. My husband was terrified. The send button had been pushed. We went into waiting mode. We waited and waited. We had gotten instantly spoiled by that quick acceptance. Where were the rest of the answers? We waited.

When we could stand it no longer, we very innocently opened up the application website. We just wanted to see if, maybe, there were already responses on the website. There weren't. We scanned her application, breaking our promise not to look. The parental panic was back as we read, in her own words, that she was a performer in a fairly time-consuming band. Odd, we'd never heard a whisper of that before. Perhaps none of the schools would ask to see a recording of her performances. Should we have ignored her wishes sooner? Should we have at least helped with the numerous grammatical errors without her knowledge? Why did we suddenly feel like another shoe was dropping?

Mom's intuition struck shortly after the discovery of the embellished activities tab. It was on a random Tuesday when Amelia came home from school early feeling sick. A pit of *something's not right* formed in my stomach and I started obsessing over the possibilities of what could have gone wrong. I came down to the idea that she had heard from the other schools and that it was probably bad news. *Oh gosh,* I thought, *I'll just pop back into the application software and check, really quick, just in case.* I noticed an Additional Questions section that we'd missed before. *Maybe just a quick peek.*

And with the click of a button, my world collapsed beneath me as I read paragraph after paragraph about a child who had been living with an abusive stepmother for nearly a decade and needed a place to escape to in order to start her life over. I felt like I'd had a concrete slab dropped on my head. And my heart. And across my face. I was gutted. Was this really what she thought of me? Was this really how broken our relationship had become? Was this really happening? I wanted to sneak upstairs and pack a suitcase, throw the dogs in the car, and leave. I had never wanted to leave anywhere so badly in the entirety of my life. I did not belong here anymore. Was this really what I had signed up for when I went on that first date years before with a man who I knew had children from a previous marriage? Was this really happening?

The anger started forming, filling my head with the warmth of seeing red. I wanted to march into my husband's office and scream *SEE!!!!! SEE WHAT THIS CHILD HAS DONE!!! WAS THIS WHAT YOU WANTED ALL ALONG???* I couldn't. The hurt outweighed. And why, what was the point? We knew this child embellished her life story. We'd witnessed it before, though not to this magnitude. Or maybe, yes. Maybe this was why the school was slow to return my calls or why the parents of her friends had little interest in getting together. Her essays were laced with venom. Her hatred was so extreme. It became instantly obvious that this surface-level tiff that I'd been imaging on my side of the relational fence was actually a deep chasm filled with hurt on her side. These were not words that were thrown together on a paper for the sake of overdramatizing a college application. They were the words of someone who had been trying to find them for years and years. They were the words of someone desperate for an escape.

We were not complete idiots. With a walk into Amelia's room at nearly any moment, we could open a random notebook and find a page dedicated to my shortcomings. We could find the same in text strings to her friends. We could find the same with eavesdropping, accidentally or intentionally. The content, while much more vicious with the inclusion of the words Child Abuser, was not new. This child did not like me. This child longed for the days when her family was intact. This child placed all that was wrong in her life squarely at my feet.

My husband naively assumed that those notebooks were left out in the open intentionally. *Maybe they were*, I'd think, *but why?* In an effort to see if he would insist that I leave? In an effort to see if I wouldn't go without any insistence? In a weird attempt to see how far she could push me before I just went away? I had developed a thick skin, but there were many holes that the jabs could sneak through. Those words were private to us. They lived under her bed or on her phone. They were not displayed to the world, or at least we'd always assumed they were kept in-house. Now they were displayed to the world, or at least to universities up and down the East Coast.

When I saw that this was not at all the private matter we'd gotten used to tiptoeing around, yes, I was ready to pack some bags. I just wasn't sure if they would be mine or hers.

One of the hardest parts about this accidental finding was managing my own emotions in a way that would also allow my husband to feel his. The history of our relationship, thus far, had included my meltdowns overshadowing any chance he had to react and feel. One of the silver linings here was that I was so blown away and shocked that there was no major meltdown. I had read the entries and sped by the meltdown stop and straight into a state of near silence. While I spent time staring into space trying to figure out how grades and SATs and dysphoria and insomnia and trauma were all pieces of the pie I'd made my child, Rich was finally seeing what Amelia and I had been hinting at for years. We were broken. It hurt him. His Dad Divorce Guilt fired up, but now it was combined with his Remarried Husband Remorse. He filled his griefcase with all of the things that had bubbled up when he did the best thing he had done in years: fall in love. How had his discovery of such joy translated into misery for the two women he loved most in his life?

We signed on with yet another therapist—the poor man. This, per Rich, was to be a family journey with all four of us stuffed into a room to hash our life story out. It was brutal. We went further into the mud. The accusations flew back and forth from parent to child to other parent to other child to therapist and then started over. The kids were urged to start taking responsibility for their own paths. The adults were urged to start taking responsibility for their own paths. We started breaking down the breakdowns, learning that in many cases, it did not matter what one's intent was but how it was received. For months we'd make baby steps of progress and see a possible light at the end of this dark tunnel, but then we'd get thrown back as we neared the topic that I felt had all but destroyed me, the allegations of child abuse.

There was no child abuse. Verbal, physical, sexual—there was no child abuse. I knew that, and maybe that should have been enough. Yet the thing that kept creeping into my head (and still does today) is that my child was so absolutely positive that I had, in fact, abused her. She was so positive that she thought nothing of sharing the trauma of it with who knows how many people. She was so sure of it that she insisted that it was not even her who coined the accusation; it was another one of her counselors. Even when that counselor denied her role, the crushing blow did not dissipate from my body.

We continued rotating around each other for months. Trying. Failing. Trying. Flailing.

We continued therapy. We explained to the kids (again) that they were thrown into my lap and that it was an *impossible* situation and how we knew it wouldn't go very well at times and how we had no choice and how we were sorry that it was so hard on them. This was not a new topic. We'd talked about it often in our home's open forum. I was beginning to understand the effects of childhood trauma and how it causes a lack of understanding until one is ready to understand. This apology-laced history of our lives may have been relayed fourteen times an hour, but would still need to be repeated another dozen in order for it to stick.

We'd drive home from therapy in a mostly silent car. Rich would pontificate on how well the session went while the rest of us counted down the miles until we could flop on our beds, lights off, with depressing music filtering through our earbuds. I felt guilty as I knew I wasn't alone in my sorrow, but I also felt like I was hardly there for myself, let alone there for Rich.

Was this another of the universe's tricks? Put so much space between you and your child at such a high rate of speed that when it comes time for them to leave the nest, you are ready to push them? No tears, just anguish? A pat on the back for good luck as you drop them off on a random street corner near a dorm? I felt like my child was the focus of all the therapeutic answers while I was getting none. When was I going to feel better?

The chasm between Amelia and me did not shrink, despite the therapy. Trust was destroyed, and feelings were annihilated. We had an unspoken agreement to coexist, putting on a happy face for Rich while knowing that nothing was actually resolved. And that is how we dove into the first eighty-four days of the 2020 pandemic quarantine.

On day eighty-five, Amelia told me she loved me.

*Amelia told me that she loved me? I thought it was probably a mistake, but then I realized that it was sent in a format in which she actually had to think and use her thumbs. She would have had time to backspace nine times rather than pushing send. She might have added a lol or a wink or well, anything, to make it less **right there** in digital black and white.*

The fracture that couldn't be fixed by anything at all only needed the minor insertion of forced interaction that only a pandemic could provide. An addendum to our unspoken agreement was that neither of us would survive an indefinite amount of isolation with anger boiling just under our skin. We had to start *trying* to like each other again. We had to start getting to know each other again. We had to try to forgive each other. The baby steps began, and we had eighty-four days to keep taking them, at our own pace. We eye-rolled any accolades from our housemates that we weren't ready to hear. A step here, a step there. A leap back. Another step forward. We started having spontaneous morning meetings to find out what each was up to that day. It took weeks for either of us to trust that those spontaneous morning meetings were not filled with suspicion or mistrust. We started offering assistance to each other. We started talking about **other** things, normal parent-child things, instead of wondering which page of The Great Book of Parent/Stepchild Mysteries we were going to reference later. A step forward, a leap forward, two steps back, a step forward. We were each still able to send the other into a spiraling meltdown with a wrong word or a wrong look or a shrug or side-eye. We started bouncing back from those events more quickly, even acknowledging the hard work we'd done and promising that the hard work doesn't get erased by a hiccup. And, as the world opened back up, we started slowly immersing ourselves in each other's lives while before we tried to remain on our own side of the fence.

Trust?

It's still a work in progress. I've never had a relationship with a person whom I had a hidden trust meter for.

Much of me still believes that Amelia will follow through on the oft-repeated threat to never return home again if I am still living here. A year prior, I would have been fine with that and likely would have forwarded her luggage, which made me feel so sad and conflicted as I knew what that would do to my husband. The idea that she would just go, forever, hurts me as it would mean that opening myself up again was a mistake. I don't think she will. I hope not anyway. I want her to go, but I also want her to come home. I want to hear about her adventures, I want to see her grow into someone I enjoy being with. I want her to find a first love and a second and learn that adult relationships are difficult. I want her to experience having a daughter. I want her to understand just how difficult the role of a (step)mom is.

I'm told that many of these hopeful revelations will not

show themselves until Amelia's frontal lobe finishes forming. I'm told that I will have to be patient and not to actually expect to learn of these revelations that would surely all point to what an impossible situation I took on and how, despite everything, I handled it all with grace.

But today, for the first time in a year, today she told me she loved me.

Unsolicited.

Just because.

Via text.

Where she actually had to think about it and use her thumbs and had a chance to backspace rather than push send.

But she pushed send.

WHO RESCUED WHOM?

It was probably the most amazing moment in my young parenting life though it hardly registered at the time. As the months and years progressed, that moment would enter my thoughts at unexpected moments with a signal as to just how important it was. Each time I recalled it, I would become more emotionally attached to it. The moment, a statement really, was so innocent. It was spoken by a small boy whom I barely knew but would eventually become the successful yin to my perceived failed yang in parenting.

We were watching *Harry Potter*. It was Max's first time seeing the movie and was the result of a deal we had. If he read the book, he could see the movie. He was just eight years old, after all, and I knew enough not to introduce the series via the television. For one, there was so much more depth in the books and, for two, the books can be a bit scary. We'd never had a movie date together, whether in the theater or at home.

I'm not even sure, at that point, that I would have been confident enough to take an eight-year-old to the movies. What do you do if they get bored? Or what if they have to go to the bathroom? Or what if they cry?

For those unfamiliar with the books, they tell the story of a young Harry Potter and his path from living with a pretty terrible adopted family to being a star student at Hogwarts School of Witchcraft and Wizardry. In the very beginning, Harry received letter after letter from Hogwarts indicating the date and time of his expected arrival. His family is adamantly opposed to this, so much so that when the volume of letters became nonstop, they stole Harry away to an island to hide. There, in the middle of a dark and stormy night, a loud knock woke all from sleep. When the door opened, it was to a half-giant/half-human named Hagrid. Hagrid, the gamekeeper at Hogwarts, had tracked Harry down and quickly had him pack up and leave with him to start his new, and presumably, more pleasant life. As Harry began to realize that he would be leaving his terrible situation, a look of relief began to drift across his face as hope was born into his eyes.

Just as Harry was departing the rain-soaked house into Hagrid's care, a small voice next to me on the couch whispered, *You're my Hagrid.*

It was so soft and subtle that I might have missed it had there not been an accompanying quick squeeze from the sticky hand that was holding my own. Yes, that had just happened.

You're my Hagrid.

Truthfully, I was so wrapped up in worry that the movie might be too scary or too confusing or too long for an eight-year-old that I heard it without really hearing it. I knew it was a sweet thing to say, but it wasn't until later that I really started to pick it apart. *Did he really say that? Did he understand what he was saying? That by declaring me his Hagrid, he was declaring me his rescuer? That he was elevating me to a position enveloped with trust? Me?* It was terrifying. I knew that I had done nothing, at that time, to deserve such accolades. As I began to recognize the importance of those whispered words, I made a promise to myself: that I would do all that I could to be worthy of them. I didn't know, at the time, that the reality of offering a safe haven for a child was actually fairly simple. Love. Acceptance. Time. Compassion.

I will not be so brazen as to declare whether either of my children needed to be rescued. Of course, yes, I have my own thoughts, but that is something I want to leave to them to work through as they grow. The divorce was incredibly difficult for them. The divorce was also necessary in order to divert their paths back towards happiness. I've no doubt that my arrival into their lives during a time when their emotional snow globe had been shaken and shaken and shaken did offer a light at the end of a long, dark tunnel. Here was someone who was not involved in the chaos. Here was someone who did not carry lines of stress on her face. Here was someone who didn't have to stop and start sentences in an attempt to avoid cutting tales with regard to life changes. Here was someone who was not present during the benchmarked bad nights.

Here was someone who only wanted to get to know a seven- and ten-year-old. Here was someone who wanted to earn a place in their hearts.

You're my Hagrid.

This came when the kids and I were really still feeling each other out. I do believe there was a higher power involved who could sense my trepidation as the magnitude of my new assignment was beginning to sink in. I needed those words at exactly that time. Nearly ten years later, I still hear them—a whisper—when I need to check myself. They pop into my head spontaneously as a reminder of the importance of my role in the kids' lives. They pop into my head spontaneously, but exactly when I need to hear them.

Am I Max's Hagrid? Or is he mine? As our years together progressed, our roles flipped on occasion. Often, during my more tumultuous times with his sister, Max would pull me aside to offer kind and encouraging words. These were in no way a backhanded effort to help me pick sides. They were only to re-expose the goodness that he has always seen in me. The wisdom in his words has always been beyond his age. I have tried so hard not to put this child on a pedestal for his ability to bring me back down to earth during an emotional uptick but, really, he deserves all available accolades. I am vigilant in having zero expectations from him when it comes to righting my ship. I understand that he is a child and will always remain in that position for me. But I am also willing to set aside my need to be right (or my need to be miserable) when he appears with a cache of comfort. As he has matured, I have seen the same cadence with his friends, always available to help someone work through a problem by listening and offering his own take, in that order. He is the safety net. He is the touchstone. He is the calm eye that sits in the center of a hurricane.

He is my Hagrid.

Which Way's Up?

Swai Flu

One of the bigger adjustments to my new living arrangements was bathroom space. In my townhouse, I had two and a half bathrooms all to myself. I could doody in a different potty than I peed and have a third place to do makeup. This didn't seem like a big deal until the first time I had to doody in this one-bathroom home. Oh jeez. I didn't know, until I moved in with a seven- and a ten-year-old, that there was no such thing as a closed door, including the one and only bathroom door. There was nowhere to hide. If I had to go, everybody knew I was going. I immediately started researching ways to add on a second bathroom.

Mornings provided an adventure that I was not prepared for. Kids and adults would arise simultaneously and there would be thirty minutes of Jenga-like movement surrounding the bathroom sink for teeth brushing, hair brushing, and makeup. The toilet was approximately zero inches away from the sink, so often that was used in sync with the sink. Oh, my Gawd.

Desperation led me to get up prior to everyone else one morning in an effort to be in and out of the bathroom before anyone else. In what I now know as a "nothing should surprise you" moment, I strolled into that bathroom full of confidence ... only to find a seven-year-old standing over the toilet, brushing his teeth while peeing. What? Yes. There was one hand on the toothbrush. There was one hand leaning against the wall.

WHO WAS HOLDING HIS WEINER?

No one.

If you have not watched a seven-year-old brush his

teeth, you have not seen the full-body wiggles that it entails. The wiggles were sending his penis back and forth, back and forth, back and forth, spraying urine across both sides of the toilet seat and onto the floor. What was happening? What was I witnessing? I believe it was the shriek that woke the rest of the house up.

I vowed to kick up my research on that additional bathroom.

I had no idea that this was peanuts compared to what was just around the bathroom corner.

It started out innocently enough.

Only a few nights later, Rich offered to cook dinner, as he knew I was struggling with the whole "being the head chef" thing. He was going to make Swai, which turned out to be a fish. Dinner was fine, I felt pretty relaxed. Off to bed we all went, yadda yadda.

Six hours later, Rich sat straight up from a dead sleep with an ominous, "I don't feel so good," before sprinting to the bathroom. I wasn't sure what to do. I don't really handle sick people (especially those who require a sprint to the bathroom). I was trying my hardest to go back to sleep, but it was super, super, super clear that he was calling my name. Well, damn. He wasn't just throwing up; he was also shooting liquid from his ass. Man, what a bummer for him. And what a relief for me to learn that all he really wanted from me was a wet washcloth. Delivery complete, check!

I have no idea how long it was until he came back to bed but, just as he was lying down, my body returned the favor. My stomach flipped, my head spun, the sprint ensued. This was not a quiet trip to the lone bathroom in this tiny house. In the lucid moments of what was clearly an exorcism, I prayed that the rest of the family would be moved out by the time I came out. Fortunately, all were sound asleep when I emerged.

But then the real hell began.

It was a big leap to take in the course of twelve hours, to go from the "new, dainty, lady who rarely farts" to one exploding from both ends. As soon as the first light hit the kids' windows, that is exactly the transition that took place. They took turns bopping into the bathroom to witness the scene: two adults sharing buckets while draining whatever was left into either toilet or the tub, depending on where they were in the rotation.

It was Saturday. My plans to spend the day lying on the bathroom floor now involved two under ten. How was this going to work? Who would prepare breakfasts or lunches or dinners? And what if one of those tiny tots had to use the bathroom? Where would I go? Back to my townhouse? How was this going to work?

We did make it back to bed via a route that included opening two Pop-Tarts, finding a SpongeBob marathon, and instilling a rock/paper/scissors system of child coverage. I knew there was no way it could get any worse when ... did I just hear Rich ask his mother to come over? Does the universe hate me? I was not ready for this. I was not ready for this woman who was not happy with my mere presence to see me in such a state. She was bringing Pepto? Sweet.

We somehow survived the Swai Flu. They'd spent the day with their grandmother and came home well fed, happy, and mostly unaware of anything they'd seen earlier. Surely, things were looking up.

The following day, we felt well enough to suggest a drive—just to get some air and get the kids out of the house again. Max was locked into SpongeBob and balked at the idea of leaving, even for a few minutes. He feigned illness, eyes never leaving the TV. We insisted and turned it off. He feigned a bellyache and Rich packed a small bucket just in case while winking at me. "He's fine, he said, just doesn't want to stop watching TV."

Oh, okay, good. I really hate it when other people throw

up.

We got approximately two miles from the house when a tiny voice came from the back seat.

"I don't feel so good."

That was it. No time for a sprint. No time to pull over. No time for me to head to the airport.

Behind me, a retching sound followed by a heinous smell. Okay, well, clearly it was hot dogs.

Well, maybe things weren't looking that far up.

CHAPTER TEN

To Be Continued

NATURE VS NURTURE

A neat way to answer the nature vs nurture questions is to have (step)kids. You will spend your '"getting to know each other" years attributing anything you don't really like in the kids to their (bio)mom. And then one day, at a moment that will stay with you forever, your child will do or say something that you do not like, and midway through telling yourself that they are *just like their mother*, you will realize that whatever they've said or done was picked up straight from your characteristics. And, just as that kick to the gut is leaving you, you will be kicked again by the memory of your own mother's words ... *I hope you have a child just like you one day* ...

I thought I had avoided my mother's wish by gaining my children via the (step)children route. I have since learned that "nurture" does hold more weight than I'd anticipated. The follow-up to the two kicks to the gut? A warm, fuzzy, full-of-love feeling of bliss, for it is that moment that will represent the first inklings of *these children belonging to* **me**. Suddenly, emotional gaps will begin to fill, and as they do, you will exhale with relief while simultaneously thinking, "*I did not even know I needed this.*"

I had those inklings first with Max. Once the floodgates

were cracked, the appearance of traits clearly inherited from me seemed to come in a constant stream. He is as funny as he is stubborn, as kind as he is determined, as soft as he is tough. He is the definition of love and compassion while also being very clear about where you stand in his life at any given time. I never planned on falling for either of my (step)children. In the beginning, my son was just an extension of Rich whom I would see on a regular but not all-the-time basis. Within days of our first meeting, I got the first lament of *you're not my mother!* and I was like *oh for sure, I'm cool with that, no worries.* I thought that was where we would stay. I didn't even notice when it happened, but soon I began to look forward to spending time with him.

Then, one day, something very sticky and slightly wet landed in my hand while walking to the car from the mall. My logical brain thought, *"Oh dear lord, what the eff is that? Pull away!"* at the exact same moment my heart-brain screamed, ***"He's holding your hand!! Do NOT abort!!"*** Oh. So, this was what it felt like to be wanted by a grimy eight-year-old boy. It was probably the first time in my life that I prayed for the car to be parked farther away just to give me another minute to decipher the weird feeling erupting through my chest.

That was nearly a decade ago.

When I look at my youngest, I see someone who grew in parallel *with* me while I navigated this new parenting world. He stood patiently by my side as I figured out momming, and I stood patiently by him as he figured out what to do with this completely unqualified second mom. It was easy and it was a nightmare. I was bitten and I was cuddled. I was stared down in anger and I had his head resting on my shoulder. I have launched myself toward anyone who has tried to hurt him, and I have debated launching him off a cliff. I have come to grips with saying *Pick up your underwear/towel/shoes* over and over. I have wondered why there were rocks in the dishwasher or a sword at the dinner table or half a dozen, half-filled glasses of water. I have learned that boys require constantly changing and always available ways to release energy. I have learned that, for boys, sitting still is, in fact, impossible. I have traveled with a purse full of Legos, little green army men, books, and an occasional Gameboy.

All of these were signals to the outside world that what they were seeing was absolutely a mother and son. No, his birth certificate does not include my name. But he is mine in all other senses.

As Max begins to leave boyhood behind and dabble his foot in beginner manhood, he has grown six inches and resembles a college freshman. The societal queues of whose child he is are long gone. There is no more hand holding or riding in the shopping cart or running over my feet while walking next to the (now) Max-pushed shopping cart. He lives on a bridge that spans the space between a careless youth and a responsible adult, moving forward and backward as he navigates this new *this is me* while I try to figure out how to keep that stamp of, *he's mine* visible. If I slow down and listen, though, I can hear it present. His deeper voice may resemble that of a stranger, but the words and tones and phrases he uses sound very much like a mix between his father and me.

We have started having conversations about his future, as Max has begun to discover his intelligence and potential. We have (selfishly?) ignored the school for years as they've pushed him to create a learning path, a career plan, skip ahead to this, map out that, instead insisting that he be allowed to be a kid for as long as possible. But now, it seems, he is beginning to sense his gifts and has developed a quiet determination to grow them. That has me written all over it, something I have no fear of repercussion in saying. Max comes from two parents who were not, and will never be, planners on the scale that I am. When I hear my son talk of goals and paths to getting there and see him taking notes on his phone, I know that these are my organizational talents showing themselves in the next generation.

Yet he is still my little guy.

I often hear him farting and giggling to himself in the next room. He and I have both been reprimanded by his grandmother for inappropriate bodily outbursts and, while I agree there is a time and a place, I appreciate our back-and-forth quest for a symphonic rear-end record. He's discovered dramatic knuckle cracking and, in turn, how much the noise makes me cringe. He enjoys my full body shudder at the noise; I enjoy that he often turns away to protect my ears. We talk about girls and Nerf guns and body odor and favorite novels and hair in weird places and memes and the benefits of a good face wash. Our relationship is happily all over the place and in so many categories that are traditionally reserved for a real mom.

As much as Max is my example of how a nurturing influence trickles down, Amelia is my example of nature holding firm. The jury will always be out as to whether that has more to do with their ages at the time of my insertion into their lives (ten and seven) or whether it is a gender thing (girl versus boy) or whether it is a baggage thing (Amelia remembers every detail of the divorce, Max remembers very little). One of the most difficult bits of (step)momming is seeing traits of the (bio)mom in the kids. And I don't mean negative traits, I mean both the positive and the negative. On a very basic level, my (step)daughter is her mother's twin. There is no question that, when she and I are out in public, we are not blood related. She is pale skinned with deep, gray eyes and nearly black hair as thick as noodles. I am olive-toned with hazel eyes and scraggly blonde hair. She is tall. I am short. She has almost always been taller than me. Oddly, Max does have my skin tone (we attribute it to years together at the pool) and dark blond, curly hair (from his father). It was not uncommon to be out getting doughnuts or coffee and for Max to hear, "*Oh, you look just like your mother,*" and then, to Amelia, "*You must look just like your father.*" I can't tell you how long it took me to understand how awkward that must have been for her.

As similar to me as Max is, Amelia is not. We have tried, she and I, to find common interests, common likes, and common ground. And while, for quite some time, it was easy to attribute our inability to fully gel on her being a smaller version of her mother (whom I also have zero in common with), I eventually began seeing past that and seeing that Amelia was just Amelia and that I wasn't the only one trying to gain entrance to her orbit. I recognized my own jealousy in those items that she seemed to latch onto with her (bio)mom. Yes, Amelia loved all things music. I did not. Yes, Amelia was creative and artistic. I was not. Yes, Amelia had a super unique style and ignored the social norms of fashion. I did not. I would hear stories about her (bio)mom's artistry and turn away for an eye roll. I would watch as she and her mom would go to concert after concert after concert. I would secretly wish that Amelia wanted to go to, well, anything at all with me, that we could have a "thing" as well. I'd see the two standing together in ripped jeans and Doc Martens and feel self-conscious in my own clothes. And then, epiphany 732. It wasn't that Amelia had *let* her (bio)mom into her orbit, it was that her (bio)mom had punched her way in. This was the way that she had found to be included in her child's life, picking up her habits, her musical tastes, and sometimes her paintbrushes.

It wasn't so much that Amelia was doing her darndest to be the opposite of everything I was nor was it that Amelia was truly a mini version of her mother. I began to see how many of Amelia's traits were actually a straight line from her *other* parent, my husband. He keeps our home stocked with musical instruments, check. We have a basement basically dedicated to arts and crafts, check. He prefers his clothes in the same monotones as she does, check. This child was as much her father's twin as she was her mother's. And it wasn't that she wouldn't pick up various, random traits from me. It was that no amount of nurture was ever going to cancel all of the others that she had already picked up from her parents.

This was, perhaps, the most important thing I learned in being her (step)mom. I'm not proud to say this, but I spent years "seeing" Amelia as a version of the woman who had turned my husband's life upside down, kids included. It was not intentional. It was also not uncommon. I would spend an hour with my husband, discussing his ex's latest shenanigans and then walk into the next room only to find a pint-sized version of her. It took effort and reflection and the retraining of my thoughts to finally stop putting the two into one basket. Did I say "two"? Now that our son is nearing baby adulthood, I find myself throwing him into that basket as well.

It is a constant struggle for me not to attribute any icky characteristics that my kids exhibit on being inherited from their (bio)mom. It is the same for them, the kids. Any icky characteristics coming from me are often attributed to the "step" in my title. Of course, the reality is that the "step" typically has nothing to do with any of our shared behaviors. I've learned to embrace the snark as something they would really only allow to emerge with someone whom they really trusted to love them regardless (me). They've learned that my frustrated tones typically emerge when I have worn myself out in running fourteen different directions while doing things for people I deeply love (them). In speaking with other moms, I've learned that we all sit in the same exhausting boat at just about every stage of child-rearing, no matter if there is a "step" involved. I found that I was putting way too much thought into *why* the kids were behaving as they were instead of recognizing that they were actually just being regular, run-of-the-mill kids.

Nature or nurture, in most cases, actually has nothing to do with the happenings in our home.

Still, if I really need to shut down a snowballing *"They are just like their (bio)mother!"* thought pattern, I remind myself of the cringe that wells up in my soul when someone suggests that my own less-than-pleasant traits are similar to those of my mother. And I adore my mother.

But, as with every daughter on the planet, I was never going to "become" her.

My kids are exactly who they are.

Themselves.

And mine.

I WISH I HAD KNOWN

I wish I had known (and also believed) that almost everything I would deal with as a (step)mother were the same things that "regular" moms dealt with. I cringed when I first heard the proclamation of, "I hate you!!!" So much so that I immediately told my own mother, who immediately congratulated me for reaching the pinnacle of parenting so quickly. Kids hate doing chores regardless of their biological connection. Kids hate most items on the dinner table. Kids fight bedtimes. Kids sass. Kids are cranky and unpredictable and a bit insane. There does not need to be a biological connection to experience any of this. I was told many times that the crankier and more unpredictable the kids were with me, the more likely it was that they were really latching onto me as a "real" mom. That seemed stupid, until recently. It's taken nearly a decade, but what's finally convinced me is my teenage son's emerging hormones coinciding with a growing disinterest in his (bio)mom. When he gets a bit on the asshole-y side, I recognize it as him feeling safe enough to be asshole-y to *me*. He knows that I am not going anywhere and that I will love him just the same if he ever comes back down to earth. Had this not coincided with his disinterest in his (bio)mom, I don't know if that would have been so clear to me.

I wish I had known not to be so overanalytical or paranoid about emotional breakdowns. Or mental breakdowns. Or communication breakdowns. I didn't realize that there would always be a long list of reasons to make someone cry (myself ... the kids ...). Evidently, this is the status quo for regular families. When I finally learned to treat these meltdowns as Status *Whoa,* things improved. I had to stop greeting these breakdowns as a personal response to my inability to be this amazing, perfect mother. Instead, I learned to greet these meltdowns with a giant stop sign. When the tears began to flow, whether mine or the kids', I had to **stop**, put the brakes on whatever it was that was causing the breakdown, and table it for later. There are no rules demanding that misunderstandings be resolved at the time of their occurrence. Learning to allow all parties to retreat to their corners or quiet spaces (or even just another topic) prevented a hop on the hamster wheel. I said that very confidently. The truth is, I could list a thousand arguments that I wished I had tabled for later. The truth is, there will probably be a thousand more to come.

I wish I hadn't spent so much time leveling myself down by calling myself an outsider. I joined a family of three. My go-to argument enders were, *"It's always three against one!"* or *"I'm never going to be like the rest of you!"* or *"Stop ganging up on me!"* Did I really think a ten- and six-year-old knew anything about gangs? The reason I felt like an outsider was because I *was* an outsider. My mistake was in my insistence that I would never be one of them because they didn't want me to be. These declarations were often produced in a loud, yelling barrage. Maybe that's why they were slow to give me the secret handshake. Eventually, I settled into the idea that, yes, I was a unique piece of this puzzle and came to appreciate it. I would never be one of them because I wasn't. They *chose* me to be in their lives. They saw my value. They wanted to make me a part of their family. They loved me and all my un-like-them ways. As I began to embrace those thoughts, I found myself lessening my subconscious push to make *them* want to be more like *me*. Once I stopped trying to push a square block into a round hole, we started to meld together into a gang. I started picking up the positive traits that they offered, and I began to see glimpses of my own traits coming out in the kids.

I wish I had known just how much biology breeds blinders. I will always see things slightly differently than my husband because of that missing genetic link. Those biological blinders were reinforced by my husband's Dad Divorce Guilt. I often made the mistake of, um, flipping out when my husband did not see a problem related to one of our children with the same urgency that I did. His blinders were to blame. I do not have those blinders, so I can often see further down the road to Consequenceville. I have learned that raising my voice or engaging my tears of frustration do not help his future vision. The only consistent method in bringing us closer to the same page is time. Quiet time. The time during which I am not screaming or taking jabs in an effort to bring his anger level up to mine. I learned to use a much softer, matter-of-fact approach to reporting the icky stuff and then to slowly take my leave. Sort of like just dropping off a package of bad news and leaving it with him to process in silence. Sometimes the processing takes a few hours, sometimes it takes a few weeks. We often don't end up on the exact same page, but this approach has gotten us much closer. When I stopped being so adamant, I was better able to hear his thoughts. I have learned that what

I viewed as a Code Red often related to that position as an outsider. I do not have the kid crisis time under my belt that he does, and that often creates anxiety born from my own lack of experience. This is why one of the most common pieces of advice in stepparenting is to let the biological parents handle the discipline. It's not because the kids will get to take an easier road. It is because the road they should take maybe doesn't need to include minefields planted out of panic.

I wish I had known that my primary role should be that of my own cheerleader. My priority (now) is advocating for my own wins and encouraging myself through the difficult times. It took me a long time to believe that my blended family did not have buyer's remorse when choosing me as a teammate. When I finally understood that, and that every child hates their parents at some point and that kid behavior is pretty much kid behavior (biological or otherwise), it became much easier to believe in myself. I started seeing my abilities with the same confidence that my husband had for years. It was like I'd been given a gold star that could be used to overshadow all of those moments when words like failure or faker tried to creep in. Nurturing my self-worth just created a better life for the entire household.

I wish I had known that my secondary role should be that of my husband's cheerleader. My secondary priority (now) is advocating for my husband. He picked me. He believed in me. He knew I was coming in green and he believed that my presence would benefit our family anyway. It may sound very 1950s, but he had a whole lot of relational garbage to handle and throwing mine into the mix unnecessarily made our road more rocky than necessary. He has so many relationships to juggle. He maintains a relationship with his kids and maintains a relationship with their mom and maintains a relationship with their (step)mom and maintains relationships with relatives on his ex-wife's side and, and, and. I had the choice of either giving him the mental space to manage all of those relationships or the choice of taking a stab at being a total control freak and doing it myself. No surprise, I went in guns blazing to the control freak side. I should have allowed my role in the circus to form more organically. He actually suggested that multiple times. I should have listened.

I wish I had known to protect our relationship as a couple first and always from the very start. We are a team. We have to feed our relationship in a way that will make it last long after the kids are gone (and, in turn, all of those other relationships). In those times when we are split, we are learning to keep that split to ourselves. Kids (all kids) will pounce on split parents. We are now able to kick off pre-determined boundaries immediately upon sensing a breach in the parenting wall. In our home, that means a thirty-minute limit per day on the heavy stuff. In times of turmoil, without those boundaries, I lean toward being obsessive, droning on and on about the topic at hand. This has caused my husband to sneak around the house like a character in *Mission Impossible*. An imposed time limit eliminates the droning as the discussions become more of a punch list than a Reason the Kids Drive Me Crazy list.

I wish I had known to always keep the magic alive. When we first moved in together, we thought nothing of talking about the kids or the kids' (bio)mom or my husband's mother or, or, or ... while in the bedroom. Eventually, we realized that we were talking about the kids or the kids' (bio)mom or my husband's mother in the bedroom. We made a rule to leave them all on the first floor. Their presence did not need to cross our marital threshold. We now treat our bedroom as a couple-only zone where we can retreat for rejuvenation. And, no, I don't mean the dirty kind (well, not always). And, no, I don't mean the kids can't physically come into the bedroom, they are welcome (well, not always). We just leave all the grime out of the bedroom. Beds are for snuggles, both kids and adults, not for problems. Bathrooms are for cute notes on the mirror, not for arguments while drooling toothpaste onto the counter.

I wish I had known to follow my husband's early lead more consistently in relation to his ex-wife. The kids already had a mom. That was a bruising fact while I was trying to settle in. It was extra difficult to acknowledge as, in our case, the kids' (bio)mom really took no interest in the raising of the kids. All of the "things" happened via our house (and typically at my prodding): shopping, doctors' appointments, school visits, vacations. We got to do the hard things and then passed much of the fun stuff to their (bio)mom. If I had totally ignored my husband, I'd likely have spent the last decade telling her precisely how that made us feel. I'd have rolled my eyes anytime the kids brought her up. I'd have made feeble attempts to sabotage their time together. It all sounds awful, yes, but that was how high my level of frustration was (and is, at times).

My husband was always adamant that we never, ever disparage his ex-wife in front of her kids. He was adamant that, if the kids disparaged her, we would not jump into the mud puddle with glee. We were to be a sounding board, not a cohort. Biology breeds blinders. He was adamant that if I tried to knock those blinders off the children, I would be the one who lost the most. This was almost impossible in the beginning, but I have made amazing strides. I have tapped into my husband's words and stayed on the side of grace, even while gritting my teeth in anger. Grace. That is still my aim. When our kids are old enough to look back at their upbringing, I want them to think of me, this woman put in a near-impossible situation, as someone who always handled every situation with nothing but *grace*.

BUT THEN, HAD I KNOWN

There were many times over the last decade in which I've been asked whether I would have jumped into the deep end of the blended family pool if I had known all that it would entail. I've asked myself the same question, probably many *more* times. When I'm really suffering, I go back through time to mentally mark the moments that I could have (should have?) labeled a "red flag, run!!" and then usually I just bang my head against the nearest wall because, really, what's the point?

The verdict?

Had I known all that this crazy life would entail, yes, I would have jumped into it, anyway.

Had I not, I would have missed so many good things—and there are **so many good things**.

On a very basic level, I would have missed this growing opportunity to share my own parenting story with other moms (step or otherwise) as they endure the rough seas of finding their sea legs. I have been shocked at how much relevant and important advice pours from my (step)soul. And while much of it is relevant to probably any "type" of a parent, my soft spot is for the (step)moms. I hope my advice is worthy of reflection but not necessarily a signal to flee. Because there is good. So much good.

- If you are lucky, your kids' (bio)mother will be Mary Poppins. There will be no gaps to span, no holes to fill, and no broken pieces to slide back into place. She will be perfect. If she, however, is not Mary Poppins, you will likely be responsible for two roles: yours (as a (step)mother) and hers (in providing whatever she leaves unfilled as their mother). You will need to make your kids feel safe. You will need to show unconditional love. You will have to have deep talks with them and then be chastised for having deep talks with them without their (bio)mom's blessing. When she leans to the side of disappointment or lack of responsibility, you will have to commit to the side of consistency and security. You will need to be the representative of a woman they *can* depend on. Oh, and you will never be thanked.

- Rather than focus on being able to have a relationship with *him*, your significant other, focus on whether you can maintain a relationship with *her*, the mother of his children. It is that relationship that will bring you the most stress. Because of these shared children, this woman will be in your life forever. She will be at every important event: graduation, weddings, the birth of grandkids. Your (step)kids will not know who to give their attention to, her or you. She will be at many less important events: games, school plays, wisdom teeth extractions. And your (step)kids will not know who to go to *first*. You will want it to be you, but you will acquiesce, offering to take your turn later. You will be second, always, regardless of which mother the kids spend the most time with.

  Learn everything you can about this woman before you commit to blending into her family. Is this someone you can interact with forever? Is she kind? Is she a train wreck? Who or what does she prioritize? How much does she rely on your significant other? How does she feel about you being with him? And with her kids? Are you wondering if the stories you've heard are accurate? Will you be able to endure more stories firsthand? Will this be high conflict, or will it just be a constant roller coaster? Will you both (your partner and you) be able to handle the pangs of unwarranted jealousy that pop up in your stomach at random moments? Will you be able to handle always being second? I write this as we near the drop-off of the last child at college, knowing that I'll have to take my spot in the back seat and watch as his (bio)mom weeps on my husband's shoulder as they watch *their* baby walk away. This relationship with your kids' (bio)mom is the one you really need to weigh before you move forward down this path.

- You will get zero credit for most of what you do. Because the kids are with us 99 percent of the time, all parental duties land with us, and, because I'm also the house manager, many of those duties fall to me. If that will not work for you, be clear from the start. The role of the mother traditionally includes the roles of the chauffeur, the cook, the contact for the schools, the nurse, the maid, and more. If there's a hat to wear, we mothers typically own it and in multiple colors. Are you willing? The kids will not see any of those things. They will mostly see you as just their dad's wife. You will be someone whom they live with because their dad chose to bring you into their home. They will love that you make their dad happy, not because you are doing all of those things that keep their lives running. You will fill all of those roles above, just not the role of "mom." That role is already filled. There will be no drawn-out thank-yous or revelations as to who is doing the real work. Which, yes, is a very mom-sounding situation ... except that's not you.

- Are you prepared to do all of the above and still be met with anger, non-acceptance, and hate? You will need to be. You will also need to believe their father (and your counselor) when you hear, "*It's not you that they are angry with*" or "*It's not you that they think they hate.*" You will feel emotionally beaten. Any animosity towards their actual parents will be placed at your feet by your (step)kids. You will be the only one they can safely despise. You will be the only one they can safely hurt. You will be the only one seen as dispensable. Can you take all of that and persevere? Yes, you will carry a glimmer of hope that maybe, *maybe* somewhere down the line they will realize that it was never you whom they were actually angry with. Can you carry on with the knowledge that will likely never happen?

- Don't wait for support from your community as it will come too slowly. The schools, doctors, dentists, and even other parents will not jump at the chance to have an additional contact for the children. They will not trust your promise to be a real participant with a real desire to be involved for really great reasons. Your husband will sign forms, make phone calls, and send emails approving participation, but it will have to be reiterated over and over and over. *Yes, she can come and have lunch at school. Yes, she can be the adult present when they get a shot. Yes, she's able to drive a carpool. Yes, she is here for the long haul. Yes, we love her.* We are oddities, those of us who do stay for the long haul. Schools, doctors, dentists, and even other parents will assume that you will be gone after a few months or years. They all expect diminishing levels of involvement because they have seen it before. If that is you, if you are not committed to being fully committed, be honest with yourself from the start. There is no shame in not wanting to carry your fair share of the parenting bucket. In fact, being honest about your lack of interest is preferable to offering false expectations.

- Creating a blended family means creating a new circle of friends, typically born of the parents of your (step)kids' friends. This group will have known each other since kindergarten (or maybe preschool or from the labor and delivery ward). You are new and missing years of history. These new parental friends will have their own kids, though likely biological or, perhaps, adopted. They will not have advice for a struggling (step)mom. In fact, they will hear (step)mom and assume yours is a part-time, easy life, devoid of their level of difficulty with your part-time children. Or worse, they will hear your difficulties and think, *"Oh, right, evil (step)mom, didn't I see this in a movie?"* Those who are not in the blended family pool have no understanding of how different it is than years ago, when the second wife was just a stand-in. History hasn't been kind to the role of the (step)mom. If you can find someone who doesn't cringe when you blurt out, *"Oh my god, I don't think I even like these kids,"* never let them go.

- If you do find someone who is understanding of your role, bring them into your world as often as you are able. This person will lift you up and won't be afraid to agree with you that maybe she doesn't always like her kids, either. This person should care about you *in addition* to the kids. You will never be short of people wanting to know how your (step)children are doing in relation to the divorce and shift in living arrangements and your arrival. Finding someone who will want to know how **you** are doing? It's a bit of a journey.

Does that all sound gloomy? It can be.

But it *is* also so good. The good bits have meant so much more to me because of all that gloom. The good means more because, despite it all, there will also be warm hugs and deep conversations and thoughtful blips that will turn my heart fuzzy. The appreciation may have not been clearly verbalized and certainly not written down, but it revealed itself in small looks or handholds or smiles.

I have learned that the title of "MOM" is fluid. Some people have it while being undeserving. Some people will earn the pants off of it and never receive it. When I speak to others, I rarely refer to myself as a (step)mom. I have earned the rights to the title of "MOM." When I speak to others, I tend to refer to my children's biological mother as just that. I have earned my title and I use it. I also respect my kids' wishes to refer to their mom as "Mom" and refer to me by either my first name or the nickname they've given me, "Bear." It does sometimes bother me, but then I remember that the title of mom, for us, often refers to someone who is a bit scattered and irresponsible and unstable. I remind myself that she carried that name before I did and that she should keep it. (Step)mom does carry a connotation that you are just a parenting sidekick. (Step)mom indicates that you are more of an observer than a participant. It is not something that sits well in my vocabulary, so I skip it.

I have earned that right.

I am a Mom.

Which Way's Up?

Barking Spiders: The OG List (sorry, Mom ... it's Rich's favorite story ... he deserves this win)

In case you haven't gathered yet, being a (step)mom can be frustrating.

Being a second wife can also be frustrating.

Also being a regular wife or a regular mom or a regular person or just trying to get through the day can be frustrating.

And often, I find that simply (ha!) diverting my frustrations can reduce them enough to be stuffed down until later. Okay, that doesn't sound healthy now that I see it on paper.

But anyway.

There is a common technique when dealing with panic attacks in which one names five things they see and five things they touch. The idea is that the brain redirects to a calmer place. I've found that redirecting my brain during moments of frustration works the same way, and I do that via lists. It's like I reward my anxiety with my OCD.

The lists represent moments of joy that have passed through my life, now documented, so that I might reach for them rather than leaping off a bridge. These are not lists about fields of flowers or the sounds of ocean waves. These are lists of moments when I made other people (mostly my husband) super uncomfortable, but not so uncomfortable that we didn't laugh about it (eventually).

I have lists titled: Jokes at My Husband's Expense, Places I Scared People and How, Words that Should be in the Dictionary, and (the original list), Top Ten Best Farts Ever.

And yes, I do whip out any of the above when I need to laugh. And I do share the list when I need my family to *laugh with me. And it stinking works.*

Eventually, I thought I'd expound on the OG List and jot down the specifics of the Top Ten Best Farts Ever (mainly because the kids wanted to retire the conversation and I was afraid the tales would be forgotten). So, without further ado:

The Barking Spiders: My Top Ten Farts Ever So Far (age forty-eight):

I don't actually know why I thought my gift for gas was list worthy, but I often (no, really) pull it up on my phone on occasions when I'm feeling especially cranky or sad or frustrated or misunderstood. So, basically, every other day since iPhone Notes was invented. It always, always, always makes me laugh. Did I mention "always?" It always makes my husband laugh, eventually. It always makes our kids ~~laugh~~ roll their eyes as they realize we are going to retell a minimum of two of these stories and typically closer to five or six. After said eye roll, their eyes dart around, searching for an exit.

Sure, I could go the adult route in these moments of frustration and talk through what I'm feeling, but that doesn't always work. It just doesn't. Sometimes a better route is to use your safety word (or list) and exit from the conversation to a safer place that you know will eventually end up in laughter. Should I be embarrassed by this? Maybe. Mortified? Probably. But what I mostly feel is:

Proud.

While my list is titled Top Ten Farts, it will likely never reach completion as I always hope for something list worthy whenever I sense (scents?) an opportunity looming. I hope I never cap it off. What would I have to look forward to if I found my Anal Opus? This catalog is in no particular order as any witnesses may offer a higher rating to one event than someone else may to another.

But yes, in this case, I will toot my own horn about my own toots. From my horn.

At the least current top eight.

Nine and Ten ... TBD. Or rather, SBD.

Ikea, Potomac Mills, VA, December 2013*: Two weeks after I'd moved to the Ville, Rich and I made a road trip to Ikea. I'd discovered that he'd never had the Swedish meatballs and he'd discovered that I didn't want to live with hand-me-down furniture, so off we went. We are typically late starters, and this day was no different. We arrived starving and made a beeline for the food court. And then we made a beeline to the Swedish meatballs. One helping? Ha! We both ordered two, pretending our children were somewhere saving a table. Did I mention we were starving? We may have inhaled those meatballs quicker than medically recommended. Delicious. Lunch, check! Let the shopping begin!*

If you've not been to Ikea (monster), here's how it works: You are taken through a maze of showrooms where you oooh and aaah at the displays, perfectly laid out, dust-free, no clutter, and you make notes of what pieces you then want to buy when you leave the maze and enter the shopping areas. Typically, by the time you get to the shopping, you have somewhere around three thousand four hundred and twelve dollars in ideas that you then have to pare down to a number that will fit in your trunk. You are handed a tape measure and tasked with guesstimating what size that trunk is and digging into your memory as to how much junk is currently living in it (did I take those bags to Goodwill?). Right. We arrived at display number ONE. Beautiful setup with a white couch as its centerpiece. We both sat down, happily full, happily on our first real couples' furniture trip. Gurgle. Gurgle. Gurgle. Were those butterflies of bliss? Oh. No. Those were meatballs bouncing around in my stomach. Yep. Oooof.

Now, I wasn't too, too worried—although Rich and I had maybe just passed the mark of farting in front of each other. And by "passed" I mean, he entered the relationship at this mark. I was still pretending it was not something I did. I also knew the old cushion trick: letting your tush exhale into a cushion, slowly rising, then leaving the evidence deep in the foam until you were well out of sight of whoever sat down next.

Gurgle, gurgle. I pushed my feet into the ground, leaned forward, and slowly started standing/exhaling. My timing was off. I did not leave anything in the cushion. Instead, (and you've got to believe me, it happened so quickly) nothing escaped until my escape hole was at the exact height of Rich's nose. At which point, a honking sound came out. I glanced over to see his eyes as wide as terrified saucers before I continued out of the display.

He came out shaking, sweating, and possibly questioning his months-old invite to bring me into his home. There was silence and shuffling as other customers moved along while trying to land on a culprit as I sat calmly in the next display wondering if anybody had noticed.

Everybody had, in fact, noticed.

It was the first time I'd heard Rich say to a room of strangers, "There is something wrong with her."

It would not be the last.

Goodwill, Richmond, VA, October 2014: *Let me reiterate, these are in no particular order. But they do mostly include Rich. Because that's when I started keeping track. Maybe it was my coping mechanism. We were on our first-ever get away from real-life weekend. We hadn't quite learned how to do nothing all day, so we were poking around Richmond, making stops on a whim. One "whim" was the string of thrift shops on Broad Street as we both* *liked to hunt for fun finds. We went into the second or third shop. Rich went one way; I went the other. Somewhere between the entrance and the coat section, I slowed enough to let out a silent scream from my stern end and meant to keep walking. Except that I realized something terrible was following me in the form of a (green? it had to be green) terrible odor. Holy hell. Did I do that? Did I just destroy the T-shirt section? I diverted and parked myself two aisles over, aimlessly moving hangers in the jeans section.*

At this moment, Rich appeared next to me and asked what I was watching.

"Oh," I said, "Just wait. Look over there in the T-shirts." We watched as a very innocent shopper started down the afflicted aisle, stopped suddenly, and crinkled up her angelic nose to a look of complete horror.

"What did you do??!!" Rich said, unsure of what he should be feeling. I'm not ashamed to say that we watched at least two more people unknowingly brave the aisle. I'm also not ashamed to say that we then had to move on because the cloud had finally reached us.

West Chester, PA, Winter, year unknown: *At some point in your dating-to-marriage life, you have to introduce your intended to your best friend and, possibly, her spouse (whom you may not know well enough yet to know if you like him). Thus, Rich and I made the trek to West Chester for a long weekend of uncomfortable questions and best-friend ratings. These are important friends. These are the friends who will tell you yay or nay on potential suitors.*

My first stop for years, when visiting, was for cheesesteaks and this time was no different, though we added Scotch eggs in as an appetizer. I've loved them forever, and I rarely see them on a menu. I'm zero percent sure if anybody else liked them, but I'm relatively sure I'll never be able to order them again (mainly because it's not been at least five years and Rich will still not let me order them again).

After eating we all piled into the car, boys in front, girls in the back and, as we hopped onto Route 3, the ghost of Scotch eggs past flew out of my fanny with a howl and permeated the entirety of Amy and John's brand-new Nissan. I immediately lost my ability to breathe because of both the spirit of the smell and the hysteria that was causing me to laugh so hard. The windows were thrown down into a twenty-degree night in an effort to clear the tarnished air.

I then watched Rich go through the "I don't know about this girl, but her friends are really cool" stage of relationship grief.

Busch Gardens, Williamsburg, VA, Date Unknown, first "big" outing with the kids: On my second trip to Busch Gardens, I had a second run-in with a Clydesdale. The first was during my sixth-grade field trip when I opted to ignore the security fencing to get a close-up picture with my Kodak Funsaver. What returned was a photo of two large brown nostrils as my model pulled its head up to snort on me.

Now, a whole adulthood later, I found myself at an amusement park with children and no clarity on how to space meals versus rides. We'd hit a snack shack, eat whatever was the worst for us, and then jump on something spinny or flippy. It seemed sensible. We then worked our way to the barns where the Clydesdales were kept, whereas it was nearing dark, we couldn't actually see any horses. We could smell them, however.

I'd wanted to get a present for our neighbor and led our group into the plush horse-lined gift shop. It seemed overheated. Gurgle. Was it hot? Why was I sweating? Gurgle. As I picked up various horses, I realized the "hot" was a signal from my stomach that a missile was loading in the chamber and that OH MAN it was about ready. I also realized that since we were right next door to the barn, I'd scored a pass on anyone noticing.

Aaaand fire!

The barn full of manure did not hide the evidence. Rather than gracefully exiting, I called Rich over to "give me his opinion on a gift." We've all done that, right? Invited a loved one into your vapor lock? It's a glorious bonus. He walked into the haze, his entire face cracked, and he scurried to the door while exclaiming, "You should be ashamed of yourself!"

The store cleared instantly, clearing a path to the register where a very uncomfortable employee rang me up. I probably should have written a note to Busch Gardens applauding her as it was clear that she was following all the protocols gifted to her by her employer while holding her breath the entire time.

Berwyn, PA, Christmas 1997: I often think about this moment with a smile and a wish that my husband or my own children had been there to witness it. However, the next most important child in my life at the time was there, my nephew. The moment probably solidified our relationship going forward. He was only three at the time and we had just finished a huge Christmas dinner involving lots of chicken and some kind of sauces. We were settled into the living room opening presents with my parents, visiting from North Carolina. I sat on the floor, relegated to the kids' zone, and gurgled.

There was an assortment of candy floating around the room, including Raisinets. While not a fan, I did see an opportunity and grabbed a half dozen or so. Gurgle.

The moment came and I let it rip, bringing silence to the room. As all turned to stare at me, I slowly stood up, unveiling a neat little pile of Raisinets under my butt. To *which my sweet little innocent nephew exclaimed, "Reindeer Poop!!" Yes. On Donner, on Dasher, on Vixen, on Oh Holy Shite.*

To this day, if you ring up my nephew and ask what my greatest fart ever was, he will immediately reply "Raisinets!"

June 9, 2019: *I actually have no idea what happened on this date, but it made the top ten. I really should go back through my calendar and see where I even was. It must have been good, but I must not have had time to document it very well.*

Sad.

Mechanicsville, VA, Spring 2019, The Gym: *Why is it that working out makes some of us sweat profusely and look like we ran through a sprinkler (me), while others come out as fresh as a dang daisy (my husband)? Or some come out of the gym feeling invigorated and ready to take on the world (me) while others feel they cannot get to the couch quick enough (my husband). And why is it that sometimes when I work out, it makes all air pockets in my entire body migrate to my keister? As a woman, I'm already at a workout disadvantage in relation to anything involving jumping. As a bubbly person, I also have to beware of anything involving squeezing my storage end too aggressively.*

For several years, our family of four took a personal training class together at the local gym each week. It was an odd way to bond, but we were struggling to help our kids burn off some anger issues with methods that didn't involve lashing out at, well, me. So, there we were, following the cruel instruction of a trainer right smack in the middle of all the other folks working out, coming in for yoga, or leaving spin classes. It was awkward in the beginning with the paranoia of looking ridiculous or like we were torturing our children. Eventually, we settled into the routine though and the nights were pretty much surprise-less.

Except on this day.

We were beginning our workout, warming up with fifteen minutes of core work when I got the first zing in my seat. Oh, boy! A few more spasms came and went, but I'm not a quitter, especially in front of my kids, so I carried on. We lined up for a minute-long plank and approximately zero seconds later I was like, "Nope, that is not going to hold itself in."

Despite a few quick passes at Lamaze breathing, the bubbles lined up. Truly, I thought I could keep things sealed enough to force whatever left me to be silent. It was not silent. It was more like a machine gun. I remained in my plank, staring at the floor while I noted the quieting of the room except for my husband's quick, "There is something wrong with you!" announcement.

I'm 100 percent sure the head trainer has yet to make eye contact with me.

Glen Allen, VA, Star Wars: The Rise of Skywalker:
When I moved to Virginia, I moved straight into a family of Star Wars nerds. A term I use gently ... I'm a nerd in some ways as well ... I just don't have the order of the trilogies memorized nor do I know which ones are sequels and which ones are prequels. But I do love Chewbacca and was sad when Han Solo died (he died, right?). I have sat through many a galaxy-driven movie and have even been sent ahead on opening nights to ensure that we got the best seats (there was no danger of a sellout, mind you, as we live in the sticks). It has become the norm that if there is another movie coming out, we will be seeing it, will likely discuss the disappointment of it, and will then be back in a year for another round. Still not a huge fan—although, if I'm being honest with myself, I'm just not a huge fan of

movies in general. What I am a huge fan of is movie theater popcorn. I will latch myself onto just about any movie trip to get myself a big bag of fresh, warm, and buttery popcorn. Which means just after the credits, when I reach the bottom of said bag, I am often destined to sit for a few hours wondering what exactly is going on in this DC Universe or that Marvel Universe or this Galactic Universe or whichever universe I have committed myself to in the name of a good snack. But the point being ... I almost did not make it past the first ten minutes of *The Rise of Skywalker*. Not because I wasn't trying, but because my husband stopped just short of demanding that I leave. The thing is that my love of popcorn sometimes has a noisy side effect. Please note, it typically does not bring a scent with it. As we tend to attend movies in which there are aliens and explosions, such outbursts are easy to hide when timed correctly.

This incident was not timed correctly.

I was so sure the Alderaan Diplomatic Envoy's retreat from the Imperial Star Destroyer would be a long drone of noise that I didn't think twice about letting the cat out of my pants bag. Therefore, I was shocked to hear the sound of zero ships in movement at the time of my own launch and see the, now common, look of horror on Rich's face. Mind you, I'm sure it matched the look of surprise on my own face as reality hit. Oh dear. This was not proper universe protocol. "Uh, you need to take that right on out of here," he whispered from my left. "Great," I thought, "I'm on his good-hearing side." No chance for any more hidden launches. I again pledged my allegiance to the resistance and sat in silence. Except for the giggles that kept escaping.

Which covered up the continued laughing farts.

Mechanicsville, VA, April 2021: *I'd been working on an interior renovation of our motorhome for about two months when I dropped this unintended surprise. I am a* professional messer-upper of important projects due to a lack of patience and ability to slow down. With the reno, I was very careful about only working for about an hour at a time, measuring, cutting, sewing, gluing, hanging, all very slowly and intentionally, and never continuing if I felt that feeling of "I should stop now" creeping in.

One area where this approach was super important was in making slipcovers for the arms of the couch, which involved lots of measuring and cutting and sewing as there was no pattern. I was also using a very fancy, very borrowed sewing machine, so I had to spend a week digging through its manual just to understand how to drive it.

In summary, this part of the renovation took forever.

When complete, I leerily walked out to the RV, a bit nervous that the slipcovers would not fit or would look terrible. I was beside myself with glee when I realized they actually looked professionally made. I was also bummed that my husband was in a meeting and could not come out to offer me accolades or pats on the back.

I was also a little gassy. So, I farted and left, closing the door behind me.

Side note: We do not keep the window open in the RV nor do we run the fan unless we are not actively using it. It is too easy to forget about, which tends to cause puddles of forgetfulness.

The next day, when I remembered my glee at the same time, I saw my husband wandering through the house. I grabbed him for a quick trip out to see my handiwork. Upon stepping into the RV, we both slowed slightly as we were met by ... what? Something ... what? We weren't using the toilet, the black water tank was empty, and we were fairly sure that there were no dead animals hidden under the seats.

What was that??

As he oohed and aahed and also gagged, I remembered the vapor deposit I'd left the previous day.

Oh.

Yes.

I blocked the exit while I explained, "Oh, I know what that is ... I farted yesterday when I was in here and then closed it up before I left."

OH MY GOD, THAT WAS YOU?!?

"Yes, my love, that was me."

AND YOU CLOSED IT IN HERE?!? TO STEW OVER-NIGHT?!? IN THE VIRGINIA WEATHER?!?!

"Yes, my love, that was me."

Mind you, while this conversation was happening, he was also trying to leave the RV while I remained firmly planted in the doorway.

I did let him leave, eventually. I'm not a total monster.

*****

Final Fart Thoughts (again, sorry, Mom)

The irony in the sufferings of Rich is that on our very first sleepover at my townhouse (after eating Mexican food for dinner) I was so incredibly paranoid that I might fart in my sleep, that he would hear me fart in my sleep, that I would be mortified that he heard me, that I would have to break up with him because I was so mortified, that, well, I did my best to fake sleeping for hours.

Our relationship was new enough that I couldn't really gauge whether or not he was asleep, so I just lay there, eyes closed, squeezing my lower cheeks with full intention of remaining that way until morning. I could also grab a nap sometime during the day, right? Anything to keep the virtue of my bum intact.

Way down the relationship road, when I was perhaps too comfortable with my flatulence, I told Rich that "gosh, those were cute times" story. As I was telling him, I saw a smirk begin to grow across his face. What was that look?

Why was he smiling?

Finally, after a few moments of delighted silence, he pulled me close and whispered, "Well, you eventually did fall asleep ... and I've known of your talents ever since ..."

AUTHOR'S NOTES

So ... That's What Was in the Box.

THIS ISN'T A LOVE STORY.

No. It is clearly so much more.

I am brazen enough to suggest that, in our home, the love is much stronger than in a traditional family home that started with two parents who raised their children from infancy. Here, we have been through a war together. Here, we know there will be more wars and we are prepared to face them.

This book covers my first eight-ish years of my role as a (Step)mom, ending with 2020. I chose to stop there mainly because I needed a stopping point for the actual book while continuing to write my blog (i.e., therapy) and with plans forming for the next book. Yes, somewhere in the midst of writing this book, I *did* start thinking, "*Oh, shit ... I'm going to have to write a second book **for sure** or everyone is going to think I'm still navigating the turbulent waters that are my relationship with my mother-in-law.*"

Well, yes, that is totally accurate, but one of us has definitely grown beyond some childish behavior.

I also did not know, when I planned to stop with 2020, that the whole world would also stop with 2020. I did not know that with that stoppage, everyone with a keyboard, pen, or stone tablet would opt to write a book. Still, I kept at it with mantras of, "*If I can just save one (step)mom from some of the strife ... if I can just give one (step)mom something to laugh at ...*" then it will have been worth it. Though I am still learning to parent (apparently that just goes on forever), my (step)children are both alive and thriving. Our family is, in fact, thriving.

In other words, I am probably a normal, everyday, regular mom.

I am enough ... and more.

Thank you for your support!

What did you think?
Please share your review
on Amazon.com.

Jyl Barlow

JYLBARLOW.COM

ACKNOWLEDGMENTS

Well, this is petrifying. I've put off writing my acknowledgments primarily for fear that I would forget somebody important. For a gal with both OCD and anxiety, that's terrifying. Should I just go with a simple, *"To anyone that I've spoken with in the last ten years (including strangers at Target, thank you."*

But seriously, if you're not featured, do not despair. My editor has already yelled at me three times for writing a book that is too long, so definitely let's assume she was the heavy.

Rich: Let's admit that there is no way to express my love for you in a tiny blurb. I am lucky. I am so, so lucky. Without you, I mean sure I'd be fine, but, my goodness, I am a better person for knowing you. You have taught me what unconditional love really looks like. You have supported me in so many wonky ideas, including the one where you sat me down in front of a new Mac and simply said, *"Write."* I love you is not big enough. I do love you more, though, so that's settled.

Amelia and Max: How do you thank your children for being your children? You had no choice (ha!) in the direction of your young lives. I have learned so much from both of you, both as a mother and a person. You have made me better at both. I will forever be proud of all that we have endured together. I will always claim you proudly as my own. I love you until the end of the earth.

Amy: If I had a dime for every time I've cried on your shoulder ...You've been a part of my life since we were baby adults. I'm still not convinced that we won't end up roommates again, reverting to washing down raw cookie dough with beer. Until then, I know you will always be firmly planted in my corner. You lift me up endlessly. You also bravely advise me to stand down when I am going emotionally rogue. You are far more than a best friend. I don't deserve you.

Karen and Jimmy. The universe threw us a golden bone (that's what she said) when it placed us next to each other, years ago, on the soccer field. To say that the two of you center us, as both parents and spouses, is an understatement. You are our touchstone. There are no words to express the safety net you have generously offered us so many times. I only hope that we have been half as helpful to you. You are our family, forever.

Jenny. Did we really only meet because I boldly signed up as a very unqualified Reading Olympics Coach? I had no idea that putting my name on that paper would spark the formation of a lifelong friendship. I follow your paths so enthusiastically because they are so worthy. To know a mom who has sat on both benches (biological and step) has been invaluable. You have given me some of the best advice I've ever gotten—yet the most important is always, "Oh, yeah, that's just a normal kid thing. It has nothing to do with being a stepmother." You are the Flight Attendant on my Momming Trip. As long as you aren't panicking, neither will I. And, thank you, for not panicking thus far.

Mom and Dad: Mom, I cannot remember how old I was when you first started telling me that I would write a book one day. You have been a fan of my word work since I first learned sass. Dad, thank you for following along and never telling me when I've written something that grosses you out. To the both of you, I do think I stalled on marriage and children because the example you offered was just too good to top. Your resilience, your ability to laugh, your deep love for each other has inspired me for years and even more so when I realized all that it takes to make this family shit look easy. Thank you is not enough.

Aunt Tonie: My second Mom. You boomeranged back into my life when I needed you the most. Since then, you have become a most trusted source of guidance (and the occasional shove back on course). Thank you for stepping in, without missing a beat, when my own mother couldn't. You're stuck with me forever now.

Jeff and Karen: Jeff, I knew when I met Rich that our plan to build a compound away from the annoyances of the world was falling to the wayside. Thank you for welcoming him as a brother, anyway. Karen, thank you for sweeping my brother off his feet. You have both been the recipients of many tearful conversations having been in some of my shoes. Your wisdom and advice will never be forgotten (also, I'm probably not done needing it yet).

Actual Max: Max. Oh goodness. Sometimes think you were put on this earth specifically to tell me, without fail (every Monday night for three years straight), *"You are such a good (step)mom, Jyl! I love my (step)mom so much and you are just like her!"* I miss you, Max, and I will never forget your encouraging words.

Rachel, Jenee, Donna, David, Alex, etc., etc. ... no, really, I'm sure there are more counselors to thank (or from whom to get my money back, depending on the day). Thank you all. Rachel, you are the one who has been with me through the muddiest bits. I **know** our family would not be intact if it weren't for you. Never forget that what you do **matters.**

(Bio)Mom: It took me a minute to understand the trust you blindly put in me with our shared children. Thank you for letting our relationships develop organically. I know that, well, we both could have been awful to each other. I am so glad that you taught me, from the start, to separate our feelings for each other from those for our children.

The Atmosphere Team:

+ **Marie:** Your enthusiasm earned Atmosphere my work. I knew right away that you really did "see" something in my book. You were also brave enough to announce that there was more work to do. You gave me the shot of confidence needed to *keep going.*

+ **Tammy:** You had the unpleasant task of being the first person ever to look beyond my story and at the actual words. I suppose this is like seeing a beautiful home and then being asked to grade the quality of the carpets. Each revision improved my writing tenfold. Thank you.

+ **Proofreader Guy:** I'm sorry I didn't understand formatting dots or squiggly dashes

The Angus Barn: Weird to acknowledge a whole restaurant? Probably, but don't judge it until you've been there. This restaurant holds my heart. This restaurant is run by my extended family, people who have watched me grow and then watched my family form, enthusiastically welcoming my husband and children into their fold. Van, I'll never forget the day you promised me that I'd meet the love of my life in the Wild Turkey Lounge. I thought you were kidding. Love wins, again.

And also....

✢ To all the shoulders I've cried on, thank you.

✢ To those who have shown me that people really can change, I am in awe.

✢ To those who have chosen not to, thank you for showing me the path to walking away, emotionally.

✢ To the wine section of any grocery store, thank you.

✢ To Wednesday Martin, reading your book *Stepmonster* was like cleaning smudged glasses. Finally, so much made sense to me.

Oh, yes—and **Reed.** The only person brave enough to insist on an acknowledgment. Thank you for finding the house that we would make a home. Even though I found it first. Right? Not important. You were my first Richmond friend. Thank you.

Not listed in the acknowledgments, but wanted to be? No worries! Fill in spaces here:

_____ was also essential in my day-to-day survival. Without _____, there is simply no way I would be here today, on the other end of this crazy decade.

ABOUT ATMOSPHERE PRESS

Atmosphere Press is an independent, full-service publisher for excellent books in all genres and for all audiences. Learn more about what we do at atmospherepress.com.

We encourage you to check out some of Atmosphere's latest releases, which are available at Amazon.com and via order from your local bookstore:

Finding Us, by Kristin Rehkamp

The Ideological and Political System of Banselism, by Royard Halmonet Vantion (Ancheng Wang)

Unconditional: Loving and Losing an Addict, by Lizzy and Adam

Telling Tales and Sharing Secrets, by Jackie Collins, Diana Kinared, and Sally Showalter

Nursing Homes: A Missionary's Journey Through Heaven's Waiting Room, by Tim Eatman Ph.D.

Timeline of Stars, by Joe Adcock

A Boy Who Loved Me, by Wilson Semitti

The Injustice in Justice, by Charmaine Loverin

Living in the Gray, by Katie Weber

Living with Veracity, Dying with Dignity, by Alison Clay-Duboff

Noah's Rejects, by Rob Kagan

A lot of Questions (with no answers)?, by Jordan Neben

Cowboy from Prague: An Immigrant's Pursuit of the American Dream, by Charles Ota Heller

Sleeping Under the Bridge, by Melissa Baker

The Only Prayer I Ever Have to Say Is Thank You, by M. Kaya Hill

Amygdala Blue, by Paul Lomax

A Caregiver's Love Story, by Nancie Wiseman Attwater

ABOUT THE AUTHOR:

Jyl Barlow navigates life as a (second)wife and (step)mom
with inappropriate laughter and near-perfect hindsight. Jyl resides just outside of Richmond, VA (home of the original "bless
your heart") with her family and as many pets as her husband
will allow. Besides writing, Jyl enjoys travel, forming plans to
become an Olympian, and watching Carolina beat Dook. Jyl is
a contributing writer to Today.com, FunnyPearls.com, and
Grown & Flown. Get to know her at JylBarlow.com and follow
her blog at WhichWaysUp.Blog.